Ca

Graphi
Proce

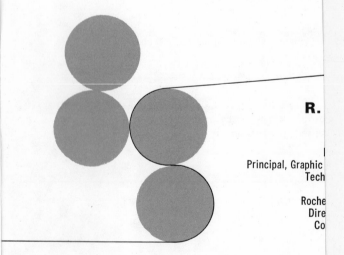

R.

Principal, Graphic
Tech

Roche
Dire
Co

American Technical Society

CONTENTS

You and the Graphic Arts

A WIDE RANGE of talents and skills are demanded by the Graphic Arts. Whether you are artistically talented, or more interested in the mechanical and technical phases, you can be sure that there are dozens of fine positions open for you in the Graphic Arts. Furthermore, there are hundreds of related careers where a knowledge of printing processes is either a requirement or an extremely important advantage. Advertising, commercial art, manufacturing paper and equipment, and professional writing are just a few of the occupations where a knowledge of the Graphic Arts is essential. And there is hardly a business executive in any industry who does not need to know something about the Graphic Arts in order to plan and buy printing intelligently.

This great demand for efficient printing recently has stimulated many new developments in the industry. For instance, the typesetting machine operator, with his specialized skill and modern equipment, is now expected to turn out a volume of printing that could never be attempted before. He has not displaced the talented and accurate compositor who still sets type by hand, since many jobs cannot be handled by a machine. But scientific research has lately developed such speeds that machines can now set more letters per minute than a person could even count. These machines select type at a speed which excels the retentive power of the human eye, while *at the same time* placing the type neatly and precisely into its proper place.

It might seem incredible, yet the only work of the operator of this machine is often limited to the supervision and repair of his machine. Many of the latest type composing machines are activated by streams of perforated tape, and are otherwise untouched by human hand. And the tapes they receive are often perforated by wire or radio from the other end of the world! *Time* magazine, for instance, is "set" by a staff of "typists" in New York. The tapes they punch are transmitted by electrical impulses to Chicago and California, where rows of machines are waiting to receive them. Similarly, newspapers in cities all over the world employ machines which set type in response to cabled signals which have been received from their central units.

Perhaps the most astonishing instrument to the newcomer, as he surveys some of the modern equipment in the Graphic Arts, is the photocomposition machine. This photographs and reduces copy automatically and can even allow for corrections. The speed and electronic controls of this, and of other processes, should impress any engineer with the profitable and exciting developments that automation has brought to the printing trades.

For example, there are robot converters which transmit electrical impulses instantaneously into halftones, and electromagnetic scanners which can read and set 2500 lines of type per minute. (Hence, they could "read" the Bible from cover to cover in a quarter of an hour!) And there is a film-compositor which mounts 1408 different characters on a matrix the size of a shoe box top! These are some of the developments which the electronics age has brought to the Graphic Arts, and which have thrown wide open the opportunities for any young trainee who is about to enter.

Naturally, the trainee must begin by learning something about the basic techniques and machines of his trade. He must know how each job is handled and how he can learn that flawless and expert skill which will adapt him to a responsible place in the team. And this book has been written for just that purpose.

The printing trades are described carefully and each of their techniques are explained with plenty of illustrations. The basic printing processes are analyzed, the differences in type faces are portrayed, and the methods of display and layout are outlined. After looking at the setting and proofing of type, the technical chapters conclude with a description of the making, engraving and, finally, the printing of the finished plates. The last chapters in the book describe bindery and paper-making.

The book closes with a chapter, on "Careers in the Graphic Arts," which should help the now informed and understanding newcomer to put his knowledge to work. And to help him, a glossary of printing terms has been arranged so that this book can still guide him when he goes out to start his practical work in the Graphic Arts.

Many of the laymen who visit printing plants find neither the time nor the ability to find out how *everything* works. They are curious and would usually like further information. In the Graphic Arts, for instance, there are always inquiries from such interested specialists as journalists, publishers, advertising men, or commercial artists, whose activities often take them into printing establishments. Since too many of them have found difficulty in obtaining clear and simple information, this book has also considered their problems. Not only has it been designed to guide and instruct trainees and apprentices in the printing trades, but it is also aimed to answer many of the non-technical queries which are so often brought to the printer.

The last chapter, on "Careers in the Graphic Arts," should dispel much of the confusion which still lingers about the printing industry. Certainly, the high wage rates and the fine prospects for expansion should be known to a wider audience than at present. And, similarly, the false notion that printers have to work like devils, against impossible deadlines, and under unhealthy conditions, should be exposed to the cleansing sweep of reliable information. Such facts must be brought before the public that they may better appreciate the vital and efficient contribution which the Graphic Arts now make to modern society. There is hardly one activity in contemporary life which does not depend upon printed products. The birth of a child is heralded with a printed announcement, and in between reading books, time tables and display ads, the child grows up to handle printed packagings of food or fabrics, and to write his own checks or to sign his marriage license. And then he calls it a day with a published obituary.

The printing industry is big business. Almost every village and town has a printing shop. The value of receipts for printed products, printing and publishing, in 1968, was over 21 billion dollars and rising at over a 6 per cent annual rate. The prospects for the future of the industry are undeniably encouraging, but it must be the skilled trainee who stands to gain the greatest benefit.

The first steps in learning are always the most difficult and challenging. If this book can help to excite and guide the trainee further in his studies it will have served its purpose.

THE PUBLISHERS

CHAPTER 1

How to Understand Printing Processes

PRINTING, or the laying of ink on paper for a variety of purposes, is accomplished through several different processes. Most of the printing done today is one of three major processes: letterpress, offset-lithography, or gravure. Three other minor processes in use are copperplate engraving, collotype, and screen process. Each of these processes is explained briefly in the following paragraphs.

"Relief" Printing: Letterpress

Letterpress printing is 500 years old, having been first done in a practical manner by Johann Gutenberg, in Germany, about the year 1450.

Letterpress printing is done from a *relief* surface, cast, cut or etched from metal and other substances. The surface of the type or illustration plate extends above the body of the type or plate. When this surface is coated with a pasty substance called printer's ink and pressed against paper, printing results.

Kinds of Work Done by Letterpress. Typical examples of letterpress printing used in everyday life are the newspaper, some school textbooks, theater tickets, and most letterheads and envelopes. This process in printing is generally used for the following kinds of work:

1. Jobs not illustrated but printed in type, in quantities from 100 copies up, particularly in sizes too small for printing on presses by other processes.

2. Jobs needed in a *hurry*.

3. Jobs requiring fine detail in illustrations.

4. Jobs requiring the blackest impression from type, and a good, even, black color through the entire piece of printing.

1

Advantages and Disadvantages of Letterpress. There are certain advantages, and disadvantages, in letterpress printing:

1. No process is faster, as evidenced by the several editions of a daily newspaper.

2. Jobs not illustrated, but only type matter, are usually cheaper to produce by the letterpress process.

3. Details of illustrations are better in letterpress than in the gravure process, and sometimes better than in offset-lithography.

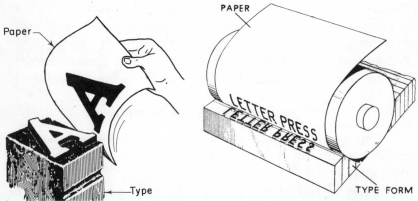

Fig. 1-1. Letterpress Printing from Type

Fig. 1-2. Letterpress: Printing from Line Slugs and Plates

4. Presswork is slow to get started in letterpress on large forms with *halftones* (varying shades of gray or color), with the exception of newspaper machines, because much time must be spent in adjusting height to paper of various parts, requiring *makeready* (see glossary for definition). However, on small work such as letterheads and envelopes, press set-up time is less on letterpress than on offset.

5. With the exception of newspaper and magazine printing, flat-bed letterpress speeds are usually slower than either offset-lithography or rotogravure presses.

6. Illustrations cannot be printed well in halftone on rough-finished paper on letterpress printing machines.

7. Letterpress is usually the best process to use when the type matter for a repeat job is "standing"; that is, ready to use again.

Plane Printing: Offset-Lithography

The word *lithography* is derived from two Greek words: *lithos,* a stone, and *graphein,* to write: hence the word means stone writing, or writing on stone. Lithography was discovered in 1796 by Alois Senefelder, a Munich playwright. For many years all lithography was done from calcareous stones. The design to be printed was drawn or transferred on the stone in a greasy ink. Then the stone was dampened, and water adhered to the parts not covered by the design. Then the stone was inked, and the ink adhered only to the image, and not to the dampened sections of the stone. Senefelder had discovered the principle of lithography: that grease and water do not mix. Between the years 1881 and 1906 the lithographic *offset* press was developed. On this new machine the ink impression is transferred from a plate, which is drawn about a cylinder, to a rubber-blanketed cylinder. The paper receives its impression from the rubber blanket. Great speeds are possible on this rotary-type offset-lithographic printing press.

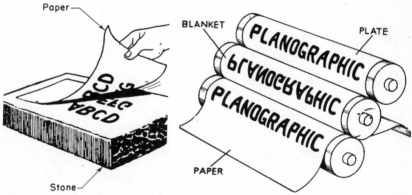

Fig. 1-3. Old Stone Lithography　　　Fig. 1-4. Modern Offset-Lithography

Dry Offset. The *dry offset* process (letterset) eliminates the need for moistening rollers on presses by printing from a shallow etched plate (.015-inch image on a .030-inch thick plate) onto a rubber blanket which transfers the image to the paper. No indentation of the paper can occur in this process which makes it desirable for printing on rough-surfaced paper. Revenue stamps are often printed this way, because the plates last for millions of impressions.

Wrap-Around Presses. New plate developments have enabled press manufacturers to design new presses which print from the new, flexible, "wrap-around" plates, Dycril or relatively thin (.025-to .030-inch thick, etched for relief printing from .006- to .010-inch). The plate is wrapped around the impression cylinder, hence the name. See Figs 1–5 and 1–6.

Fig. 1-5. A Harris 36″ x 49″ Two-Color "Wrap-Around" Letterpress

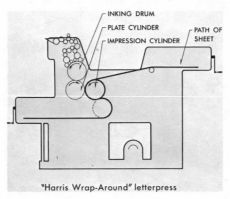

Fig. 1-6. A Diagrammatic View of the Harris "Wrap-Around" Press

Kinds of Work Done by Offset-Lithography. Typical examples of work done by offset-lithography are bank checks and deposit slips, the advertising matter on cans printed directly on the metal of the container; paper labels; children's books, especially in colors; text books with halftone illustrations; printed billboards; many kinds of advertising matter; weekly newspapers and "shoppers."

Advantages and Disadvantages of Offset-Lithography.

1. Generally speaking, when the halftone illustrations are *many,* offset-lithography is the best process.

2. Difficult type forms to compose, if already printed, can be photographed and run offset, thus saving on resetting the type.

3. Crayon drawings and those with delicate stipples and vignettes are best printed by offset. (A *vignette* is an illustration in which the tone of gray fades off into nothing at the edges.)

4. Storage facilities of plates are usually better with offset compared to letterpress.

5. Blank work, with many rules and cross-rules, makes a better job if printed offset; in letterpress, there is a tendency of the rules (or lines) to punch into the sheet of paper, which makes the pad or pile of paper bend upward at the edges. Also, rules can be made to join perfectly in offset; a hard job in letterpress.

6. Offset-lithographers sometimes have a difficult time, especially in type work, to keep all pages of a form in a uniform density of ink.

7. Halftones, or plates having varying shades of gray tones, can be printed on rough paper. This cannot be done well by letterpress.

Intaglio Printing: Gravure and Engraving

The invention of the process of gravure printing, an intaglio process, is credited to Karl Kleitsch, of Vienna, in 1879. In 1894 he developed a rotary method of printing from etched copper cylinders in his workshop in Lancaster, England. By 1905 a gravure plant was set up in New York City, and by 1914 *The New York Times* established its own rotogravure plant.

The term *gravure* is from the French, and means cutting or engraving. "Roto" and "sheet-fed" are two prefixes usually to the word gravure in its present usage. It refers to a process of printing in which the ink adheres to paper upon great pressure, coming from very small etched-out sections of a copper cylinder. The ink therefore comes from an *etched-out* portion of the cylinder, and the surface ink, on the gravure press, is scraped away.

Kinds of Work Done by Gravure. Typical examples of gravure printing are found in paper money, postage stamps, bonds, magazines, newspaper weekly supplements, and food and candy wrappers.

Advantages and Disadvantages of Gravure.

1. Rotogravure is suited for long runs on the press, 25,000 or above, in which illustrations comprise over one-third of the area.

2. Rotogravure printing cylinders may last as long as a million impressions, far more than are found in letterpress or in offset.

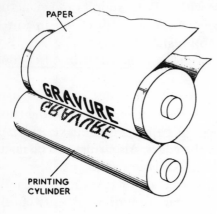

Fig. 1-7. Gravure Process

3. Fine detail is lacking in gravure printing in illustrations, but gravure has a much softer value than any other of the processes. The *screen* of gravure illustrations is not so apparent as that found in other processes.

4. Rotogravure presses are set up to print faster than letterpress.

5. All type faces are screened in gravure printing, which makes the type faces thicker, roughening the edges. This makes the use of fine-lined types difficult, and narrows the selection of type faces.

6. Cheaper paper stock can be used on gravure presses compared with the paper stock used on letterpress machines and offset presses.

7. Rotogravure presses have greatest speeds, and many print four or five colors on both sides of the sheet (or continuous *web* of paper) at one time through the press.

Copperplate Engraving. Maso Finiguerra is said to be the inventor of the copperplate engraving process. He discovered the art of etching on a copper plate about 1446, in Florence, Italy. From his work the present process of engraving has grown.

The engraving of copper plates is done largely by hand, but often by machine, on a copper plate which is well polished.

How to Distinguish The Graphic Arts Processes

	LETTERPRESS	OFFSET-LITHOGRAPHY	GRAVURE
Rotary Methods of each Process	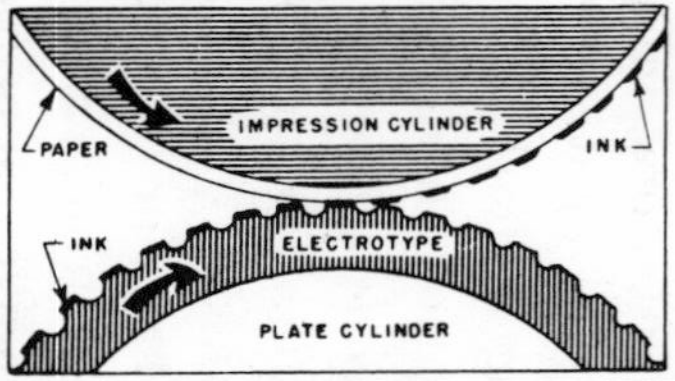	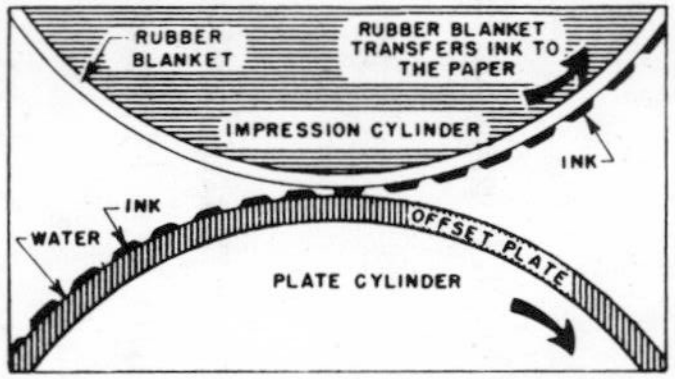	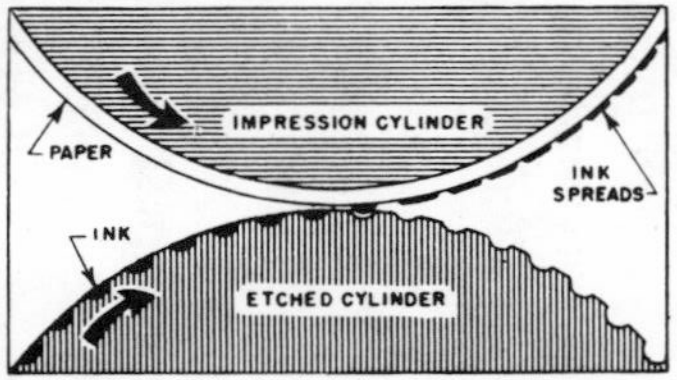
Examine Type	Often shows a slight impression on back of sheet—hold at an angle to light	Never shows an impression on the back of sheet—hold at an angle to light	All type is screened the same as illustrations—examine with a magnifying glass
Examine Line Engravings	Impression may show on back of sheet—hold at an angle to light	Never shows impression on back of sheet	Illustrations which appear as line are actually screened
Examine Ink	Usually appears as an intense black. Detail is sharp	Solid blacks usually appear gray when compared with letterpress. Detail usually less sharp than letterpress	Smooth, blending tones. Detail not as good as in letterpress or lithography
Examine Halftone Dots	Highlight dot Shadow dot  Usually 120–133 line	Highlight dot Shadow dot  Usually 80–133 line	Highlight and shadow screen  Usually 150 line; ink tends to fuse and obliterate screen

Because of the extreme differences in quality of work done in letterpress and offset-lithography, it is often difficult to distinguish one process from another. Offset often looks like letterpress.

Fig. 1-8.

Ink is rolled over the plate to fill the cut-out lines of the printing matter. The surplus ink is wiped off the surface of the plate, leaving the ink in the cut-out portions. The paper is then pressed against the plate in the press, and the ink leaves the recesses and adheres to the paper. In so doing, the ink has a decided raised effect that is felt easily with the fingers.

Steel plate printing is similar to that of copperplate printing. However, steel plates are usually run on power presses, which lessens the cost of the printing.

Kinds of Work Done by Copperplate Printing. Typical examples of the copperplate and steelplate processes are name cards, wedding and society printing, letterheads and envelopes, and greeting cards.

Fig. 1-9. Copperlate Process

Advantages and Disadvantages of Copperplate Engraving.

1. Copperplate engraving is a slow and costly process, more expensive per piece than any other process.

2. The elegance of the work cannot be matched by other processes with regard to dense black type, illustrations, raised surface.

3. Social custom often demands this type of work for certain types of announcements, such as wedding invitations.

Imitation Copperplate Engraving. Imitation engraving is known by several names, among which are *raised-letter printing, process embossing, thermography, and virkotyping.* The process is letterpress or offset. A slow-drying ink is used, and immediately after printing, the sheets are either dusted by hand or by machine with a resinous powder. The sheets are then run through a heater, where the ink fuses and swells, giving an engraved appearance. This process is chiefly used where customers do not choose to pay for the costlier genuine copperplate engraving. Genuine engraving usually has an indention on the back of the printed sheet. Imitation engraving does not have this indention, and is often of a less dense black.

Paint Printing: Screen Process

The process on which screen printing is based is probably the oldest form of printing. It is attributed to the Chinese and Egyptians for its origin, although the present process is the one used in ancient Japan. Samuel Simon patented the process in Manchester, England in 1907. John Pilsworth of San Francisco is credited with developing the present multicolor process.

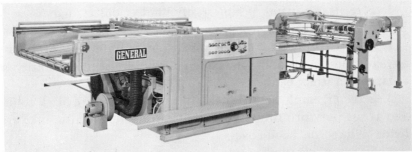

Fig. 1-10. The General Screen Process Press

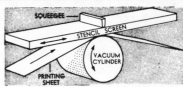

The process is simply that of squeezing paint through a stencil which is mounted on a screen stretched tightly over a frame. The stencil may be hand cut from paper, painted on the screen itself, or photographed on the screen. Paint is poured onto the screen, and is pushed through to the object being printed with a rubber blade.

Kinds of Work Done by Screen Process. Typical examples of screen printing are the lettering on milk bottles and vacuum cleaner bags, designs on lamp shades, some kinds of decorated oilcloth, signs on streetcars and buses, and designs on furniture. Felt pennants; advertising signs, large, and in color; and designs on children's toys are often done by screen process.

Screen Process Presses. In the early days of the screen process, presswork was done largely by hand. Now presswork may be done mechanically, as shown in Fig. 1–10. This press screen processes sheets up to 44 to 64 inches at about 2,000 impressions per hour. A revolving, perforated vacuum cylinder holds and moves the material across a stationary squeegee during the printing cycle. Both chase and cylinder are reciprocal in action so both move at the same speed. Material and stencil touch at a straight line beneath the squeegee. Sheets are fed and printed flat. The squeegee lifts and the chase moves back to starting position after each impression.

Advantages and Disadvantages of Screen Printing. Some advantages and disadvantages of the screen process are listed below:

1. Screens can print on almost any kind of object: paper, cardboard, cloth, felt, glass, wood, and metal.

2. The screen process can be used to print on objects of almost any size and shape—thick like bakelite, cylindrical like a bottle, or as large as a street banner.

3. Screen is employed to lay a pure white over a pure black color, and is the only printing process that can do it. Metallic inks are being printed on book covers.

4. Screen work is adaptable for short-run work.

5. Screen presses run slowly, and much of the production is done by hand methods.

6. White ink can be laid on black paper—very difficult by other methods.

7. Short runs of color printing on heavy boards is good by the screen process.

Screenless Illustration Printing: Collotype or Photogelatin

Photogelatin or collotype printing is attributed to Joseph Albert, of Munich, who experimented in 1870 with sensitized gelatin on glass plates. At first only art masterpieces were reproduced.

Collotype and photogelatin printing is called by many different names, some of which are phototype, albertype, lichtdruck, artotype, and heliotype. The process reproduces illustrations in *continuous tone;* that is, like the photograph would appear, without the screen used in letterpress, offset-lithography, and gravure.

Plates for the collotype process are made in either plate glass or aluminum similar to those used for offset-lithography. The plates are etched, however, to give a gravure-like intaglio plate.

Kinds of Work Done by Collotype. Typical examples of work done by the collotype process are the large moving picture advertising posters and placards found in theater lobbies, artwork such as paintings and drawings usually purchased already framed, window hangers and display boards, and the better kinds of picture postcards.

Advantages and Disadvantages of Collotype.

1. The process is best for short-runs, from 100 to 3,500 copies.

2. Collotype is the only process in printing that gives continuous tone printing, without a screen of any sort.

3. Platemaking cost of collotype work is low-priced, compared with any printing process other than screen process.

4. Presswork in collotype is slow when compared with other printing processes.

5. Three colors of collotype are said to be as good as four colors printed by any other process.

Pressureless Printing: Electrostatic

The electrostatic or pressureless printing process is being developed for commercial use. This new method allows text and pictures to be printed on irregular surfaces, such as corrugated board; fragile surfaces, such as an egg; soft surfaces, such as a wad of cotton; and rough surfaces, such as a brick.

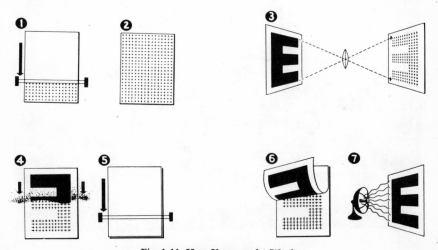

Fig. 1-11. How Xerography Works

The process utilizes a fine screen with a coated image. The material to be printed is interposed between the image element and a ground in an electrical field. Ink particles are metered through the image openings and electrically propelled to the object. There is no contact between the screen and the subject receiving the image.

Xerography devices make copies of business papers and also make offset plates. Figure 1–11 shows how Xerography works: 1. The surface of a specially coated plate is being electrically charged as it passes under wires. 2. The plate is charged with positive electricity. 3. Copy (E) is projected through a camera lens. The plus marks show the projected image with positive charges. The positive charges disappear in areas exposed to light as shown by white space. 4. A negatively-charged powder adheres to the positively charged image. 5. Paper is passed over the plate and receives a positive charge. 6. The positively charged paper attracts the powder from the plate, and a direct positive image is formed. 7. The print is heated for a few seconds to fuse the powder and to form a permanent print.

Fig. 1-12. The Xerox Offset Platemaker

Figure 1–12 illustrates the Xerox electrostatic copying device. At the left, a camera makes an enlarged or reduced electrical plate image. Center, a processor prepares the plate. At the right, a fuser uses heat to fix the image on the plate.

Xography provides three-dimensional printing which can be seen without benefit of special reading glasses. This recent development uses a special screen which is placed before the film in process. The screen divides the film into many small vertical "strips." Plates are made in a conventional manner. A special press applies a coating to the printed surface. The screen focuses upon the small "strips" and gives the illusion of depth. Thus far the process is used for advertisements which are specially printed and inserted in magazines.

Electronic Stencil and Offset-Plate Makers. Several devices make stencils and offset plates. Copy is placed on one cylinder of the machine and offset plate for a mimeograph-type stencil on the other, adjustments are made, the device started, and in minutes the plate or stencil is ready for production. See Fig. 1–13.

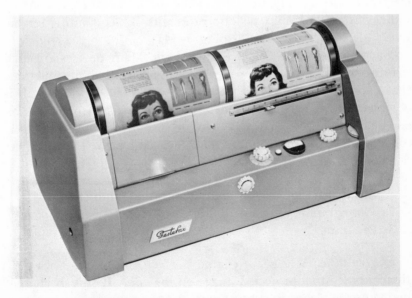

Fig. 1-13. The Gestafax Electronic Stencil and Offset Platemaking Device

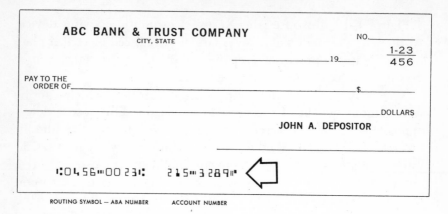

ROUTING SYMBOL — ABA NUMBER   ACCOUNT NUMBER

Fig. 1-14. "Magnetic" Ink Printing, Arrow Points to Printed Numbers

Magnetic Ink Reading Machine Printing. Specially-designed figures printed at the bottoms of bank checks are printed with ink capable of being magnetized and read by electric reading machines for routing the checks to the proper places. Over 14 billion checks are processed annually in the U.S., and *MICR,* as it is called, allows electronic sorting. The printing of the special numbers is done by either offset-lithography or letterpress with ink containing ferrous oxide (derived from iron). See Fig. 1–14.

Office Copiers and Offset Platemakers. Many devices are used in business and industry to make single or multiple copies of letters, charts and the like as well as offset plates for small duplicators. It is obvious that if one copy is needed it is less expensive to make it on one of these devices than to typewrite, proofread and correct the copy. The devices make copies for a few cents each. These devices can be categorized as follows:

1. Electrostatic
2. Photographic
3. Facsimile

4. Diffusion Transfer
5. Dye Transfer
6. Infrared or Thermographic

Electrostatic. A negative charge is given to the plate, which is then exposed to a projected image on the copy. Positively-charged pigments are placed in contact with the paper, and the negatively-charged latent image receives the pigment; heat fixes the image. A re-usable plate is used on the Xerox machine. These devices are automatic in operation. They include Apeco Electro-stat, Copytron, Statimatic, Electricon and Xerox.

Photographic. Special paper masters are exposed automatically to the copy and negative and master are combined in making the plate. They include: Verifax, Itek, and Addressograph-Multigraph.

Facsimile. Entire page proofs of publications are being transferred miles to satellite printing plants by electrical transmission. The original, including type and illustrations, is scanned one elemental area at a time by specific electrical current. The usual device has 96 scanning lines per inch, a rectangular elemental scanning area $1/96$ x $1/138$ inches, and 90 scanning lines per minute.

The current is used at the receiving end to receive the image, or exposed on plate or on film. Land lines, FM radio, microwave and coaxial cable are used. An entire newspaper page can be transferred in about five minutes.

Diffusion Transfer. Copy is exposed on a paper negative which is placed in contact with the offset plate or paper and run together through a developer. This type copier includes: Agfa, Apeco, A. B. Dick, Photorapid and Copycat.

Dye Transfer. This process is similar to diffusion transfer except that a developed gelatin image (silver haloids) plus dye is transferred. Included are: Verifax and Kenro.

Infrared or Thermographic. Plastic coated film or special paper react to infrared heat and the image is developed and exposed at the same time. Thermofax is an example.

SELF-TEST

This self-test will serve as a review of this chapter. The questions are either true or false, or multiple choice. The numbers following each question refer to the page number on which the correct answers can be found.

1. The three major processes in the graphic arts are: (1)

   a. Gravure
   b. Letterpress
   c. Collotype

   d. Offset-lithography
   e. Screen Process
   f. Copperplate engraving

2. The three minor processes in the graphic arts are: (1)

   a. Gravure   d. Offset-lithography

   b. Letterpress   e. Screen Process

   c. Collotype   f. Copperplate engraving

3. Offset lithography was the first process to be discovered. (1)

4. Letterpress printing is done from relief surfaces. (1)

5. The best process to use for the fastest job is offset-lithography. (1)

6. The finest detail in illustrations is secured through the gravure process. (1)

7. Most school textbooks are printed letterpress. (1)

8. Newspapers are usually printed by gravure. (1)

9. Letterpress cannot print halftones as well on rough paper as offset-lithography. (2)

10. Straight type matter jobs are best printed by letterpress. (2)

11. Offset-lithography is an older process than letterpress. (1–3)

12. The first lithography was done from stones. (3)

13. Offset-lithography is done from a smooth, plane surface. (3)

14. Letterpress printed jobs can be rerun by offset-lithography. (5)

15. Vignette illustrations are best run letterpress. (5)

16. For small jobs, offset presses are set up faster than letterpress. (5)

17. Gravure printing is done from etched-out images. (5)

18. Gravure is best suited for very long press runs. (6)

19. The finest detail is possible in gravured illustrations. (6)

20. Type faces in gravure compare very well with letterpress for clarity and design. (6)

21. Copperplate engraving is usually used for social printing. (7)

22. Copperplate engraving is closely allied in process to gravure. (8)

23. Thermography is an imitation gravure process. (8)

24. Screen process is the only one that can lay white paint on a black object. (10)

25. Screen process can print on almost any object, no matter what shape it might have. (10)

26. Screen process is adapted only for short run printing. (10)

27. Collotype illustrations carry a screen like letterpress. (11)

28. Plate making in collotype work is very expensive. (11)

29. What kind of printing process provides the illusion of depth, or three-dimensional printing. (13)

31. The invention of letterpress printing is attributed to: (1)
   a. Alois Senefelder   d. Maso Finiguerra
   b. Johann Gutenberg   e. Samuel Simon
   c. Karl Kleitsch

32. The invention of offset-lithography is attributed to: (3)
   a. Alois Senefelder   d. Maso Finiguerra
   b. Johann Gutenberg   e. Samuel Simon
   c. Karl Kleitsch

33. The invention of gravure is attributed to: (5)
   a. Alois Senefelder   d. Maso Finiguerra
   b. Johann Gutenberg   e. Samuel Simon
   c. Karl Kleitsch

34. Typical examples of letterpress printing include: (1)
   a. Theater displays f. Billboards k. Theater tickets
   b. Daily newspapers g. Billboards l. School books
   c. Paper money h. Wedding invs. m. Picture books
   d. Glass bottles i. Tin cans n. News supplem'ts
   e. Bank checks j. Magazines o. Lamp shades

35. Typical examples of offset-lithography include: (4)
   a. Theater displays f. Postage Stamps k. Theater tickets
   b. Daily newspapers g. Billboards l. School books
   c. Paper money h. Wedding invs. m. Picture books
   d. Glass bottles i. Tin cans n. News supplem'ts
   e. Bank checks j. Magazines o. Lamp shades

36. Typical examples of gravure include: (5)
   a. Theater displays f. Postage stamps k. Theater tickets
   b. Daily newspapers g. Billboards l. School books
   c. Paper money h. Wedding invs. m. Picture books
   d. Glass bottles i. Tin cans n. News supplem'ts
   e. Bank checks j. Magazines o. Lamp shades

37. Typical examples of copperplate engraving include: (8)
    a. Theater displays   f. Postage stamps   k. Theater tickets
    b. Daily newspapers   g. Billboards   l. School books
    c. Paper money   h. Wedding invs.   m. Picture books
    d. Glass bottles   i. Tin cans   n. News supplem'ts
    e. Bank checks   j. Magazines   o. Lamp shades

38. Typical examples of screen process printing include: (9)
    a. Theater displays   f. Postage stamps   k. Theater tickets
    b. Daily newspapers   g. Billboards   l. School books
    c. Paper money   h. Wedding invs.   m. Picture books
    d. Glass bottles   i. Tin cans   n. News supplem'ts
    e. Bank checks   j. Magazines   o. Lamp shades

39. Typical examples of collotype printing include: (11)
    a. Theater displays   f. Postage stamps   k. Theater tickets
    b. Daily newspapers   g. Billboards   l. School books
    c. Paper money   h. Wedding invs.   m. Picture books
    d. Glass bottles   i. Tin cans   n. News supplem'ts
    e. Bank checks   j. Magazines   o. Lamp shades

40. How does Xerography work? (12)
41. Progress in what field made the wrap-around press possible? (3)
42. Screen process presses print on flat surfaces. (10)
43. What allows ink to be magnetized? (14)

CHAPTER 2

How to Know Various Type Faces

The History of the Alphabet

PICTURE WRITING began 5,000 years ago, and gradually developed into symbols which represented words instead of objects. A further development, about 1,500 years later, was the alphabet. One such alphabet was created by the Semites, near Egypt, about the year 1600 B.C. This alphabet, consisting of about 21 letters, each representing a consonant, was adopted by the Phoenicians and Armenians. The Greeks added letters to the Phoenician alphabet, which came to us via the Latin.

There has been but little change in the form of the Latin letters of the alphabet of 2,000 years ago and our present letters, as shown in the square alphabet of the Romans in Fig. 2–1.

MANVSCRIPT

Fig. 2-1. Square Capitals of the Romans

Gradually, by the year 200 A.D., some letters extended below the line, and others above the line. Still others took on a more round form. This new writing was called *uncial*, and is shown in Fig. 2–2.

MANUSCRIPT

Fig. 2-2. Uncial Letter Form

19

Through a slow process of development, the letters of the alphabet took shape in two forms, as practiced by the scribes or writers of books in both northern and southern Europe. In this way two styles of letter designs were born: the *Gothic* of northern Europe (see Fig. 2–3), and the *Humanistic* of southern Europe (see Fig. 2–4). When the first type faces were designed in movable types, they were patterned after either one or the other of these two letter forms.

manuscript

Fig. 2-3. Gothic Letter Form

The First Printing in China

Printing in its earliest form was done from wooden blocks, on which both reading matter and illustrations were carved by hand. The first printed book was the *Diamond Sutra,* printed by Wang Chieh on May 11, 868, in China, in memory of his parents.

There is some reason to believe that the Empress of Japan, in 770 A.D., caused a million impressions to be made from a carved block of wood. The copy was a quotation from Buddhist scripture.

manuscript

Fig. 2-4. Humanistic Letter Form

Wooden blocks were carved in reverse and in relief by hand, "inked" with water color, and paper was placed over the block. A brisk rubbing transferred the ink to the paper or parchment.

The first movable types were made of china by Pi Sheng between the years 1041 and 1049. Although the first movable types were thus invented by the Chinese, their language was not suited to their use, and so the invention died aborning. It is not known that the art of printing found its way to the West from China, or whether printing from blocks and from movable types was discovered later in Europe.

Fig. 2-5. St. Christopher Woodcut

Block Printing in Europe

Block-printed playing cards were found in Europe as early as 1377, when they were so plentiful that even the working men could afford to buy them. The earliest wood-block prints of which we have dated record in Europe pictured the Buxheim St. Christopher (see Fig. 2–5), and were printed in the year 1423. The quality of the prints shows years of experimentation, indicating that block prints were actually made as early as 1400. After movable types came into use in Europe, the block printing practice disappeared because the new invention outmoded its use.

Invention of Movable Type

It is generally accepted that Johann Gansfleisch, who took his mother's name of Gutenberg to keep it alive, was the first European to use movable types. Records of lawsuits show that Gutenberg, with his two partners, Johann Fust and his son-in-law, Peter Schoeffer, were developing the art of printing from movable types in Mainz, Germany, in 1450. It is also accepted that Gutenberg was developing the art as early as 1439. It is not known whether Gutenberg conceived the idea of movable types by himself, or whether he heard of the art as practiced in China.

Fig. 2-6. Ancient Wood-Block Cutter

Although the famous 42-line Bible (see Fig. 2–7) has been largely heralded as the first book printed by Gutenberg, it was probably not his first work. The perfection of its printing was no doubt the result of perhaps ten years of experience in making other works.

The first dated printing work from movable types appeared in 1454. This was an "indulgence" granted by Pope Nicholas V to

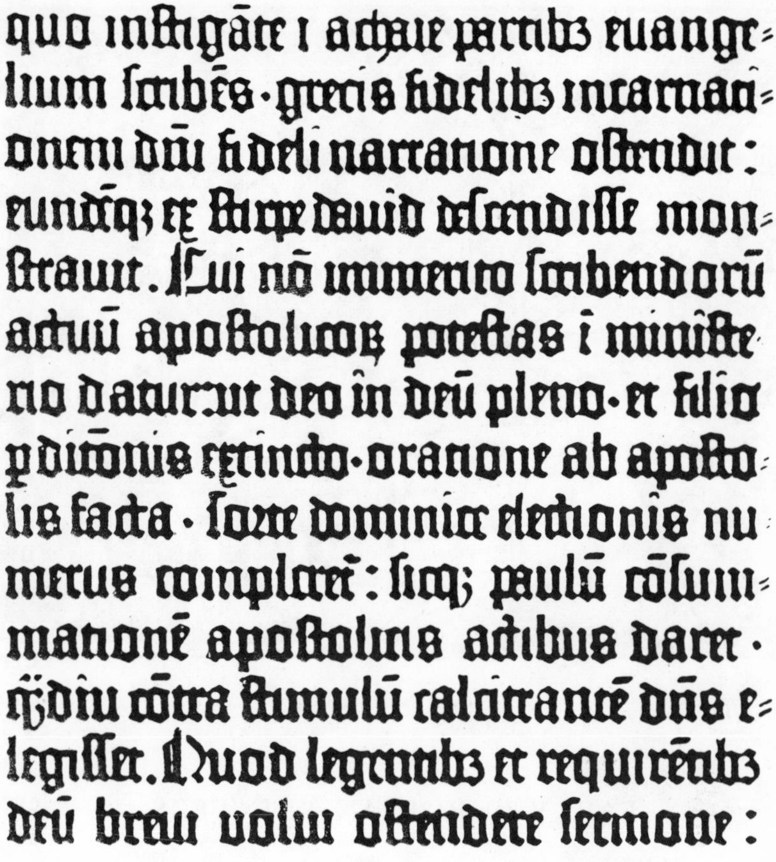

quo inftigate i achate partibz euange=
lium fcnbes · grecis fidelibz incarnad=
onem dui fideli narratione oftendit :
eundiqz et ftirpe dauid defcendiffe mon=
ftrauit . Cui no immerito fcribendorū
actuū apoftolicoz poteftas i minifte·
rio datur:ut deo in deū pleno · et filio
p ditonis returdo · oratione ab apofto·
lis facta · forte dominice electionis nu·
merus complere : ficq; paulū cōfum=
matione apoftolicis actibus dare ·
fjdiu contra ftimulū calcitrance dns e=
legiffet. Quod legentibz et requirētibz
deū breui uolui oftendere fermone :

Fig. 2-7. Section from a Page of the Gutenberg Bible
(A copy can be seen in the Library of Congress at Washington, D.C.)

those who aided in the war with the Turks. The Pope's emissary
went to Mainz to enlist the aid of the printing press to eliminate
the necessity of writing each indulgence by hand. Evidence points
to the fact that Gutenberg was one printer of these indulgences.

Spread of Printing in Europe

The art of printing soon spread to other cities of Germany, and
to other countries of Europe. Historians have listed the following
printers who set up shop in certain cities on the dates noted:

Ancient Printing Shop

EARLY EUROPEAN PRINTERS

DATE	PLACE	PRINTERS
1460	Strasburg, Germany	Johann Mentelin
1464	Strasburg, Germany	Heinrich Eggestein
1465	Subiaco, Italy	Conrad Sweynheym and Arnold Pannartz
1467	Rome, Italy	Ulrich Han
1468	Basel, Switzerland	Berthold Ruppel
1469	Venice, Italy	Johann of Speyer
1470	Venice, Italy	Nicholas Jenson
1470	Paris, France	Michael Friburger and Martin Crantz
1473	Nuremburg, Germany	Anthony Koberger
1473	Utrecht, Netherlands	Gerardus Leempt and Nicholous Ketalaer
1473	Lyons, France	Guillaume Leroy
1494	Venice, Italy	Aldus Manutius
1497	Paris, France	Henri Estienne

First Printing in English

The first book to be printed in the English language was the *Recuyell of the Histories of Troy,* printed at Bruges, in what is now Belgium, about the year 1475. The printer was William Caxton, who was helped by Colard Mansion. Caxton later returned to England, and near Westminster Abbey printed the first book in England, *The Dictes* and *Sayengis of the Philosophers,* in 1477. By the time Caxton printed Chaucer's *Canterbury Tales* in 1478, printing was firmly established in England. Before Caxton died in 1491 he had printed almost 100 different books.

First Printing in America

Nineteen years after the Pilgrims landed in what is now Massachusetts, the Reverend Jose Glover, of Sutton, England, arrived with a printing press. Stephen Daye, of Cambridge, England, and his printer son were employed by Glover. The press was established in Harvard Academy in 1639. The first work of the new press was entitled the *Freeman's Oath.* No copy exists. *The Whole Book of Psalms* appeared in 1640. The title page of this book appears on the next page.

Two attempts were made to publish newspapers in the British American colonies, one in 1689 and the other in 1690. These attempts were suppressed by the government.

Ancient Typecasting

Ancient Presswork

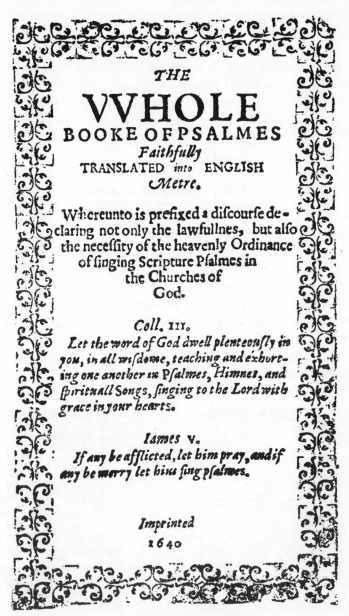

Fig. 2-8. One of the First American Books

The first regularly published newspaper in America was established in Boston in 1704 by John Campbell. The *Boston News-letter* continued publication until 1776, and was printed by Bartholomew Green.

Spread of Printing in America

Printing spread in British North America similarly to the way it prospered in Europe many years before. The following table gives some of the first dates of the establishment of printing presses:

EARLY AMERICAN PRINTERS

DATE	PLACE	PRINTERS
1639	Cambridge, Massachusetts	Stephen Daye
1660	Boston, Massachusetts	Marmaduke Johnson
1685	Philadelphia, Pennsylvania	William Bradford
1693	New York, New York	William Bradford
1717	Boston, Massachusetts	James Franklin
1728	Philadelphia, Pennsylvania	Benjamin Franklin

Present-Day Letter Designs

The approximately 2,000 type faces of today have roots in the type faces of the past. The historical significance of these type faces is brought out on the following pages, which explain the basic type designs now in use in the printing plants of the United States.

Eleven Type-Face Classifications. For the purpose of study, the present-day type faces are divided into eleven classifications (including their italics) based on both their origin and general characteristics:

1. Venetian
2. Oldstyle
3. "Modern"
4. Transitional
5. Sans Serif
6. Square Serif
7. Text or Blackletter ("Old English")
8. Script
9. Twentieth Century
10. Contemporary
11. Newspaper

This classification of eleven type-style designs may coincide in part with other type-face classifications taught in schools of printing and in art schools. Some difference in thought will be noted. It is difficult to get complete agreement on the matter.

Tag
A Venetian Face:
Cloister

Tag
An Oldstyle Face:
Caslon

Tag
An Oldstyle Face:
Garamond

Tag
A "Modern" Face:
Bodoni

Tag
A Transitional Face:
Baskerville

Tag
A Sans Serif Face:
Futura

Tag
A Square Serif Face:
Beton

Tag
A Text Face:
Engravers Old English

Tag
A Script Face:
Coronet

Tag
A Twentieth Century Face:
Bookman

Tag
A Contemporary Face:
Egmont

Tag
A Newspaper Face:
Regal

Fig. 2-9. Typical Examples of the Eleven Type-Face Classifications

Each classification is discussed on the following pages, and a particular type face exemplary of each general classification is shown in the roman, italic, and bold designs, where most are available. In many instances other designs are available in the type "family" group, such as the bold italic, medium and medium italic, extrabold and extrabold italic, etc.

Following a discussion of each type classification, and in addition to a showing of an example of each classification, the names of the most used type faces are listed with the makers. It should be remembered that foundry type faces are American, Amsterdam, Baitimore, Berthold, Stempel, Bauer, Haas, and Klingspor.

Machine-set faces are those of Intertype, Linotype, Monotype, and Ludlow.

Fig. 2–9 presents three distinguishing characters of each classification. All faces except Regal are 24-point design size, but are blown up here to show their distinguishing features. Fig. 2–10 presents type-face parts.

Printing students should learn type-face parts to discuss them intelligently.

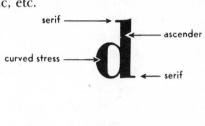

serif — ascender — curved stress — serif

vertical stem — bowl — descender

thin stroke — serif — thick stroke

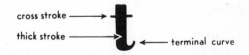

cross stroke — thick stroke — terminal curve

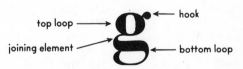

top loop — hook — joining element — bottom loop

Fig. 2-10. Parts of a Type Face

VENETIAN TYPES: ORIGIN OF THE ROMAN TYPE FACE

The Venetian letter design in type faces was established by Nicholas Jenson, a Frenchman, whose work in Venice, Italy, made him the world's first great type designer. Jenson cut the first roman letters, similar to the roman letters cut in stone during the Roman Empire of the first century, and he printed almost 100 books about the year 1470 on theology, medicine, and the classics.

The present Cloister type faces are based on Jenson's designs and were patterned by L. B. Benton in 1914 to compare well with the originals when printed on hard-surfaced papers. In the beginnings of the art of printing, all papers were soft, not hard as book papers are today.

Distinguishing Features. Venetian letters have serifs which are triangular at the top and flat and blunt at the bottom. As exemplified in Cloister Oldstyle, little difference is found in the weight between the hairlines and the main strokes of the letters. On the lowercase g, the lower loop is small, and the hook is blunt and points right. The cross-strokes of the lowercase e are angular rather than horizontal. The lowercase k has no serif on the bottom right. Generally speaking, the face is relatively small for its point size because of its long descenders and high ascenders.

Venetian Group of Letter Designs. The following type faces, both hand and machine-set, are the most popular of the Venetian group:

NAME	MAKE	NAME	MAKE
Benedictine	Linotype	Jenson	Monotype
Benedictine Book	Linotype	Jenson Oldstyle	American
Cloister	Linotype	Italian Oldstyle	Monotype
Cloister Oldstyle	American	Kennerley Oldstyle	Monotype
	Intertype	Kenntonian	Intertype
	Monotype	Medieval	Intertype
Cloister Wide	Linotype	Old Roman	Linotype
Eusebius	Ludlow	Weiss Roman	Bauer
Goudy	Intertype		Intertype
	Monotype		

CLOISTER OLDSTYLE: A VENETIAN TYPE FACE

ABCDEFGHIJKLMNOPQR
STUVWXYZ
abcdefghijklmnopqrstuvwxyz

CLOISTER OLDSTYLE

ABCDEFGHIJKLMNOPQR
STUVWXYZ
abcdefghijklmnopqrstuvwxyz

CLOISTER OLDSTYLE ITALIC

ABCDEFGHIJKLMNOPQRSTU
VWXYZ
abcdefghijklmnopqrstuvwxyz

CLOISTER OLDSTYLE BOLD

OLDSTYLE TYPES

The term *oldstyle* refers to two primary type faces, Caslon and Garamond, and also many others designed later which bear similar characteristics. William Caslon designed the types, which now bear his name, in England about 1722. He modeled his type faces

CASLON: AN OLDSTYLE TYPE FACE

ABCDEFGHIJKLMNOP
QRSTUVWXYZ
abcdefghijklmnopqrst
uvwxyz

CASLON

ABCDEFGHIJKLMNOP
QRSTUVWXYZ
abcdefghijklmnopqrst
uvwxyz

CASLON ITALIC

ABCDEFGHIJKLMNOP
QRSTUVWXYZ
abcdefghijklmnopqrst
uvwxyz

CASLON BOLD ITALIC

after Dutch types then in vogue, and greatly improved them. Caslon has been a popular type face in this country since early historical days. The Declaration of Independence was first set in this type-face design. Caslon type was first imported, and then manufactured in this country in 1857. It was called oldstyle until renamed Caslon by Henry Lewis Bullen. In its various sizes and weights, there are 26 members of the type family. Through the years, Caslon has been up and down in popularity. It was practically eclipsed for five decades until its revival in 1814.

Distinguishing Features of Caslon. Caslon looks better in mass than when examined letter by letter. It has pleasing weight. It is readable because the letters are open, round, and wide. The lowercase e features a wide-open eye. The lowercase g has a narrow-bottomed loop, and its hook has a right-pointing ball. The cross-stroke of the lowercase f is shorter at the left than at the right. Caslon is more sturdy than its sister oldstyle, Garamond, and appears best when printed on rough-finished paper.

English Oldstyle Group of Letter Designs.

NAME	MAKE	NAME	MAKE
American Caslon	Monotype	Hess Oldstyle	Monotype
Binny Oldstyle	Monotype	Italian Oldstyle	Monotype
Bruce Oldstyle	Monotype	Janson	Linotype
Caslon	Intertype		Monotype
	Linotype	Jenson	Monotype
	Monotype	Jenson Oldstyle No. 2	American
Caslon Light	Ludlow	New Caslon	American
Caslon No. 2	Linotype		Monotype
Caslon No. 3	Intertype	Oldstyle No. 1	Intertype
	Linotype		Linotype
Caslon No. 137	Linotype	Oldstyle No. 3	Linotype
Caslon No. 540	American	Oldstyle No. 7	Intertype
Caslon Oldface	Intertype		Linotype
	Linotype	Oldstyle No. 9	Intertype
Caslon Oldstyle	Monotype	Original Oldstyle	Linotype
Caslon Oldstyle No. 471	American	Recut Caslon	American
Caslon Oldstyle No. 472	American	Ronaldson Oldstyle	Monotype
Century Catalog	American	Schoolbook Oldstyle	American
Century Oldstyle	American	True-Cut Caslon	Ludlow
Farmers Oldstyle	Monotype		

FRENCH OLDSTYLE TYPES

Garamond is the French oldstyle letter design, and is a contrast to Caslon, the English oldstyle. It was designed by Jean Jannon about 1530. It is said that Jannon redesigned Claude Garamond's original type face, and was also probably influenced by Geoffry Tory and Nicholas Jenson. This is why the type face carried the name of Garamond. Garamond has more grace than its sister oldstyle, Caslon. It has more delicate shading than Caslon. The serifs are spur-like, and carry a decided French feeling of design.

Distinguishing Features of Garamond. The capital letters of Garamond feature long and pointed serifs. The cap A has a rather high cross-stroke, and the lower angle of the cap N extends well below the usual alignment of the other characters. Spurred serifs form the bottoms of certain lowercase letters: f, h, i, l, m, n, p, q, and r. Oddly, spearheaded serifs top the lowercase letters i, j, m, n, p, and q. The lowercase g has a large lower loop and a long, straight hook that points to the right. The lowercase j has no ball, but points to the left at the bottom and is quite pointed. The loop of the lowercase e is generally small and tight, as is the upper portion of the cap A.

French Oldstyle Group of Letter Designs.

NAME	MAKE	NAME	MAKE
American Garamond . .	Monotype	Garamond No. 2 . .	Linotype
Garamond	American	Garamond No. 3 . .	Intertype
	Intertype		Linotype
	Linotype	Garamont	Monotype
	Ludlow	Granjon	Linotype

GARAMOND: AN OLDSTYLE TYPE FACE

ABCDEFGHIJKLMNOPQRST
UVWXYZ
abcdefghijklmnopqrstuvwxyz

GARAMOND

ABCDEFGHIJKLMNOPQRST
UVWXYZ
abcdefghijklmnopqrstuvwxyz

GARAMOND ITALIC

ABCDEFGHIJKLMNOPQRS
TUVWXYZ
abcdefghijklmnopqrstuvwxyz

GARAMOND BOLD

ABCDEFGHIJKLMNOPQR
STUVWXYZ
abcdefghijklmnopqrstuvwxyz

GARAMOND BOLD ITALIC

MODERN TYPES

The term *modern* when designating a style of type-face design refers not to time, but to a particular design originated by Giambattista Bodoni, in 1789, in Parma, Italy. For this type design he is known as the "father of the modern type face." There is some indication that Bodoni was influenced by Pierre Simon Fournier, the French type founder. Bodoni types were introduced into this country about the year 1912. A sister face to Bodoni is Bodoni Book, which has the same general characteristics, but is thinner of body.

Distinguishing Features of Bodoni. The most pronounced feature of Bodoni is the extreme contrast between the very thin hairlines and the thick stems, which give a "sunlight and shadow" effect to the type face. The serifs are not bracketed, but are straight and thin. Bodoni has very long ascenders and descenders. The ball hook on the distinguishing lowercase g has a flat right side, and the lower loop is large.

"Modern" Group of Letter Designs.

NAME	MAKE	NAME	MAKE
Bodoni		Bodoni Campanile . . .	Ludlow
Bodoni Italic		Bodoni Light	Ludlow
Bodoni Bold	American	Bodoni Modern	Intertype
	Intertype		Ludlow
	Linotype	Modern	Monotype
	Ludlow	Modern Roman	American
	Monotype	Nubian	American
Bodoni Black	.Ludlow	Onyx	American
Bodoni Book	American		Monotype
Bodoni Book Italic . .	Intertype	Palisade	Intertype
	Linotype	Poster Bodoni	Linotype
	Monotype	Ultra Bodoni	American
Bodoni Black	Ludlow		Monotype

BODONI: A "MODERN" TYPE FACE

ABCDEFGHIJKLMNOPQRSTU
VWXYZ
abcdefghijklmnopqrstuvwxyz

BODONI BOOK

*ABCDEFGHIJKLMNOPQRSTU
VWXYZ
abcdefghijklmnopqrstuvwxyz*

BODONI BOOK ITALIC

ABCDEFGHIJKLMNOPQRSTU
VWXYZ
abcdefghijklmnopqrstuvwxyz

BODONI

*ABCDEFGHIJKLMNOPQRST
UVWXYZ
abcdefghijklmnopqrstuvwxyz*

BODONI ITALIC

ABCDEFGHIJKLMNOPQRSTU
VWXYZ
abcdefghijklmnopqrstuvwxyz

BODONI BOLD

TRANSITIONAL TYPES

Around 1752 an Englishman named John Baskerville deliberately set out to improve William Caslon's type face after it had been in use about 25 years. Whether he did or not is debatable, but the fact remains that Baskerville did develop a new type face for that day which is now termed a *transitional* type. Baskerville remodeled Caslon by increasing the contrast between the hairlines and the main strokes, increasing the width of the letters, and making the letters more open. Baskerville might be named the father of smooth paper, because he was the first to print *on* the surface, rather than *into* the paper, as was the custom in his day. To do this, Baskerville made a smooth paper stock surface, which is now termed "calendered."

Distinguishing Features of Baskerville. The most distinguishing characteristic of Baskerville's type face is the open bottom loop of the lowercase g. The cross-stroke of the lowercase t is beveled at the left, but extends to the right without the bevel. The thin ball hook of the lowercase g has a downward trend. The serifs have rounded curves, and are relatively long. The cap E has perpendicular vertical serifs. On letters like the cap B and L, the vertical strokes are curved slightly where they are joined to the base of the letter. This book is composed in Linotype Baskerville, in the 11 point size.

Transitional Group of Letter Designs.

NAME	MAKE	NAME	MAKE
Baskerville		Bell	Monotype
Baskerville Bold		Benton	American
Baskerville Bold Italic	American	Bulmer Roman	American
	Intertype	Scotch	Intertype
	Linotype		Linotype
	Monotype	Scotch No. 2	Linotype
Baskerville Roman . .	American	Scotch Roman	American
			Monotype

BASKERVILLE: A TRANSITIONAL TYPE FACE

ABCDEFGHIJKLMNOPQRST
UVWXYZ
abcdefghijklmnopqrstuvwxyz

BASKERVILLE

*ABCDEFGHIJKLMNOPQRST
UVWXYZ
abcdefghijklmnopqrstuvwxyz*

BASKERVILLE ITALIC

**ABCDEFGHIJKLMNOPQRST
UVWXYZ
abcdefghijklmnopqrstuvwxyz**

BASKERVILLE BOLD

***ABCDEFGHIJKLMNOPQRST
UVWXYZ
abcdefghijklmnopqrstuvwxyz***

BASKERVILLE BOLD ITALIC

SANS SERIF TYPES

The French word *sans* means *without*. Hence the term sans serif means without serifs, which explains the type-face design. Present-day sans serifs are either *monotone* or they have thick-and-thin strokes. Monotone sans serif type faces have hairlines and thick strokes of the same weight, or thickness.

Futura, a distinguished member of the sans serif group of type faces was designed by Paul Renner, of Germany, in 1927. Futura is made in hand-set by Bauer, and machine-set by Intertype. Because the curved strokes of Futura vary in thickness as they join the stem of the letter, Futura is not a monotone sans serif type face.

Patterned after Futura, but in a monotone design, is the popular sans serif called Vogue, shown on the opposite page.

Distinguishing Features of Vogue. To distinguish Vogue from other sans serif type faces, look for the following features on the lowercase g: a flat curve on the tail, a main stem which extends above the upper loop, and a round upper loop. Another distinguishing character is the straight stem on the lowercase j, and an upper hooked stem on the lowercase f. See page 43 for a chart showing the different modern sans serif type faces.

Sans Serif Group of Letter Designs.

NAME	MAKE	NAME	MAKE
Airport	Baltimore	Metro	Linotype
Bernhard Fashion	American Intertype	Phenix	American
		Radiant	Ludlow
Bernhard Gothic	American	Sans Serif	Monotype
Erbar	Linotype	Spartan	American Linotype
Futura	Bauer Intertype	Stellar	Ludlow
Huxley Vertical	American	Tempo	Ludlow
Kabel	Continental	Twentieth Century	Monotype
Lydian	American	Vogue	Intertype

VOGUE: A SANS SERIF TYPE FACE

ABCDEFGHIJKLMNOPQRSTUV
WXYZ
abcdefghijklmnopqrstuvwxyz

VOGUE

ABCDEFGHIJKLMNOPQRST
UVWXYZ
abcdefghijklmnopqrstuvwxyz

VOGUE ITALIC

ABCDEFGHIJKLMNOPQRSTUV
WXYZ
abcdefghijklmnopqrstuvwxyz

VOGUE BOLD

ABCDEFGHIJKLMNOPQ
RSTUVWXYZ
abcdefghijklmnopqrstuvwxyz

VOGUE EXTRABOLD

The Misnomer of the Name "Gothic." An error which has persisted for years is the term "gothic" when applied to certain old-time sans serif type faces. Gothic should be applied to blackletter or text to be accurate. One such face, misnamed *Gothic No. 16,* appears below:

ABCDEFGHIJKLMNOPQRST UVWXYZ
abcdefghijklmnopqrstuvwxyz

Misnamed Gothic Group of Letter Designs.

NAME	MAKE	NAME	MAKE
Agency Gothic	American	Numbered Gothics* . .	American
Alternate Gothic . . .	American		Intertype
	Intertype		Linotype
Bank Gothic	American		Monotype
Copperplate Gothic . .	American	Lining Plate Gothic . .	Ludlow
	Monotype	News Gothic	American
DeLuxe Gothic	Intertype	Railroad Gothic	American
Franklin Gothic . . .	American		
	Linotype		
	Intertype		
	Monotype		

* Many numbers run from 3 to 578, but not inclusive. About 30 such faces exist.

MODERN SANS SERIF TYPE FACES

Type Face	Thin	Light	Med.	Demi-Bold	Bold	Extra Bold	Black	Heavy	Extra Heavy	Ultra Bold	In-line	Light Cond.	Med. Cond.	Bold Cond.	Black Cond.	Heavy Cond.	Extra Bold Cond.
BERNHARD GOTHIC American	E[1]	E	E									E[9]	E				
FUTURA Bauer		E	E[3]E	E	E		E	E	E[7]	E[8]	E		E	E			E
FUTURA Intertype		E	E[3]E	E	E								E	E			
KABEL Continental	E[2]	E		E	E		E				E[5]						
METRO Linotype		E	E				E	E				E[10]	E[11]	E[12]			E
SANS SERIF Monotype		E	E			E					E[6]	E	E				
SPARTAN American			E				E	E					E				
SPARTAN Linotype		E	E				E	E					E		E		
TEMPO Ludlow	E[13]	E	E		E			E		E	E		E	E		E	
TWENTIETH CENTURY Monotype		E	E		E	E							E				E
VOGUE Intertype		E			E	E						E	E	E			E

1. Fashion 2. Thin 3. Book 5. Zeppelin 6. Lined 7. Display 8. Othello
9. Huxley Vertical 10. Erbar 11. Erbar 12. Erbar 13. Stellar

SQUARE SERIF TYPES

The modern square serif type faces became popular shortly after Heinrich Jost, of Germany, designed Beton in 1931. Jost's square serif type face is a modernistic one, although certain oldstyle features can be found in it. Distinguishing features of Beton are the one-sided serif atop the cap A, the double serif on the lowercase t, the pointed serifs on the cap E, and the curved tail of the cap K. Beton is a thick-and-thin square serif design.

Cairo is a square serif type face designed from the Beton of Jost. It features the same masonry-like and hammered effect of all of the popular square serif type faces in use today. Unlike Beton, and much like other square serifs, Cairo is a monotone face. Cairo is illustrated on the opposite page.

Distinguishing Features of Cairo. Cairo is a pure geometrical design, therefore readable and legible. The round caps and lowercase of Cairo are true circles. The lowercase t has a serif only at the right, at the bottom of the stem. The lowercase r features a right stroke that bends downward. The cap A has a double-topped serif, unlike the A of Beton.

Square Serif Group of Letter Designs.

NAME	MAKE	NAME	MAKE
Beton	Bauer	Obelisk	Ludlow
	Intertype	Slimline	Monotype
Cairo	Intertype	Square Face	Monotype
Karnak	Ludlow	Stymie	American
Memphis	Linotype		Monotype
		Tower	American

A comparison of the many popular square type faces now in use can be studied on the chart on page 46.

CAIRO: A SQUARE SERIF TYPE FACE

ABCDEFGHIJKLMNOPQRST
UVWXYZ
abcdefghijklmnopqrstuvwxyz

CAIRO

ABCDEFGHIJKLMNOPQRS
TUVWXYZ
abcdefghijklmnopqrst
uvwxyz

CAIRO ITALIC

ABCDEFGHIJKLMNO
PQRSTUVWXYZ
abcdefghijklmnopqrst
uvwxy

CAIRO BOLD

MODERN SQUARE SERIF TYPE FACES

Name of Type Face	Light	Inter-mediate	Medium	Wide	Bold	Extra Bold	Black	Heavy	Open	Light Cond.	Medium Cond.	Bold Cond.	Black Cond.	Extra Bold Cond.
BETON Bauer	E		E		E	E			E		E	E		
BETON Intertype		E	E	E	E	E								
CAIRO Intertype	E		E		E			E			E	E		E
KARNAK Ludlow	E	E	E				E				E¹		E	
GIRDER Continental	E		E					E						
MEMPHIS Linotype	E		E		E	E	E				E	E		E
STYMIE American	E		E		E	E	E				E²	E		
STYMIE Monotype	E		E		E	E	E³			E⁴	E	E		E

1. Obelisk   2. Tower   3. Squareface   4. Slimline

TEXT OR BLACKLETTER TYPES

Blackletter and text are names denoting a type face modeled and designed on the old original types of the gothic period. They resemble the original types of Gutenberg, shown below:

quo inſtigāte i adue partibʒ euangelium ſaibēs · gretis fidelibʒ incarnationem dūi fideli narratione oſtendit :

This type face is called *gothic* by bibliographers. It is called *text* also because it was the first type face used for the body matter, or text, of books printed in ancient times. Another name given to the face is *Old English*. The more modern version is reproduced below, named *Engravers Old English*.

ABCDEFGHIJKLMNOPQR STUVWXYZ

abcdefghijklmnopqrstuvwxyz

Text or Blackletter Group of Letter Designs.

NAME	MAKE	NAME	MAKE
American Text	American	Lino Text	Linotype
Cloister Black	American Monotype	Old English	Ludlow
		Shaw Text	American
Engravers Old English	American Intertype	Typo Text Shaded	American
		Waldorf Text	American
Goudy Text	Monotype	Wedding Text	American Monotype

SCRIPT TYPES

Script is a term denoting a style of type designed in imitation of handwriting or hand-lettering. These types have good display value, and are currently popular in advertisements as well as in all kinds of commercial printing.

Present-day script faces are enumerated here as either *joining* or *nonjoining* for the purposes of study. The joining scripts, in hand-set types, are fully "kerned"; that is, part of the face extends over the side of the body. These types are therefore quite fragile, and care must be taken in their use, especially when "planing down" the types on the imposing table preparatory to presswork. The machine-set faces are, of course, more sturdy, because they are cast on a line, and serifs are a part of the body of the slug-line.

Long press runs of hand-set full-kerning scripts are often either electrotyped (duplicated), or photoengraving plates are made from the proof of types to keep them from becoming worn out on the press.

Joining Script Group of Letter Designs.

NAME	MAKE	NAME	MAKE
Adonis	American Intertype	Interscript	Intertype
Ariston	Berthold	Kaufmann Bold . . .	American
Bank Script	American	Kaufmann Script . .	American
Bernhard Brushscript . .	Bauer	Mandate	Ludlow
Britannic	Baltimore	Royal Script	American
Broadstroke	Monotype	Signal	Berthold
Brush	American	Stylus	Monotype
Commercial Script . . .	American	Swing Bold	Monotype
Mistral	Amsterdam	Typo Script	American
Embassy	Fotosetter	Typo Script Extended	American
		Typo Upright	American

Nonjoining Script Group of Letter Designs.

NAME	MAKE	NAME	MAKE
Artscript	Monotype	Lydian Cursive	American
Civilite	American	Linoscript	Linotype
Coronet	Ludlow	Park Avenue	American
Coronet Bold	Ludlow	Palette	Berthold
Flash	Monotype	Phyllis	Bauer
Rondo	American	Piranesi Italic	American
Gillies Gothic	Bauer	Raleigh Cursive	American
Grayda	American	Romany	American
Hauser Script	Ludlow	Stationers Semiscript	American
Keynote	American	Stylescript	Monotype
Legend	Bauer	Trafton Script	Bauer
Liberty	American		

ABCDEFGHIJKLMNOPQR
STUVWXYZ
abcdefghijklmnopqrstuvwxyz

LUDLOW CORONET

ABCDEFGHIJKLMNOPQR
STUVWXYZ
abcdefghijklmnopqrstuvwxyz

AMERICAN GRAYDA

TWENTIETH CENTURY TYPES

The beginning of the twentieth century saw now type faces to replace the old faces which had been in use for generations. A type face known as Oldstyle Antique was redesigned by A. C. Phemister, a Scotchman. After this type face reached the United States about 1912, it was again redesigned, and named Bookman.

Distinguishing Features of Bookman. Bookman is a rugged, businesslike type face having strong lines. Its ascenders and descenders are short, which makes the body larger, and therefore quite readable. The lowercase g has a down-slant on the lower loop, and its teardrop hook points right. Bookman is a good bookface type, especially for children's books. It is still a popular type face. See the opposite page.

Cheltenham, designed by Bertram G. Goodhue in 1902, was the most used American type in its 30 versions. It is easily distinguished by its tall ascenders and short descenders, and the open loop of the lowercase g with its peculiar joining element. Its serifs are thick and short.

Twentieth Century Group of Letter Designs.

NAME	MAKE	NAME	MAKE
Antique	Intertype Linotype	Century Oldstyle . . .	American Monotype
Bookface	Intertype	Century Schoolbook . .	American Monotype
Bookman	Linotype Monotype Ludlow	Cheltenham	American Linotype Ludlow Monotype
New Bookman	Monotype		
Bookman Oldstyle . . .	American		
Century Expanded . . .	American Intertype Linotype Ludlow Monotype	Cheltonian . . . . . Cooper . . . . Clarendon . . . . . . Craw Clarendon . . . DeVinne	Intertype American American American Intertype

ABCDEFGHIJKLMNOP
QRSTUVWXYZ
abcdefghijklmnopqrst
uvwxyz

BOOKMAN

ABCDEFGHIJKLMNOPQRST
UVWXYZ
abcdefghijklmnopqrstuvwxyz

CHELTENHAM

ABCDEFGHIJKLMNOPQR
STUVWXYZ
abcdefghijklmnopqrstuvwxyz

CENTURY EXPANDED

ABCDEFGHIJKLMNOP
QRSTUVWXYZ
abcdefghijklmnopqrstuv
wxyz

CRAW CLARENDON

CONTEMPORARY TYPES

Since the 1930's matrix manufacturers have brought out interesting book type faces. Eight of these are illustrated on the opposite page. In this study of type we will call these *contemporary types*.

Waverley was designed by Intertype Corporation in 1941. It has sharp, contrasting hairlines, thickened strokes, bracketed serifs, and a large lowercase. It is reminiscent of the Scotch face.

Weiss Roman, designed by Emil Rudolf Weiss, was issued in 1931 by Bauer and somewhat later by Intertype. It reflects modernism, but holds its own with the traditional types. It can be distinguished by its reversed cap S.

Egmont, an Amsterdam and Intertype face, was designed in 1936 by S. H. deRoos. It is distinguished by tall ascenders and short descenders, and variations between light and heavy strokes.

Electra was designed by W. A. Dwiggins in 1937 for Linotype. It is an original modern body type face, and lacks sharp contrast between the thick and thin strokes.

Fairfield, the work of Rudolf Ruzicka, was designed for Linotype in 1939. It has straight-cut serifs. Fairfield is narrow, with long ascenders and descenders.

Caledonia is the work of W. A. Dwiggins, who made it in 1939 for Linotype. This type has good weight that makes for readability, and has a Scotch type flavor. The lowercase height is large.

Deepdene is a Frederic W. Goudy face, made for Monotype in 1934. It has very long ascenders and descenders, and a good, warm color.

Contemporary Group of Letter Designs.

NAME	MAKE	NAME	MAKE
Caledonia	Linotype	Electra	Linotype
Centaur	Monotype	Fairfield	Linotype
Cochin, Nicolas	American	Primer	Linotype
Cochin	Monotype	Times Roman	Linotype
Deepdene	Monotype		Monotype
Emerson	Monotype	Waverley	Intertype
Egmont	Bauer	Weiss Roman	Bauer
	Intertype		Intertype

A FEW CONTEMPORARY TYPES

Waverley
ABCDEFGHIJKLMNOPQRSTUVWXYZ
ABCDEFGHIJKLMNOPQRSTUVWXYZ
abcdefghijklmnopqrstuvwxyz
abcdefghijklmnopqrstuvwxyz

Weiss Roman
ABCDEFGHIJKLMNOPQRSTUVWXYZ
ABCDEFGHIJKLMNOPQRSTUVWXYZ
abcdefghijklmnopqrstuvwxyz
abcdefghijklmnopqrstuvwxyz

Egmont
ABCDEFGHIJKLMNOPQRSTUVWXYZ
ABCDEFGHIJKLMNOPQRSTUVWXYZ
abcdefghijklmnopqrstuvwxyz
abcdefghijklmnopqrstuvwxyz

Electra
ABCDEFGHIJKLMNOPQRSTUVWXYZ
ABCDEFGHIJKLMNOPQRSTUVWXYZ
abcdefghijklmnopqrstuvwxyz
abcdefghijklmnopqrstuvwxyz

Fairfield
ABCDEFGHIJKLMNOPQRSTUVWXYZ
ABCDEFGHIJKLMNOPQRSTUVWXYZ
abcdefghijklmnopqrstuvwxyz
abcdefghijklmnopqrstuvwxyz

Caledonia
ABCDEFGHIJKLMNOPQRSTUVWXYZ
ABCDEFGHIJKLMNOPQRSTUVWXYZ
abcdefghijklmnopqrstuvwxyz
abcdefghijklmnopqrstuvwxyz

Primer
ABCDEFGHIJKLMNOPQRSTUVWXYZ
ABCDEFGHIJKLMNOPQRSTUVWXYZ
abcdefghijklmnopqrstuvwxyz
abcdefghijklmnopqrstuvwxyz

Times Roman
ABCDEFGHIJKLMNOPQRSTUVWXYZ
ABCDEFGHIJKLMNOPQRSTUVWXYZ
abcdefghijklmnopqrstuvwxyz
abcdefghijklmnopqrstuvwxyz

NEWSPAPER TYPES

The designing of newspaper type faces for regular column reading is different from designing types for general use in other fields of printing. Legibility and readability are the foremost considerations in small sizes of type. Because newspaper type faces are seldom made over the 14-point size, no consideration need be made of how such a face would look in the larger sizes.

Newspaper types are generally stereotyped; that is, a duplicate plate is made from type slugs assembled in pages. Some detail of a type face is lost in this process. Because newspapers are printed on the roughest kind of paper, called newsprint, and with a cheap grade of ink, the body type used must be designed with care.

A good newspaper type face used for column matter must have a good color in mass, and have an abundance of white space not only between the letters and lines, but also within the letters themselves. The bowls or loops, found on lowercase letters like e, b, d, p, and q must be open so they will not fill with ink.

Particular attention must also be paid to the design of letters which might be confused with one another. The lowercase c must never be taken for an e, or an a for an s.

To make the body types of newspapers more readable, the *x-height,* or the normal height of the lowercase letters without consideration for the ascenders and descenders, must be large. This is accomplished by making the ascenders and descenders shorter than the usual types.

Several popular newspaper type faces are shown on the opposite page. Note their particular design to suit their purpose.

Newspaper Group of Letter Designs.

NAME	MAKE	NAME	MAKE
Corona	Linotype	Opticon	Linotype
Excelsior	Linotype	Paragon	Linotype
Ideal	Intertype	Rex	Intertype
Imperial	Intertype	Regal	Intertype
Ionic	Monotype	Textype	Linotype
Ionic No. 5	Linotype		

A FEW NEWSPAPER TYPES

Ideal

ABCDEFGHIJKLMNOPQRSTUVWXYZ
ABCDEFGHIJKLMNOPQRSTUVWXYZ
acdefghijklmnopqrstuvwxyz
acdefghijklmnopqrstuvwxyz

Regal

ABCDEFGHIJKLMNOPQRSTUVWXYZ
ABCDEFGHIJKLMNOPQRSTUVWXYZ
abcdefghijklmnopqrstuvwxyz
abcdefghijklmnopqrstuvwxyz

Rex

ABCDEFGHIJKLMNOPQRSTUVWXYZ
ABCDEFGHIJKLMNOPQRSTUVWXYZ
abcdefghijklmnopqrstuvwxyz
abcdefghijklmnopqrstuvwxyz

Textype

ABCDEFGHIJKLMNOPQRSTUVWXYZ
ABCDEFGHIJKLMNOPQRSTUVWXYZ
abcdefghijklmnopqrstuvwxyz
abcdefghijklmnopqrstuvwxyz

Corona

ABCDEFGHIJKLMNOPQRSTUVWXYZ
ABCDEFGHIJKLMNOPQRSTUVWXYZ
abcdefghijklmnopqrstuvwxyz
abcdefghijklmnopqrstuvwxyz

Opticon

ABCDEFGHIJKLMNOPQRSTUVWXYZ
ABCDEFGHIJKLMNOPQRSTUVWXYZ
abcdefghijklmnopqrstuvwxyz
abcdefghijklmnopqrstuvwxyz

Imperial

ABCDEFGHIJKLMNOPQRSTUVWXYZ
ABCDEFGHIJKLMNOPQRSTUVWXYZ
abcdefghijklmnopqrstuvwxyz
abcdefghijklmnopqrstuvwxyz

How to Recognize Type Faces

To most people type faces look very much alike, especially the faces in the smaller sizes. But type faces are not alike; they just seem to be! Few, if any, persons who have spent the greater part of their lives working with type faces know *all* of them by sight. Many type faces are quite similar in many respects, and even the experts must study them closely to differentiate between them. However, it is common practice to identify type faces from the over-all visual impression they make; you proceed then to check their distinguishing details.

The Lowercase g as a Distinguishing Character. To help in distinguishing between types faces—body type faces in particular—the lowercase g is one of the most distinctive characters to examine. Fig. 2-11 presents five letter g's, blown up in size so that the characteristics of each can be examined. Note how they differ!

Caslon　　　Bodoni　　　Cheltenham　　　Granjon　　　Cloister

Fig. 2-11. Differences Found in the Design of the Lowercase g

Fig. 2–12 shows how the lowercase letter g can be broken down into its elements to help in distinguishing one type face from another. These elements are (1) the size and shape of the top loop, (2) the position and shape of the hook, (3) the angle of the joining element between the top and bottom loop, and (4) the size and shape of the bottom loop. The charts on the following pages will help to name the various type faces.

Top Loop—size and shape　　*Hook*—position and shape

Angle of joining element　　*Bottom loop*—size and shape

Fig. 2-12. Characteristics of the Lowercase g

How to Use the Body Type Recognition Charts. To find the correct name of a body type face, examine it under a good magnifying glass:

1. Find a lowercase g.
2. Note the position and shape of the hook (see Fig. 2–12).
3. Find the letter g on the chart which matches it.
4. Look for other characteristics of the lowercase g: the size and shape of the lowercase g loops; the joining elements.
5. If the type face being examined is closely related to more than one on the chart by comparison of the letter g, find other letters shown on the charts, and compare them, also.
6. Note the lightness or boldness of the letter.

Design as a Factor in Type Size. The size of type, expressed in points, means little without reference to the *design* of the type. Figure 2–13 illustrates the factors in sizes of type faces. The type faces represented are all of the *same point size*. Because of their peculiarities of design, some seem *larger* than others. When determining the readability of type faces, consideration must be given to the face weight, width of characters, and height of lowercase.

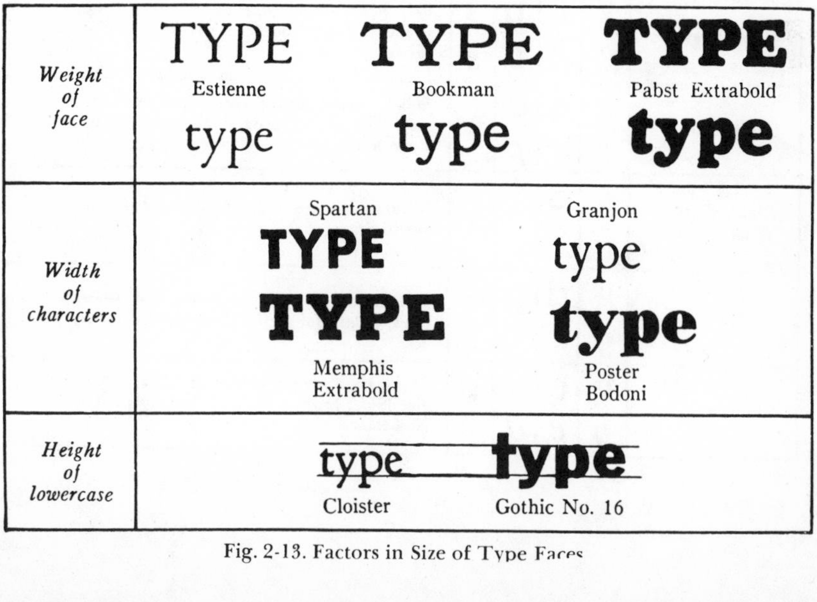

Weight of face	TYPE Estienne type	TYPE Bookman type	**TYPE** Pabst Extrabold **type**
Width of characters	Spartan **TYPE** **TYPE** Memphis Extrabold		Granjon type **type** Poster Bodoni
Height of lowercase	type Cloister	**type** Gothic No. 16	

Fig. 2-13. Factors in Size of Type Faces

Type name	Recognition Characters				Distinguishing features of g and other letters
Bodoni	g g	d d	p p	s s	Ball hook fat at right; large lower loop; straight serifs.
Bodoni Book	g g	d d	p p	s s	Ball hook round at right; large lower loop; straight serifs.
Century Expanded	g g	j j	p p	r r	Large ball hook points down; large upper loop; j fish-hooks with ball at bottom; ball on r.
Benedictine	g g	e e	i p	b b	Tapering hook points upward; large top loop; e has slanting cross stroke; i has diamond dot.
Benedictine Book	g g	e e	i p	b b	Thin hook points upward; large top loop; differentiate from Benedictine by lighter face.
Bookman	g g	b b	p p	s s	Teardrop hook points right; down slant of lower loop; note blackness of face.
Elzevir #3	g g	b b	p p	s s	Small ball hook points upward; large lower loop; note extreme lightness of face.
Caledonia	g g	b b	p p	s s	Ball hook points up; open lower loop; space between loops; p has long bottom serifs.
Cheltenham	g g	q q	d p		Short, round knob; open bottom loop; serif left of q; serifs thick, short; p has open loop.
Cheltenham Wide	g	q			Differentiate from Cheltenham by character width.
Ionic #5	g g	d d	p p	s s	Elongated knob points down; flat lower loop; blunt, flat serifs; s has vertical serifs.
DeVinne	g g	c c	d d	p p	Thick knob points down; thin bottom on flat lower loop; c features ball; serifs long and thin.

Type name	Recognition Characters				Distinguishing features of g and other letters
Scotch	g g	t t	k k	p v	Medium knob points down; wide bottom loop; t has straight cross; v has 7-shaped stroke.
Scotch #2	g g	t t	k k	p v	Differentiate from Scotch by width and lighter hook.
Textype	g g	f f	b b	p p	Right of knob cut off; f has straight cross mark and has knobbed top.
Excelsior	g g	f f	b b	p p	Right of knob cut at angle; right side of cross mark extends right of balled f.
Baskerville	g g	a a	t t	d d	Thin ball points down; slight opening of loop; cross on t to right, beveled at left.
Jenson	g g	a a	t t	d d	Thick ball droops; lopsided lower loop; a has small loop.
Estienne	g g	j j	k k	y y	Straight hook extends to right; left angle; j has slight left curve; g has short right hook.
Fairfield	g g	j j	k k	y y	Very thin short hook; open upper loop; j hooks to left; j thins before ending.
Electra	g g	j j	k k	y y	Straight hook has uptrend; open between loops; j has sharp end, turns left; k has no serif right.
Garamond	g g	j j	k k	y y	Straight long hook points right, bottom loop large; bottom of j sharpens to left.
Garamond #3	g g	j j	k k	y y	Short, thin hook points right; close loops; j has blunted left turn.
Granjon	g g	e e	j j	k k	Straight hook thick on end, points right; wide lower loop; e has very small upper loop; k has long sweep.

Type name	Recognition Characters				Distinguishing features of g and other letters
Cloister	g g	e e	k k	y y	Blunted, long, right-pointed hook; small lower loop; e cross stroke at angle; no serif on k.
Caslon	g g	f f	d d	p p	Right-pointing ball for hook; narrow bottom loop; f has ball top and cross stroke longer at right.
Caslon #2	g g	f f	d d	p p	Very small ball hook; large lower loop; f has low cross stroke.
Caslon #137	g g	f f	d d	p p	Elongated ball hook droops slightly; small lower loop; g has blunt hook pointing upward.
Caslon Old Face	g g	f f	d d	p p	Teardrop hook points slightly up; large top loop; f has longer right stroke set low.
Weiss	g g	j j	d d	y y	Blunt hook points right, round upper loop; "upside down" effect on cap S.
Egmont	g g	j j	d d	y y	Hook has cut-off effect, large top and small lower loop; y turns up at bottom.
Medieval	g g	j j	d d	y y	Flat right side; open lower loop; loop of g connected.
Deepdene	g g	j j	k k	y y	Small upper loop; blunted straight hook; large lower loop.
Kennerley	g g	j j	d d	y y	Angular, small upper loop; blunted hook; large lower loop.
Goudy	g g	j j	d d	y y	Up-pointing hook, small lower loop; j fishhooks upward; y has no up-curl.
Waverley	g g	j j	d d	y y	Round, close-fitting ball hook; round upper and tight lower loop. Tail of y turns up.

Display Type Faces

A display type face is one which contrasts sharply with the regular body type which appears in paragraph form. This contrast can be gained with increased size, change of design, boldness, color of ink, or by isolation. Over 1,400 different type designs exist in type and matrix fonts in the United States. Most foundry faces run in a series from 6 to 72 point sizes. A few of the more popular designs are shown on the following pages, and can be classified as follows:

1. Venetian
2. Oldstyle
3. Transitional
4. Modern
5. Sans Serif
6. Gothic
7. Square Serif
8. Blackletter
9. Script

VENETIAN

Cloister Bold
PACK MY BOX
Pack my box

Cloister Bold Italic
PACK MY BOX
Pack my box

Cloister Italic
PACK MY BOX
Pack my box

Goudy Bold
PACK MY BOX
Pack my box

Goudy Bold Italic
PACK MY BOX
Pack my box

Goudy Italic
PACK MY BOX
Pack my box

Goudy
PACK MY BOX
Pack my box

OLDSTYLE and TRANSITIONAL

Bookman Italic

PACK MY BOX

Pack my box

Bookman Oldstyle

PACK MY BOX

Pack my box

Century Bold

PACK MY BOX

Pack my box

Century Bold Condensed

PACK MY BOX

Pack my box

Century Bold Italic

PACK MY

Pack my box

Century Expanded

PACK MY

Pack my box

Century Oldstyle

PACK MY

Pack my box

Century Schoolbook

PACK MY BOX

Pack my box

Century Schoolbook Bold

PACK MY

Pack my box

Garamond Bold

PACK MY BOX

Pack my box

Garamond Bold Italic

PACK MY BOX

Pack my box

Garamond Italic

PACK MY BOX

Pack my box

Garamond

PACK MY BOX

Pack my box

Palatino

PACK MY BOX

Pack my box

MODERN

Bodoni 22

PACK MY BOX
Pack my box

Bodoni Italic

PACK MY BOX
Pack my box

Bodoni Bold

PACK MY BOX
Pack my box

Bodoni Bold Italic

PACK MY BOX
Pack my box

Bodoni Book

PACK MY BOX
Pack my box

Bodoni Book Italic

PACK MY BOX
Pack my box

Corvinus Italic Medium

PACK MY BOX
Pack my box

Bernhard Modern Roman

PACK MY BOX
Pack my box

Bernhard Tango

PACK MY BOX
Pack my box

Bulmer Roman

PACK MY BOX
Pack my box

Bulmer Italic

PACK MY BOX
Pack my box

Onyx

PACK MY BOX
Pack my box

Ultra Bodoni

PACK MY BOX
Pack my box

Ultra Bodoni Extra Condensed

PACK MY BOX
Pack my box

SANS SERIF

Lydian Bold Condensed

PACK MY BOX

Pack my box

Lydian Bold Condensed Italic

PACK MY BOX

Pack my box

Lydian Bold Italic

PACK MY BOX

Pack my box

Lydian Italic

PACK MY BOX

Pack my box

Spartan Black

PACK MY BOX

Pack my box

Spartan Black Italic

PACK MY BOX

Pack my box

Bernhard Gothic Light

PACK MY BOX

Pack my box

Spartan Black Condensed

PACK MY BOX

Pack my box

Spartan Extra Black

PACK MY BOX

Pack my box

Spartan Heavy

PACK MY BOX

Pack my box

Spartan Heavy Italic

PACK MY BOX

Pack my box

Spartan Medium Italic

PACK MY BOX

Pack my box

Spartan Medium

PACK MY BOX

Pack my box

Dom Bold

PACK MY BOX

Pack my box

GOTHIC

Alternate Gothic No. 2

PACK MY BOX
Pack my box

Bank Gothic Condensed Light

PACK MY BOX

Bank Gothic Condensed Medium

PACK MY BOX

Bank Gothic Bold 534

PACK MY

Bank Gothic Light

PACK MY

Bank Gothic Medium

PACK MY

Copperplate Gothic Heavy Cond.

PACK MY

Copperplate Gothic Heavy Extended

PACK MY

Copperplate Gothic Italic

PACK MY

Copperplate Gothic Light

PACK MY

Copperplate Gothic Light Condensed

PACK MY BOX

Copperplate Gothic Light Extended

PACK MY

BLACKLETTER

American Text

Pack My Box

Cloister Black

Pack My Box

Engravers Old English

Pack My Box

Engravers Text

Pack My Box

Wedding Text

Pack My Box

Shaw Text

Pack My Box

SQUARE SERIF

P. T. Barnum

PACK MY
Pack my box

Contact Bold Condensed

PACK MY BOX
Pack my box

Contact Bold Condensed Italic

PACK MY BOX
Pack my box

Stymie Black

PACK MY BO
Pack my box

Stymie Black Italic

PACK MY BO
Pack my box

Stymie Bold

PACK MY
Pack my box

Craw Clarendon

PACK MY BOX
Pack my box

Stymie Bold Condensed

PACK MY BOX
Pack my box

Stymie Bold Italic

PACK MY
Pack my box

Stymie Light

PACK MY BOX
Pack my box

Stymie Light Italic

PACK MY BOX
Pack my box

Stymie Medium

PACK MY BOX
Pack my box

Stymie Medium Italic

PACK MY BOX
Pack my box

SCRIPT

Liberty

Pack My Box

Park Avenue

Pack My Box

Romany

Pack My Box

Royal Script

Pack My Box

Typo Script

Pack My Box

Typo Shaded

Pack My Box

Typo Upright

Pack My Box

Bank Script

Pack My Box

Bond Script

Pack My Box

Brush

Pack My Box

Commercial Script

Pack My Box

Freehand

Pack my box

Grayda

Pack My Box

Kaufmann Bold

Pack My Box

Kaufmann Script

Pack My Box

Holla

Pack my box

Mistral

Pack my box

Rondo

Pack my box

Diskus

Pack my box

Murray Hill

Pack my box

SELF-TEST

This self-test will serve as a review of this chapter. The questions are either true or false, or multiple choice. The numbers following each question refer to the page number on which the correct answer can be found.

1. The alphabet is 5,000 years old. (19)
2. Our English alphabet came to us from the Latin. (19)
3. The first Roman alphabet was in lowercase letters. (19)
4. The Gothic letters came from northern Europe. (20)
5. The Humanistic letters came from southern Europe. (20)
6. Printing in its earliest form was done from wood blocks. (20)
7. The first printed book was made in China. (20)
8. The first movable types were made of china in China. (20)
9. Playing cards were printed after the invention of movable type in Europe. (22)
10. Gutenberg was the first European to use movable types. (22)
11. The first book printed from movable types was the famous 42-line Gutenberg Bible. (22)
12. Pope Nicholas V was one of the first printing customers. (22)
13. Movable types were first used in Europe in 1550. (22)
14. The first book in the English language was printed from movable type in England. (25)
15. Caxton was the first French printer. (25)
16. The first American printer was Benjamin Franklin. (25)
17. The first work printed in America was *The Whole Book of Psalms*. (25)
18. The first regularly published newspaper in America was established in 1804. (27)
19. The first New York printer was William Bradford. (27)
20. The world's first great type designer was Nicholas Jenson. (30)
21. Cloister Oldstyle is an oldstyle type face. (30)
22. Venetian type faces were first designed in Venice, Italy. (30)
23. Both Garamond and Caslon are oldstyle type faces. (32)
24. Caslon designed his first type face in 1722. (32)
25. Caslon types were modeled after the Venetian faces. (32)
26. An outstanding feature of Caslon is its long descenders. (33)

27. Garamond features spur-like serifs. (34)
28. Bodoni designed the type that bears his name in 1789. (36)
29. The most pronounced feature of Bodoni is its extreme contrast between the thick and thin strokes. (36)
30. Baskerville redesigned Bodoni's type face. (38)
31. Baskerville is a transitional type face. (38)
32. Sans serif faces are either thick and thin, or monotone. (40)
33. So-called Gothic type faces are similar in appearance to the sans serif faces. (42)
34. In the modern group of sans serif type faces, all medium faces are of the same weight. (43)
35. Square serif type faces have a masonry-like appearance. (44)
36. Blackletter type faces are quite similar in appearance to the first type face used by Johann Gutenberg. (47)
37. Script types are designed after the lettering used by the scribes before the invention of movable types. (48)
38. Cheltenham was one of the most popular type faces in American use. (50)
39. Select the contemporary types from those listed below: (52)

    a. Weiss Roman   e. Bookman   i. Scotch
    b. Cheltenham   f. Century   j. Egmont
    c. Waverley   g. Electra   k. Fairfield
    d. Caledonia   h. Deepdene   l. Baskerville

40. Newspaper types are seldom made in sizes over 14 point. (54)
41. The x-height of newspaper types is generally large. (54)
42. In attempting to distinguish a type face, one of the most distinguishing characters is the lowercase: (56)

    a. Letter a   c. Letter g   e. Letter h
    b. Letter t   d. Letter p   f. Letter m

43. All sizes of type in a given point size appear to be the same size when printed on paper. (57)
44. Egmont was designed by S. H. deRoos (52)
45. Caledonia was designed by Frederic W. Goudy. (52)
46. Deepdene was designed by Rudolf Ruzicka. (52)
47. Electra was designed by W. A. Dwiggins. (52)
48. Cheltenham was designed by Bertram G. Goodhue. (50)

TYPE-FACE RECOGNITION TEST

Determine two things about the type faces listed below: (1) To which of the eleven type-face classifications each belongs, and (2) what type face each is. Check yourself by referring to pages 34, 48, and 55.

1. Tag   5. *Tag*   9. *Tag*   13. Tag

2. **Tag**   6. Tag   10. Tag   14. **Tag**

3. Tag   7. Tag   11. Tag

4. Tag   8. **Tag**   12. 𝕿𝖆𝖌

CHAPTER 3

How to Make Layouts

Duties of the Layout Man

A *layout* is a plan of a job of printing. The arrangement of type masses, illustration, and ornamentation is *laid out* by artists in typographical work, just as plans and models are made for houses and industrial products. Layouts show how the completed printed job will look when off the press. Layouts, correctly made, indicate to the typesetter, make-up man, pressman, and binder just how he is to do his work. A layout can be okayed or changed by the customer before any actual work is done in the shop, which may result in saving both time and cost. A *dummy* is a collection of layouts, as dummy for a booklet or brochure consisting of more than one page.

The layout man first gets all data relative to the job of printing to be done. This includes size, perhaps the kind of paper to be used, the typewritten copy to be put into type, any available photographs or drawings to be reproduced in the printed piece, the number of copies to be printed, the manner in which the job is to be distributed, other pieces of printing already completed which will be seen at the same time as the piece now being planned, and any other pertinent information.

The usual first step of the layout man in planning a job of printing is to make small or *thumbnail* sketches. He selects the best of these in his opinion or in the opinion of others, and makes a *rough* layout, which is a series of blocks or elements of copy and illustrations, and an indication of the displayed words and other elements of the copy, such as illustrations.

Fig. 3-1. Comprehensive Layout Containing Blocks of Copy to Be Set in Type, Margins and Illustration, All in Actual Size and Position. The Actual Lettering of the Display Lines Simulates the Type to Be Used.

Fig. 3-2. The Finished Layout of the Comprehensive Layout Shown in Fig. 3-1. Note That the Picture Frame Has Been Removed to Achieve Simplicity. *Courtesy of Reincke, Meyer & Finn, Inc.*

If the rough layout pleases the layout man and his employer, the layout man proceeds to make a *comprehensive* layout or *visual*. The comprehensive layout is a guide for the printers who will set the type, and for the platemaker who will provide the *cuts* for the illustrations. See Fig. 3–1 on page 72 for an example of a comprehensive layout.

The comprehensive layout contains the actual sizes of the blocks of copy to be set in type, the sizes of the margins, the size and positions of the illustrations, the actual lettering of the display lines in simulation of the kind and size of type to be used. Great care is taken to see that the lettering of the proposed type faces is in correct size to be finally reproduced, although small type is indicated by drawing straight lines. See Fig. 3–1.

The *finished layout* is usually made up of photo prints of the artist's work and proofs of type pasted up to make the work appear in form as though printed. Very often the layout man gets an okay from the customer on the comprehensive layout. If not, the finished layout gets the final okay signal for printing. See Fig. 3–2.

Typographic Design

There are few rules governing the laying out of a piece of printing. When the same piece of copy is given to two, a dozen, or more than 100 layout men, and they are given their own lead in the work, each will lay out the job in a different way. Depending upon one's feelings for typographical art, each layout will be good, but none will be the same. This is demonstrated in the advertisements appearing on pages 75, 77, 82, 84, 86, and 88. These layouts were selected at random from entries in typographical contest conducted by the *Inland Printer*. The *copy* for each is identical, but the *layouts* for each are extremely *different*. One's personal opinion will designate perhaps one as the best of the group, and others in order as to excellence under it.

A close examination of these layouts will show that each layout man selected different words to display in large type, and that the layouts vary considerably in treatment not only as to illustration, but also as to the treatment of the text matter.

Layout 1

WATCH

TODAY'S

SKIES

for the first Stratoliner !

Just at noon today, the first Stratoliner to visit Chicago will make its appearance over the Loop.

As you watch it, a mile in the air, remember this:

It is the largest, newest and finest flying transport in service anywhere in the world. ● It is four-motored for greater power, greater speed and greater smoothness. It carries thirty-three passengers and a crew of five. ● It gives you the fastest and most luxurious service ever offered from Chicago to New York and to California.

T·R·A·N·S·C·O·N·T·I·N·E·N·T·A·L AIRLINES

Layout 2

Watch today's skies for the first STRATOLINER

Just at noon today, the first Stratoliner to visit Chicago will make its appearance over the loop.

As you watch it, a mile in the air, remember this: It is the largest, newest and finest flying transport in service anywhere in the world. It is four-motored for greater power, greater speed and greater smoothness. It carries 33 passengers and a crew of 5. *It gives you the fastest and most luxurious service ever offered from Chicago to New York and to California.*

Layout 3

★ *Just at noon today*
the first Stratoliner to visit Chicago
will make its appearance over the Loop
As you watch it
a mile in the air, remember this
It is the largest, newest and finest flying transport
in service anywhere in the world

WATCH TODAY'S SKIES!

It is four-motored
for greater power, greater speed and greater
smoothness. It carries
33 passengers and a crew of 5
It gives you the fastest
and most luxurious service ever offered from
Chicago to New York and to California

TRANSCONTINENTAL AIRLINES

Layout 4

WATCH
TODAY'S
SKIES

for the first Stratoliner

Just at noon today,
the first Stratoliner to visit Chicago
will make its appearance over the loop
As you watch it, a mile in the air,
remember this:
It is the largest, newest, and finest
flying transport in service
anywhere in the world.
It is four-motored for greater power,
greater speed and greater smoothness.
It carries 33 passengers and a crew of 5.
It gives you the fastest
and most luxurious service ever offered
from Chicago to New York
and to California.

TRANSCONTINENTAL *Airlines*

Harmony. This element of typographic design refers to a pleasing relation between the type faces used, with regard to their design as well as to shape and weight, and a general pleasing relation among the shapes of the various elements of the job. Generally speaking, a thin type face looks better than a wide type face in narrow confines. The reverse is also true; wide faces look well in wide panels of space.

Balance refers to equalized and pleasing elements of a printed job. This is especially important when a group of type matter is placed out of center. Elements out of balance are easily seen, because the printing looks top heavy, or seems to have the appearance of being too heavy on the left or the right.

Proportion refers to the comparative relationships between the elements of a job of printing.

Methods of Display

Display means contrast. A word or a line is displayed when it becomes more visible and readable through a contrast in weight, color, shape, or size with other type matter on the page.

Words of minor display value can be put in contrast with other type used, even in the same point size as the other type:

1. Small caps of the same type face.
2. Light caps of the same type face.
3. Italic lowercase of the same type family.
4. Bold italic lowercase of the same type family.
5. Bold caps of the same type family.
6. Bold italic caps of the same type family.
7. A type of another type family—either bold or italic.
8. A type of the same family, but in the bold condensed or the extrabold condensed versions.
9. By underscoring, if used *sparingly*.

It should be remembered that *too much* display is *no* display. Only a few elements can be displayed in any piece of printed matter. The reader's eye can be attracted only to a few elements or lines—he cannot grasp quickly the thoughts presented if his eye meets with an array of many different kinds of type display.

WATCH TODAY'S SKIES *for the first* **STRATOLINER!**

Just at noon today, the first Stratoliner to visit Chicago will make its appearance over the Loop. As you watch it, a mile in the air, remember this: √ It is the largest, newest and finest flying transport in service anywhere in the world. √ It is four-motored for greater power, greater speed and greater smoothness. It carries 33 passengers and a crew of 5. √ It gives you the fastest and most luxurious service ever offered from Chicago to New York and to California.

TRANSCONTINENTAL *Airlines*

WATCH TODAY'S SKIES For the First STRATOLINER

Just at noon today, the first Stratoliner to visit Chicago will make its appearance over the Loop. As you watch it, a mile in the air, remember this: It is the largest, newest and finest flying transport in service anywhere in the world. It is four-motored for greater power, greater speed and greater smoothness. It carries 33 passengers and a crew of 5. It gives you the fastest and most luxurious service ever offered from Chicago to New York and to California.

WATCH
TODAY'S SKIES
FOR THE NEW
STRATOLINER

→ Just at noon today, the first Stratoliner to visit Chicago will make its appearance over the Loop. As you watch it, a mile in the air, remember this:

It is the largest, newest and finest flying transport in service anywhere in the world. It is four-motored for greater power, greater speed and greater smoothness. It carries thirty-three passengers and a crew of five. It gives you the fastest and most luxurious service ever offered from Chicago to New York and to California

Watch Today's Skies

for the first Stratoliner!

Just at noon today, the first Stratoliner to visit Chicago will make its appearance over the Loop. As you watch it, a mile in the air, remember this:

● It is the largest, newest and finest flying transport in service anywhere in the world.

● It is four-motored for greater power, greater speed and greater smoothness. It carries 33 passengers and a crew of 5.

● It gives you the fastest and most luxurious service ever offered from Chicago to New York and to California.

TRANSCONTINENTAL AIRLINES

Appropriateness of type faces to the subject matter of the printing job can best be shown through example. The following are typical, and similar specimens can be found in almost any daily newspaper or magazine.

THE LONG LOOK . . . . . . Long type for a long look

Town Folks . . . Plain type for just folks

Railroad . . . . : Rugged for railroads

FAIRCHILD SONS . . . . . . The type designates age
INC.
Funeral Directors Since 1886

Citadel . . . . Building brick effect

18 Century . . . . Old script gives age

MONOGRAM BLOUSE . . Monogram-effect type

GOWNS . . . . French type for ladies

Modern Pipe . . . . Type gives "pipe" effect

THE APPROPRIATENESS OF TYPE FACES

WHAT TYPE FACES CAN EXPRESS

1. Type can be light or **heavy**

2. Type can be unassuming or graceful

3. Type can whisper or **shout**

4. Type can be monotonous or sparkle

5. Type can be **UGLY** or beautiful

6. Type can be mechanical or formal

7. Type can be *social* or ecclesiastical

8. Type can be FAT or THIN

9. Type can be decorative or plain

10. Type can be easy to read or hard to read

Key to the type faces listed above, left to right in order:

1. 18-point Bernhard Fashion and Beton Extrabold.
2. 18-point Caslon and Garamond.
3. 6-point Ideal and 24-point Vogue Extrabold.
4. 18-point Vogue and Egmont.
5. 14-point Hobo and 18-point Weiss Roman.
6. 18-point Cairo Medium and Bodoni.
7. 18-point Park Avenue and Engravers Old English.
8. 18-point Beton Wide and Palisade.
9. 18-point Rivoli and Cheltonian.
10. 14-point Regal and 4-point Century Expanded.

Hand-lettered Display. In spite of the thousands of type faces available for use in advertising and commercial printing, layout men often see the need to strive for special effects in their work. They look for something striking, and more appropriate. Examples of the resultant hand lettering are shown below.

Handlettering has been taken over in part by cold type photographic machines which can enlarge or reduce, Italicize, backslant, outline, stagger, bounce, and create many interesting effects.

Centered and Squared-Line Layout. Illustrated on the next page in numbers 1 to 5, inclusive, is a kind of layout practiced by many typographers, which we call centered and squared-line layout. In this style of typography the compositor or layout man has widest latitude in arranging the copy into lines that will fit well when squared. This necessitates some letterspacing; therefore cap letters are best to use, because lowercase looks too weak when letterspaced.

No. 1. This is a pleasing arrangement set in caps of sans serif bold face in three sizes. In the original the shield and stars on the last line were printed in red, the rest in black. The second colors of this and other cards are not shown.

No. 2. A unique effect is made on this card by printing fine red lines through the black line of the main display. Three kinds of type are used: a condensed sans serif, a cursive, and what is usually termed copperplate gothic. The typographer saw fit to display the phone number.

No. 3. Square serif type faces are used in this layout, plus what appears to be a piece of rule bent to form the curved line which accentuates the name of the mechanic. The second line and the rule appeared in red.

No. 4. Here the layout man assumed that the phone number was of primary importance. It is rather large for card typography. The ornaments simulate cash registers.

No. 5. The red rule work on this card gives a pleasing effect. Script faces and lightweight square serif types were used.

Slanted and Curved-Line Layout. Tricks in typography are often used to give special effects. This typesetting is usually not easy to accomplish, because of the difficulties encountered in locking the type for the press. See numbers 6 to 8 on the next page.

No. 6. Here a joining script in bold face is printed in red, and dominates the card. A flush left and right arrangement appears in a bold sans serif face.

No. 7. Here the mechanic's name is stressed, with the upper corner devoted to the name of the company and phone number.

No. 8. Circular typography pleases some buyers of printing. In this layout the same type is used in several sizes.

NATIONAL CASH REGISTER SERVICE

WORK GUARANTEED · ESTIMATES FREE · BUY · SELL · EXCHANGE

1304 SOUTH UNIVERSITY · ANN ARBOR · DIAL 2-1335

L. V. HANDLER, FACTORY TRAINED MECHANIC * * * * * * *

1

L. V. Handler   M E C H A N I C

NATIONAL CASH REGISTER SERVICE

1304 South University ☆ Ann Arbor

Dial 2-1335

BUY · SELL · EXCHANGE

Factory Trained, Work Guaranteed, Estimates Free

5

NATIONAL CASH REGISTER SERVICE

L. V. Handler, Mechanic · *Factory Trained*

· W O R K   G U A R A N T E E D · E S T I M A T E S   F R E E

B U Y · S E L L · E X C H A N G E

Dial 2-1335

1304 SOUTH UNIVERSITY, ANN ARBOR

2

L. V. Handler, Mechanic

Factory Trained

Work Guaranteed

Estimates Free

National Cash Register Service

Buy, Sell
Exchange

Dial 2-1335

1304 South University, Ann Arbor

6

NATIONAL CASH REGISTER SERVICE

BUY · SELL · EXCHANGE · ESTIMATES FREE

Factory Trained Mechanic · Work Guaranteed · Dial 2-1335

1304 SOUTH UNIVERSITY · ANN ARBOR

L. V. HANDLER

3

★ NATIONAL CASH REGISTER SERVICE · DIAL 2-1335

BUY · SELL
EXCHANGE

L. V. HANDLER

FACTORY TRAINED MECHANIC

Work Guaranteed · Free Estimates

★

1304 South University · Ann Arbor

7

DIAL 2-1335

National Cash Register Service

| **L.V. HANDLER** · MECHANIC |
Factory Trained · Work Guaranteed
Estimates Free · Buy, Sell, Exchange

1304 SOUTH UNIVERSITY · ANN ARBOR

4

ESTIMATES FREE   DIAL 2-1335

NATIONAL CASH REGISTER SERVICE

L. V. HANDLER
MECHANIC   WORK GUARANTEED

FACTORY
TRAINED

BUY
SELL
EXCHANGE

ANN ARBOR
1304 SOUTH UNIVERSITY

8

Centered Line Layout. This kind of typography is easiest for most beginners. In fact, most of the typography today follows this style. Generally speaking, it is not so interesting as other styles. See numbers 9 and 10 on the next page.

No. 9. Here the typographer displayed, and very large, the name of the service offered in a very bold face. The matter at the bottom is centered and squared in a square serif type face.

No. 10. A unique effect is achieved here in the use of the large letter "S" which extends well above the main display line. The other faces used are copperplate gothic.

Flush Left and Right Layout. A very popular device used by typographers is the flush left and flush right arrangement of typographic elements. Five examples of this kind of typography are shown in the examples 11, 13, 14, 15, and 16, on the next page. Note that in each instance this layout arrangement is used, the elements never look well if too near the same width. See particularly examples 15 and 16, and note the short and long squared effects used. Remember this when making layouts of this kind.

No. 11. The stressing of the word "service," large and in red, displays the work offered. Sans serif faces are used throughout.

No. 12. Square serif faces are used in this presentation, with a red double rule dividing two elements which have pleasing division of space. The job appears to be chopped off at the bottom on the right side.

No. 13. Here a red rule aligns with the main body of squared elements and *bleeds* off the card. The script line, set at a slight angle, balances well with the remainder of the copy. Sans serif types are used in two weights and two sizes.

No. 14. Placed at the lower right, this layout makes a pleasing effect. The decorative initial and the word "service" in red stress the type of work offered.

No. 15. Here the isolation of the main line in red gives good display to that element. Elements at the right are squared and well spaced for ease in reading. The rule at the bottom was in red.

No. 16. The use of an outlined, large cap line dominates the card. One family of type is used in square serif, with the addition of one line in a letterspaced condensed sans serif face.

NATIONAL
Cash Register
Service

1304 South University • Ann Arbor
L. V. Handler • Mechanic • Factory Trained • Work Guaranteed
DIAL 2-1335 • Buy • Exchange • Sell • Estimates Free

9

National
CASH REGISTER SERVICE
1304 SOUTH UNIVERSITY · ANN ARBOR
DIAL 2-1335 · L. V. HANDLER · MECHANIC

FACTORY TRAINED · WORK GUARANTEED
ESTIMATES FREE · BUY, SELL, EXCHANGE

13

BUY : SELL   EXCHANGE   DIAL 2 - 1335

NATIONAL S **CASH REGISTER**
ervice
WORK GUARANTEED
ESTIMATES FREE

L. V. HANDLER   1304 SOUTH UNIVERSITY
FACTORY TRAINED MECHANIC   ANN ARBOR

10

*N*ATIONAL CASH REGISTER
Service L.V. HANDLER, *Mechanic*
FACTORY TRAINED • WORK GUARANTEED
ESTIMATES FREE • BUY, SELL, EXCHANGE
1304 South University
ANN ARBOR · DIAL *2-1335*

14

DIAL
2-1335

Factory Trained
Work Guaranteed
Buy, Sell, Exchange

NATIONAL
CASH REGISTER SERVICE

1404 SOUTH UNIVERSITY · ANN ARBOR

Estimates Free   L. V. HANDLER, *Manager*

11

WORK GUARANTEED
ESTIMATES FREE

NATIONAL CASH REGISTER SERVICE
BUY · SELL · EXCHANGE
L. V. HANDLER
FACTORY TRAINED MECHANIC
1304 SOUTH UNIVERSITY • ANN ARBOR • DIAL 2-1335

15

DIAL 21335
•
BUY   SELL
EXCHANGE
•
FACTORY
TRAINED
•
Estimates
Free

National Cash Register Service
1304 University South
Ann Arbor

WORK GUARANTEED

L. V. HANDLER, Mechanic

12

BUY · SELL
EXCHANGE
L. V. HANDLER · Mechanic · FACTORY TRAINED
NATIONAL
CASH REGISTER SERVICE
WORK GUARANTEED · ESTIMATES FREE
1304 SOUTH UNIVERSITY · ANN ARBOR
DIAL 2-1335

16

Squared and Flush Left Layout. As exemplified in illustrations numbered 17 through 20, on the next page, the squared and flush left layouts can achieve an interesting effect. Rules in each example hold the lines together well.

No. 17. A pleasing arrangement is shown here in the treatment of the word "National" as aligned with the balance of the line as well as being squared with the element forming the left of the job. Sans serif types are used throughout, and they are letterspaced well to give the squared effect.

No. 18. This arrangement, although made "spotty" because of the addition of the diamonds, illustrates this kind of layout.

No. 19. Here the typographer used all of the space of the card, but used a very thin sans serif face for the main display, which dominates because of great size. Letterspaced italic caps, considered by some typographers as poor form, are used at the bottom.

No. 20. A dotted and plain rule divides this card into pleasing elements. The modern sans serif and joining script make a pleasing whole.

Rule Ornament Layout. Rules are difficult to use, especially when they dominate the typography of the card. It is best to give the most display to type that can be *read*. No one can *read* a series of rules which appear in example number 22. See the illustrations numbered from 21 to 24, inclusive, on the next page.

No. 21. The panel border here gives a pleasing effect. Roman faces are used throughout in what appears to be small caps.

No. 22. The rule work in the center of this job is too strong, and adds little to the typography.

No. 23. Two elements of copy are displayed in a rather unique manner on this card layout. The arrow, running from the phone number to the mechanic's name, displays these two words, even if they are not set in large type. Square serifs make up the bulk of the job, with one line set in a modern script face. The arrow appeared in red, along with the script type.

No. 24. The hanging rule work at the left of this layout gives a "different" effect. The main line is set in script, and in a good size for display. The box and its contents appear in red. A modern sans serif in light weight is well spaced.

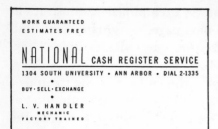

WORK GUARANTEED
ESTIMATES FREE
•
NATIONAL CASH REGISTER SERVICE
1304 SOUTH UNIVERSITY • ANN ARBOR • DIAL 2-1335
•
BUY · SELL · EXCHANGE
•
L. V. HANDLER
MECHANIC
FACTORY TRAINED

17

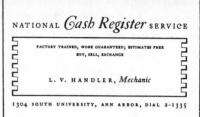

NATIONAL *Cash Register* SERVICE

FACTORY TRAINED, WORK GUARANTEED; ESTIMATES FREE
BUY, SELL, EXCHANGE

L. V. HANDLER, *Mechanic*

1304 SOUTH UNIVERSITY, ANN ARBOR, DIAL 2-1335

21

NATIONAL CASH REGISTER SERVICE

Factory Trained — Work
Guaranteed — Estimates
Free — Buy, Sell, Exchange

♦

♦

L. V. HANDLER
Mechanic

1304 South University • Ann Arbor • Dial 2-1335

18

DIAL 2-1335   Estimates Free

NATIONAL CASH REGISTER SERVICE

L. V. Handler, Mechanic   Work Guaranteed
Factory Trained   Buy - Sell - Exchange

1304 SOUTH UNIVERSITY   -   -   -   ANN ARBOR

22

1304 SOUTH UNIVERSITY, ANN ARBOR · DIAL 2-1335

NATIONAL

✳
BUY - SELL
EXCHANGE

CASH REGISTER SERVICE
• L. V. HANDLER, Mechanic

FACTORY TRAINED · WORK GUARANTEED · ESTIMATES FREE

19

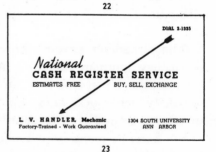

DIAL 2-1335

National
CASH REGISTER SERVICE
ESTIMATES FREE   BUY, SELL, EXCHANGE

L. V. HANDLER, Mechanic   1304 SOUTH UNIVERSITY
Factory-Trained - Work Guaranteed   ANN ARBOR

23

L. V. Handler
FACTORY-TRAINED MECHANIC

NATIONAL CASH REGISTER SERVICE
Dial 2-1335 ● 1304 SOUTH UNIVERSITY ● ANN ARBOR

WORK GUARANTEED ● ESTIMATES FREE ● BUY, SELL, EXCHANGE

20

National Cash Register Service

Factory Trained
Work Guaranteed   L. V. HANDLER, MECHANIC
Estimates Free   1304 SOUTH UNIVERSITY, ANN ARBOR
Buy, Sell,
Exchange   DIAL 2-1335

24

Illustrated Layout. Pictures are often used in advertising matter not only to illustrate the product, but to attract attention, as the examples on the next page show in numbers 25 through 28. Illustrations shown in these particular examples are either cut from rubber blocks, probably by the layout man himself, or made up of type and rule characters.

No. 25. There is no doubt in the reader's mind, without reading, about the kind of service offered. The simply designed cash register dominates the card. Three faces of type are used.

No. 26. Here the typographer has attempted to give a unique effect through the use of the bent line "service" and the simulated gun. Although the phone and service lines are displayed, the use of the gun ornament has little value except for getting attention.

No. 27. The "mechanics" of the type of service offered is displayed here through the use of a type ornament illustration of a mechanic's vise. A red rule bleeds off the top of the card, and again the modern sans serif type faces are used, with added check marks.

No. 28. The small type-made cash register and curved dollar signs set in sans serif type faces ornament this card.

Type Trick Layout. Circles, angular lines, and squared effects often used by typographers appear in examples 29 through 32 on the next page.

No. 29. Here a group of stars, printed in red, help to make a good balance on the left area of the card. The two types used in the main line are not well related, however.

No. 30. Special type characters (circles containing numbers) are used in this card to simulate the keyboard of a cash register. With the main line exception, square serif types are used.

No. 31. A slanting effect is given here with the use of many dollar signs to hold the copy together. Work of this kind is rather difficult to compose in type. The main line, set closely in condensed caps, would look better if letterspaced.

No. 32. A rather crowded effect exists in the circle of this example. The layout man has eliminated the difficulties in lockup by printing the circle in a second color, and eliminating the necessity of justifying the type in a round enclosure. With the exception of two lines set in sans serif, all type is square serif.

25

29

26

30

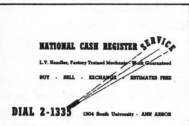

27

31

28

32

How to Mark Layouts for Type Composition

14 pica inside measure, 1-pt. rule border, 17 wide and 19 deep All Karnak family.

ONE HUNDRED AND SEVENTH

1949

ANNUAL REPORT

OF THE

TOWN OF GLENCOE

ILLINOIS

CUT

10 Light caps, full

18 Black, letterspace 4 pts, ctr.

24 Black Cond. caps, full

10 Light caps, letterspace 2 pts. ctr.

14 Black caps, full.

10 Light caps, letterspace 2 pts ctr

How to Specify Type for Composition. Full specifications are provided with the rough layout above for composition into type. Note that the measures are given (in picas) for the size of the job, and the width to set the type within the border. The Ludlow Karnak family is noted as the face to set throughout the job. Other markings mean:

"10 Light caps, full." Set in 10-point Karnak Light, in capitals, and letterspace between letters to make a full 14-pica line.

"18 Black, letterspace 4 pts., ctr." Set in 18-point Karnak Black, put four points space between letters, and center the line.

"24 Black Cond., caps, full." Set in 24-point Karnak Black condensed capitals, and space between letters to make a full line.

"10 Light caps, letterspace 2 pts., ctr." Set in 10-point Karnak Light, in capital letters, place two points space between each letter, and center the line."

ONE HUNDRED AND SEVENTH

107th

ANNUAL REPORT

OF THE

TOWN OF GLENCOE

ILLINOIS

"14 Black caps, full." Set in 14-point Karnak Black, in capital letters, and put enough space between letters to make a full line.

"10 Light caps, letterspace 2 pts., center." Set in 10-point Karnak Light, in capital letters, put a 2-point space between each letter, and center the line.

"Cut" refers to the inclusion of a photoengraved plate.

The completed job of type composition, shown on this page, has been set according to the directions given on the layout opposite. In the event that faces in other than one type family are used, each type name is designated, as "10 Light Futura Caps." The abbreviation *lc* refers to small letters, and *c&lc* to capitals and small letters.

Effect of Paper Texture on Type Faces

A factor often ignored in selection of body type faces, but nevertheless of great importance, is the effect of the texture of paper on small type faces printed by letterpress. Hard-surfaced papers do not thicken the type faces, and soft-surfaced papers do thicken them.

Baskerville on

Exacting and zealo — Antique

Exacting and zealo — Coated

Exacting and zealo — M.F.

Exacting and zealo — News

Exacting and zealo — S&SC

The examples above were originally set in the same 10 point size but they have been photographically enlarged so that the effects of the paper's texture can be seen more easily. The types were actually printed on the kinds of paper mentioned at the right and the enlargements were taken from them.

On soft papers like antique, news, machine finish (often referred to as *M.F.*), type faces appear to be heavier than when they are printed on hard-surfaced papers like coated and sized and supercalendered (often referred to as *S&SC*). Note that apparently different "weights" of type faces appear even though each one is printed on the *same* type face!

In the process of offset-lithography, and when type is to be reproduced also in photoengraved plates in letterpress, it is common practice to pull proofs of the lighter-faced types on rough-surfaced papers.

When photographed for reproduction, type faces appear heavier than when the proofs are pulled on the usual hard-surfaced papers.

Fig. 3-3A. Stock Artwork, Reduced One-Half

Fig. 3-3B. Modular Art   *Left:* Parts Are Removed from Backing Sheet   *Center:* Pieces Are Placed in Position on Art Board   *Right:* The Completed Artwork

Fig. 3-3C. Stock Art, Reduced One-Half

Fig. 3-4A. *Left:* Rule Pak Borders Are Printed on Acetate with Adhesive Backing
Right: Examples of ABC's Tapes, Useful in Creating Graphs

Fig. 3-4B. The Formliner Allows Small, Accurate Adjustments Between
Lines to Be Drawn on Paper or Scratched into the Negative

Copy Preparation for Offset-Lithography

The techniques of preparing copy for offset-lithography may
vary from the techniques for letterpress. For offset, "camera-ready"
copy is needed. Display and text matter lines may be either hot or
cold type. Reproduction proofs are needed if the hot type is used.
Cold type is applied directly to copy. Illustrations may be original
or stock art. See Figs. 3–3A, 3–3B, and 3–3C.

Borders and spot illustrations may be reproduction proofs of
foundry material or cut-out, preprinted, adhesive backed acetate.
See Fig. 3–4A.

Rules (lines) may be hot type, ruled by hand with a pen and
T-square or scratched into the emulsion side of the negative with
a sharp tool. The Formliner is a useful device for ruling. (Shown in
Fig. 3–4B.) It has a light source beneath a rotating glass top. The

Fig. 3-5A. Eight Kinds of Shading Media

Fig. 3-5B. Positive Shading Media
Being Applied

Fig. 3-5C. Reverse Shading Media
Being Applied

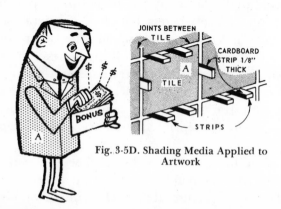

Fig. 3-5D. Shading Media Applied to
Artwork

accurate ruling of horizontal and vertical lines is made easier. The machine can be set to space equally between lines. When hot type reproduction proofs are used for copy, it is customary to compose the horizontal lines and rule the vertical lines with a pen or scratch the lines on the negative. This method eliminates the breaks between vertical and horizontal lines which occur if both lines are composed in hot type. Shading media in hundreds of screens, stipples and other designs are commonly used to augment artwork rather than doing the shading by hand. See Figs. 3–5A and 3–5B. Fig. 3–5C illustrates the use of shading media.

Expensive airbrush work is eliminated with the use of adhesive-backed acetate film (shown in Fig. 3–6A).

Fig. 3-6A. Bourge Overlay Retouch Method   *Top:* Screened Overlay Was Placed over Entire Picture then   *Bottom:* Cut Away over Distinct Area

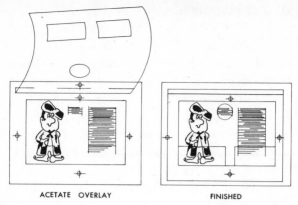

ACETATE OVERLAY   FINISHED

Fig. 3-6B. An Acetate Overlay *(Top Left)* Drawn over Black Artwork to provide Second Color for Artwork   *Right:* Acetate Placed over Black Plate Drawing

To provide color copy for artwork, it is common practice to lay matte-finished acetate over the original art and draw the second or more colors to register. See Fig. 3–6B.

"Foto-Chase" make-up is an ATF development. Photographically set copy is mounted on extremely light-weight plastic about 5/16 of an inch thick, and a special cutter is used to make desired widths and lengths. Column rules are provided in various thicknesses. The make-up of pages needing periodic revision (classified advertisements, catalogs and the like) can be accomplished faster than when hot metal slugs are used. Pages are made up in a "Foto-Chase" with the right reading material for making negatives for printing by any process.

Types to Use for Gravure

Type matter reproduced by the gravure process is always screened. This is a peculiarity of the process which must be taken into consideration to get the most legible types possible. Blowups of typical gravure type faces are shown on the page opposite. These type faces were taken from actual jobs of gravured printing.

The top example is taken from a national magazine which is produced both by letterpress and gravure. The bold fuzzy type at the left was originally reproduced by gravure. The type at the right of the center line is the type reproduced by letterpress. Note the effect of the gravure screen on this type face in comparison with the letterpress process.

Fine-serifed and thin-lined types, as well as fine and heavy-lined types, do not reproduce well by the gravure process. Bold and light-faced sans-serif types reproduce fairly well, as shown below, as does a type face with heavy, blunt serifs in a reasonably heavy text type face.

WHAT HAPPENS TO TYPE IN THE GRAVURE PROCESS

GRAVURED TYPE   LETTERPRESS TYPE

**governments have separately or col
an equal concern rest payments by**

FINE-SERIFED AND THIN-LINED TYPES

*world's best travelers, for town, for commuting
. these downy-soft, abundantly furred, all but*

FINE AND HEAVY-LINED TYPES

heat-resistant paint, and more

How to Designate Type Lines

Aids for laying out printed matter, especially for booklets and for other work including blocks of type matter, are the *type line spacers* shown on pages 98 and 99.

Lines are shown in point divisions of 6, 7, 8, 9, 10, 11, 12, 13, 14, 15, 16, 17, 18, 20, and 22.

Care must be taken in planning leaded lines; that is, lines with space between them, such as 8 on 10, 11 on 13, etc.

Also provided are typewriter line counters for single and double-spaced typing (for both elite and pica typewriter sizes), and a character counter for both elite and pica typewriter copy.

Layouts are usually made on transparent paper so that tracing of type characters in larger sizes and illustrations can be done easily. These transparent sheets of paper can be laid over these line spacers to determine sizes and leading of type lines.

single type-writer	double type-writer	6-12 points space	7-14 points space	8-16 points space	9-18 points space
1		1	1	1	1
2	1	2	2	2	2
3		3	3	2	2
4	2	4	3	3	3
5		5	4	4	
6	3	6	5	4	4
7		7	6	5	
8	4	8	7	6	5
9		9	8	7	6
10	5	10	9	8	7
11		11	10	9	
12	6	12	11	10	8
13		13	12		9
14	7	14			
15		15			10
16	8	16	14	12	11
17		17	15	13	
18	9	18	16	14	12
19		19	17	15	13
20	10	20	18	16	
21		21	19	17	14
22	11	22	20		15
23		23	21	18	16
24	12	24	22	19	
25		25	23	20	17
26	13	26	24	21	18
27		27	25	22	
28	14	28	26	23	19
29		29	27	24	20
30	15	30	28	25	
31		31	29	26	21
32	16	32	30	27	22
33		33	31	28	23
34	17	34	32	29	
35		35	33	30	24
36	18	36	34	31	25
37		37	35		26
38	19	38			
39		39			27
40	20	40			
41		41			

Type Line Spacers

10-20 points space	11-22 points space	13 points space	15 points space	17 points space
1	1	1	1	1
2	2	2	2	2
3	3	3	3	3
4	4	4	4	4
5	5	5	5	5
6	6	6	6	6
7	7	7	7	7
8	8	8	8	8
9	9	9	9	9
10	10	10	10	10
11	11	11	11	11
12	12	12	12	12
13	13	13	13	13
14	14	14	14	14
15	15	15	15	15
16	16	16	16	16
17	17	17	17	17
18	18	18	18	18
19	19	19	19	19
20	20	20	20	20
21	21	21	21	21
22	22	22	22	22
23		23	23	23
24		24	24	24
		25	25	25
		26	26	26
		27	27	27
		28	28	28
		29	29	29
		30	30	
		31	31	
		32	32	
		33	33	
		34		
		35		
		36		
		37		

12 Characters → to the inch   1234567890123456789012345678901234567890123456789 10 20 30 40 50 60 70

10 Characters → to the inch   1234567890123456789012345678901234567890123456 10 20 30 40 50 60

How to Use Reverse Plates

Reverse plates, or photoengravings made from type in which the white and black proof is "reversed," are well-known devices that bring great attention value, especially in advertisements and for special effects in other kinds of printing.

Proofs of the type matter are sent to the photoengraver with lines indicating the outside dimensions of the plate to be provided. The photoengraver then delivers the necessary plates.

Illustrated below are several typical reverse plates. At the upper left is a square serif bold-face type, and at the upper right a sans serif bold-face type. These faces are best to use for reverse plates. Thin-serifed types are difficult to use because the serifs are often lost in presswork by any reproduction method. An example of this is shown in the middle right, below.

Other interesting effects in reverse plates, shown at the bottom of the illustration, are hand-lettered, or negatives are furnished by specialists in this work.

Some photoengravers and trade compositors are equipped with special cameras and lenses to provide slanted, curved, and perspective photoprints from proofs of type matter.

How to Copyfit Manuscript

One of the most important duties of the layout man is to copyfit typewritten manuscript to type. If copyfitting is not correctly done, type matter may have to be reset, and this increases the cost of printing.

How to Find the Character Count per Pica. Although type founders and matrix makers furnish the character count per pica of their type faces, sometimes the reference material is not at hand. Here is the procedure to find out.

1. Assume that the lowercase alphabet has $28\frac{1}{2}$ characters, necessary because thinner characters occur more frequently than thick characters.

2. Divide the alphabet length in points (this can be approximated with a printer's line gauge) into 342 to find the characters per pica—$28\frac{1}{2}$ characters with an average width of one pica would be $28\frac{1}{2}$ x 12 points per character, or 342 points. Thus the alphabet length of 171 points equals two characters per pica.

3. Assume that the capital alphabet has $27\frac{1}{2}$ characters. Use 330 as a basis for figuring characters per pica for all cap alphabets.

A device for copyfitting sizes of type in 6-, 7-, 9-, 10-, 11-, and 12-point sizes in almost 600 faces and sizes of type is provided in this book. If directions are followed explicitly, anyone can determine how much space a page of typewritten manuscript will take in most of the kinds and sizes of types in use today.

In the copyfitting procedure set forth here, only one factor can throw off the estimate: the loose spacing often practiced by the typesetter or machine operator.

Ems per Line in Various Measures by Point Sizes. To determine the number of ems in a line of text, merely measure the width of the text in picas and determine the point size; then enter the table on the following page. Where the pica width and point size cross is the em count to the nearest tenth. For example, if the text width is 20 picas and the point size is 14, then the amount of ems per line is 17.1.

EMS PER LINE IN VARIOUS MEASURES BY POINT SIZES

PICAS WIDE	Point Sizes											
	6	7	8	9	10	11	12	14	18	24	30	36
10	20.0	17.1	15.0	13.3	12.0	10.9	10.0	8.6	6.7	5.0	4.0	3.3
11	22.0	18.9	16.5	14.7	13.2	12.0	11.0	9.4	7.3	5.5	4.4	3.7
12	24.0	20.6	18.0	16.0	14.4	13.1	12.0	10.3	8.0	6.0	4.8	4.0
13	26.0	22.3	19.5	17.3	15.6	14.2	13.0	11.1	8.7	6.5	5.2	4.3
14	28.0	24.0	21.0	18.7	16.8	15.3	14.0	12.0	9.3	7.0	5.6	4.7
15	30.0	25.7	22.5	20.0	18.0	16.4	15.0	12.9	10.0	7.5	6.0	5.0
16	32.0	27.4	24.0	21.3	19.2	17.5	16.0	13.7	10.7	8.0	6.4	5.3
17	34.0	29.1	25.5	22.7	20.4	18.5	17.0	14.6	11.3	8.5	6.8	5.7
18	36.0	30.9	27.0	24.0	21.6	19.6	18.0	15.4	12.0	9.0	7.2	6.0
19	38.0	32.6	28.5	25.3	22.8	20.7	19.0	16.3	12.7	9.5	7.6	6.3
20	40.0	34.3	30.0	26.7	24.0	21.8	20.0	17.1	13.3	10.0	8.0	6.7
21	42.0	36.0	31.5	28.0	25.2	22.9	21.0	18.0	14.0	10.5	8.4	7.0
22	44.0	37.7	33.0	29.3	26.4	24.0	22.0	18.9	14.7	11.0	8.8	7.3
23	46.0	39.4	34.5	30.7	27.6	25.1	23.0	19.7	15.3	11.5	9.2	7.7
24	48.0	41.1	36.0	32.0	28.8	26.2	24.0	20.6	16.0	12.0	9.6	8.0
25	50.0	42.9	37.5	33.3	30.0	27.3	25.0	21.4	16.7	12.5	10.0	8.3
26	52.0	44.6	39.0	34.7	31.2	28.4	26.0	22.3	17.3	13.0	10.4	8.7
27	54.0	46.3	40.5	36.0	32.4	29.5	27.0	23.1	18.0	13.5	10.8	9.0
28	56.0	48.0	42.0	37.3	33.6	30.5	28.0	24.0	18.7	14.0	11.2	9.3
29	58.0	49.7	43.5	38.7	34.8	31.6	29.0	24.9	19.3	14.5	11.6	9.7
30	60.0	51.4	45.0	40.0	36.0	32.7	30.0	25.7	20.0	15.0	12.0	10.0

Figuring Ems per Page. To determine the number of ems in a page of 12 point type, merely measure the page in picas. A pica is an em; Hence, a page 25 picas wide and 40 picas deep contains 1,000 ems. Factors for other point sizes help:

10 point—Multiply the 12 point ems by 1.44.
 9 point—Multiply the 12 point ems by 1.78.
 8 point—Multiply the 12 point ems by 2.25.
 7 point—Multiply the 12 point ems by 2.94.
 6 point—Multiply the 12 point ems by 4.

Copyfitting Scales. Twenty-eight copyfitting scales are provided on the following pages to correctly fit 895 kinds of type, from 6-point through 12-point. Copyfitting scales are not sufficiently accurate to copyfit type larger than 12-point. Neither can capital letters be determined with any accuracy, because of the varying widths of the letters and because fewer cap letters can be set in any line compared with lowercase letters. Estimates can be made, however, by consulting typefounders' catalogs.

Copyfitting devices, made up of charts giving characters per pica or the alphabet length of the lowercase alphabet, are furnished to users by many of the makers of typesetting machines.

How to use the copyfitting scales provided in this book is best explained in a typical problem: The typewritten copy on page 104 is to be set in 12-point Intertype Baskerville, 23 picas wide. How many lines will it make? The procedure is as follows:

1. See the Index to Copyfitting Scales (page 106). Note by the table that this type face and size calls for the use of Scale No. 7.

2. Note that each scale has *two* sides: one for elite and one for pica typewriter sizes. Measure the copy on page 104. This copy has 10 characters per inch; hence it is pica size. Elite typewriter size has 12 characters per inch.

3. Use a strip of cardboard about the size of the scale, and make sure that you have the correct *side* of the scale. Laying the card-

board scale on the scale No. 7 in the book (page 114) mark your scale at 23 picas as shown on the book scale. Twenty-three picas are at the line to the left of the line marked 24 picas.

4. Lay your improvised scale on the typewritten copy below, and measure off the lines which will set in 12-point Baskerville, by Intertype. The diagonal marks on the typewritten copy below will coincide with your measuring.

5. Note that the eight diagonal marks on the copy below indicate that the typewritten manuscript will make eight lines when set in 12-point Baskerville by Intertype. Note the proof of the statement by examining the type, actually set in the face wanted, at the bottom of page 105.

John Baskerville was the first to calender his paper and print on, not into, the sheet. His ink was intensely black. He left an abundance of white space around his type page, and leaded his lines generously, though with more restraint than Bodoni was to show. He did not use ornamentation, and achieved his dignified, "learned" effects simply by suitable arrangement of sizes. Capitals, especially on title pages, usually were letterspaced.

This copyfitting procedure is also recommended when one must determine the number of pages a given type face will take, with a predetermined width of line and leading, or space between *lines,* on a large manuscript. It is not necessary for one to measure such a manuscript page for page. Merely figure the first few pages of the entire manuscript by this method, and if the typing is uniform, a sufficiently good estimate can be made for the remaining pages.

Examine the copy carefully, and note if any adjustments should be made on any line having a preponderance of small "points"; that is, having any periods or commas.

Note that a type face like Baskerville and Garamond, in the same point sizes, do not necessarily make the same amount of copy area for Linotype, Intertype, and Monotype. One should know in advance what matrices will be used, because they do not all take the same space. Whether or not an Intertype or a Linotype is used is unimportant in typecasting. But, the *matrices* used is of primary importance. Linotype matrices can be used on Intertypes, and the reverse is also true.

Comparative Copyfitting. The section on comparative copyfitting on pages 111 through 124 will enable one to select alternate or substitute type faces when he cannot secure the kind of type that was originally specified, and when he does not choose to copyfit his work a second time to fit another type face. The type faces and sizes listed under the Copyfitting Scale headings will make the *same number of lines.*

Caution: Make sure that the *correct side* of the scale is used when copyfitting by this method. Also, make sure that you have selected the correct *manufacturer* of the type used.

John Baskerville was the first to calender his paper and print *on,* not *into,* the sheet. His ink was intensely black. He left an abundance of white space around his type page, and leaded his lines generously, though with more restraint than Bodoni was to show. He did not use ornamentation, and achieved his dignified, "learned" effects simply by suitable arrangements of sizes. Capitals, especially on title pages, usually were letterspaced.

INDEX TO COPYFITTING SCALES — *Machine-Set*

1. Find name of type in first column.
2. Find column for Linotype, Intertype, or Monotype.
3. Find point size in correct column.
4. Note scale number given under point size.
5. Turn to Copyfitting Scales (pp. 111-124).

	LINOTYPE							INTERTYPE							MONOTYPE						
Point Size	6	7	8	9	10	11	12	6	7	8	9	10	11	12	6	7	8	9	10	11	12
Baskerville	21	19	16	13	10	8	6	23		14	14	11	10	7	24	20	16	14	11	8	6
Benedictine	24	19	15	12	9	7	5														
Beton Bold										18	13	10	7	5							
Beton Extrabold										8		4		1							
Beton Medium										18	13	10	7	5							
Beton Wide										8		4		1							
Binny Oldstyle															22	17	15	13	9	7	6
Bodoni	25	19	15		9		7	25		15		9		7	22	17	15	13	10	8	6
Bodoni Book	26	21	17	13	11		8	26		17		11		8	26	21	17	15	12	10	9
Bookman, Bookface	21	17	15	12	9	7	6	20	18	13	12	9	4	4	20	17	15	13	10	8	6
Cairo, Cairo Bold								19		14		9		4							
Cairo Bold Condensed									18		13		8								
Cairo Extrabold Cond.											13		8								
Cairo Heavy								19		13		8		4							
Cairo Medium								19		15		10		4							
Cairo Medium Cond.											13		8								
Caledonia	21		15	12	10	8	6														
Caslon		20	15	13	12	8	5	22		15		12	8	5							
Caslon Oldface	27		20	15	14	11	7								25	20	17	13	10	8	6
Caslon Oldstyle															25	20	17	13	10	8	6
Caslon #2	25		17		10	8	6														
Caslon #3	22	18	15	11	10		4	22		15		8		4							
Caslon #137		21	17	13	10	8	6														
Caslon Oldstyle #137															25		17	14	10	8	6
Century Expanded	19	15	12	10	8	6	5	19	15	12	10	8		5	22	17	14	11	9	8	6
Century Oldstyle #157															22	17	15	12	9	8	6
Century Schoolbook															20		12	10	8	6	5
Cheltenham, Cheltonian		19	15	13	11		9	22	19		13			9							
Cheltenham Wide	17		13		9		6	17		13		9		6	22	17	15		10		6

	LINOTYPE							INTERTYPE							MONOTYPE						
Point Size	6	7	8	9	10	11	12	6	7	8	9	10	11	12	6	7	8	9	10	11	12
Cloister	26		19		15	13	11	27		21		15		12							
Cloister Wide	21		15		11		8														
Deepdene															27		20		14		9
Egmont Bold										17		11		7							
Egmont Light										20		13		9							
Egmont Medium								28		20	14	11		7							
Electra			16	13	11	9	8														
Erbar Bold, Light Cond.			25		20		16														
Excelsior	15	12	11	9	8	7	5														
Fairfield	21		16	13	11	9	8														
Futura Bold								20		15		8		3							
Futura Bold Cond.								28		22		14		9							
Futura Book								27		22		14		9							
Futura Demibold								24		18		9		6							
Futura Light								28		21		14		9							
Futura Medium								26		19		12		8							
Futura Medium Cond.										28		21		15							
Garamond	26		19	15	12	9	6	23	20	17	15	13	10	9	23	20	16	14	12	11	9
Garamont															28		18	13	11	8	6
Goudy Light															22	17	15	13	10	8	6
Goudy Oldstyle								24		17		11		7	23		16		10		7
Granjon	28		18	15	13	11	8										19	16	13	11	
Ideal News								16	13	12	10	8	5	3							
Ionic No. 5	16	13	10	8	7		4														
Janson			14	12	10	8	7										16	14	11	9	7
Jenson			14		10		6								22		15		10		6
Kennerley Oldstyle															28		20	15	13	10	8
Kenntonian								25		16		12		8							
Medieval								24		15	12	9		5							
Memphis Bold	19		16	12	9		4														
Memphis Bold Cond.				13			5														
Memphis Extrabold		6		4			1														
Memphis Light	19		16	12	9		4														
Memphis Medium	19		16	12	9		4														
Memphis Med. Cond.			19		13		9														
Metroblack #2	20		15		9		4														
Metromedium	23		19		12		7														

Point Size	LINOTYPE							INTERTYPE							MONOTYPE						
	6	7	8	9	10	11	12	6	7	8	9	10	11	12	6	7	8	9	10	11	12
Metrolite #2	20		15		9		4														
Regal #1								16	13	12	10	8		3							
Regal #2								14	12	11											
Regal #2a									12	10		6									
Rex								18	16	13		9		5							
Sans Serif Bold															26		17		12		8
Sans Serif Extrabold															19		13		7		4
Sans Serif Light															26		17		12		9
Sans Serif Medium															26		17		12		8
Scotch	19		14		11	9	5			15		11	9	6	25		17	13	10	8	6
Scotch #2		17	13	10	8	6															
Spartan Black	17		14		7		3														
Spartan Heavy	21		18		9		6														
Spartan Light			20		13		8														
Spartan Medium	21		20		13		8														
Stymie Bold 189															18		12		6		3
Stymie Bold 790															19		13		7		3
Stymie Extrabold															17		11		6		2
Stymie Light															23		16		10		5
Stymie Medium															23		16		10		5
20th Century Bold															23		18		10		6
20th Century Extrabold															20		15		7		4
20th Century Light															28		22		14		10
20th Century Medium															28		20		13		8
Textype	17	14	13	11	9	7	6														
Vogue								21		19		13		8							
Vogue Bold								23		19		12		7							
Vogue Bold Condensed										27		20		14							
Vogue Extrabold								21		14		8		4							
Vogue Extra Bold Cond.										27		20		13							
Waverley										15	11	9	7	5							
Weiss Roman										22	18	16	13	10							

INDEX TO COPYFITTING SCALES—
Hand-set in American

	ROMAN						ITALIC					
Point Size	6	8	10	12	14	18	6	8	10	12	14	18
Baskerville	28	21	16	9	6	2	28	22	19	12	7	4
Bernhard Gothic Light	26	20	13	10	5	1	28	22	15	11	7	2
Bernhard Gothic Medium	26	21	13	10	6	1	26	20	13	10	5	1
Bernhard Gothic Heavy		17	11	8	4	1						
Bernhard Gothic Extra Heavy				5	2							
Bodoni	26	15	10	7	5	1	26	15	11	7	5	1
Bodoni Bold	23	13	8	5	3		24	13	9	6	3	
Bodoni Book	28	18	13	9	7	2	28	18	13	10	7	2
Bookman Oldstyle	19	15	10	6	2		20	14	8	3	1	
Caslon #540	28	17	13	9	6	2	28	17	15	11	7	3
Caslon Bold	17	11	6	3			18	11	5	3	1	
Century Expanded	20	13	8	5			22	14	10	6	2	
Century Bold	21	13	8	4	1		21	13	7	4		
Century Schoolbook	20	13	8	5	1		21	13	8	5	2	
Century Schoolbook Bold	16	10	5	3								
Cheltenham Oldstyle	28	22	15	11	6	2	28	21	14	10	5	1
Cheltenham Medium	22	16	10	7	3		23	17	10	7	3	
Cheltenham Wide	22	16	10	7	3							
Cheltenham Bold	19	14	8	5	2		19	14	6	5	1	
Cloister Oldstyle	27	20	15	11	8	3	28	24	18	15	11	5
Cloister Bold	23	16	11	9	6	1	25	18	14	10	7	2
Garamond	19	16	12	9	6	1	27	21	16	12	9	4
Garamond Bold	19	14	9	7	4		23	17	12	9	6	1
Goudy Oldstyle	23	16	10	7	3		28	20	14	10	5	1
Goudy Bold	20	13	8	5	2		22	14	9	6	2	
Invitation	15	10	7	4	2							
Invitation Shaded		9	6	4	2							
Kaufmann Script									15	12	9	3
Kaufmann Bold									12	9	7	2
Lydian			11	6	4				13	9	6	1
Lydian Bold			10	6	4				12	7	4	1
Park Avenue				12	9	4						
Rivoli			18	14	9	5			16	13	9	4
Shaw Text			16	12	8	1						

Hand-set in American

	ROMAN						ITALIC					
Point Size	6	8	10	12	14	18	6	8	10	12	14	18
Spartan Medium		20	13	8	5	1				9	5	1
Stymie Light	21	16	8	5	2		20	14	7	4	1	
Stymie Medium	19	13	6	4	1		19	13	6	4	1	
Stymie Bold	17	13	6	4	1		16	12	6	3	1	
Wedding Text	28	21	14	10	8							

COMPARATIVE COPY-FITTING

Type faces listed under copy-fitting scale numbers will occupy the same space when set. Under "Make," I is for Intertype, L is for Linotype, M is for Monotype.

Scale	Type Face	Make	Size
1	Beton Extrabold	I	12
	Beton Wide	I	12
	Memphis Extrabold	L	12
2	Stymie Extrabold	M	12
3	Futura Bold	I	12
	Ideal News	I	12
	Regal #1	I	12
	Spartan Black	L	12
	Stymie Bold	M	12
	Stymie Bold 790	M	12
4	Beton Extrabold	I	10
	Beton Wide	I	10
	Bookface	I	11
	Bookface	I	12
	Cairo	I	12
	Cairo Bold	I	12
	Cairo Heavy	I	12
	Cairo Medium	I	12
	Caslon #3	L	12
	Caslon #3	I	12
	Ionic #5	L	12
	Memphis Bold	L	12
	Memphis Light	L	12
	Memphis Extrabold	L	10
	Memphis Medium	L	12
	Metroblack	L	12
	Metrolite	L	12
	Sans Serif X-Bold	M	12
	20 Century X-Bold	M	12
	Vogue X-Bold	I	12

Scale	Type Face	Make	Size
5	Benedictine	L	12
	Benedictine Book	L	12
	Beton Bold	I	12
	Beton Medium	I	12
	Caslon	L	12
	Caslon	M	12
	Century Expanded	L	12
	Century Expanded	I	12
	Century School-book	M	12
	Excelsior	L	12
	Medieval	I	12
	Memphis Bold Cond.	L	12
	Rex	I	12
	Scotch	L	12
	Stymie Light	M	12
	Stymie Medium	M	12
	Waverley	I	12
6	Baskerville	L	12
	Baskerville	M	12
	Binny Oldstyle	M	12
	Bodoni	M	12
	Bookman	L	12
	Bookman Old Face	M	12
	Caledonia	L	12
	Caslon #2	L	12
	Caslon Oldstyle 37	M	12
	Caslon 137	L	12
	Caslon Oldstyle	M	12
	Century Expanded	L	10
	Century Expanded	M	12
	Century Oldstyle	M	12
	Century School-book	M	10
	Cheltenham Wide	L	12
	Cheltonian Wide	I	12
	Cheltenham Wide	M	12
	Futura Demibold	I	12

Scale	Type Face	Make	Size
6	Garamond	L	12
	Garamont	M	12
	Goudy Light	M	12
	Jenson	L	12
	Jenson	M	12
	Regal #2a	I	12
	Scotch	I	12
	Scotch	M	12
	Scotch #2	L	12
	Spartan Heavy	L	12
	Stymie Bold	M	10
	Stymie Extrabold	M	10
	20th Century Bold	M	12
	Textype	L	12
7	Baskerville	I	12
	Benedictine	L	11
	Benedictine Book	L	12
	Beton Bold	I	11
	Beton Medium	I	11
	Binny Oldstyle	M	11
	Bodoni	L	12
	Bodoni	I	12
	Bookman	L	11
	Caslon Oldface	L	12
	Egmont Bold	I	12
	Egmont Medium	I	12
	Excelsior	L	11
	Goudy Oldstyle	M	12
	Ionic #5	L	10
	Janson	L	12
	Janson	M	12
	Metromedium	L	12
	Sans Serif Extra-bold	M	10
	Spartan Black	L	10
	Stymie Bold	M	10
	20th Century Extra-bold	M	10

Scale	Type Face	Make	Size
7	Textype	L	11
	Vogue Bold	I	12
8	Baskerville	L	11
	Baskerville	M	11
	Beton Extrabold	I	8
	Beton Wide	I	8
	Bodoni	M	11
	Bodoni Book	L	12
	Bodoni Book	I	12
	Bookman Oldface	M	11
	Cairo Bold Cond.	I	12
	Cairo Exbld. Cond.	I	12
	Cairo Heavy	I	10
	Cairo Medium Cond.	I	12
	Caledonia	L	11
	Caslon	L	11
	Caslon	I	11
	Caslon Oldstyle	M	11
	Caslon #2	L	11
	Caslon #3	I	10
	Caslon 137	L	11
	Caslon Oldstyle	M	11
	Century Expanded	L	10
	Century Expanded	I	10
	Century Expanded	M	11
	Century Oldstyle	M	11
	Century Schoolbook	M	10
	Cloister Wide	L	12
	Electra	L	12
	Excelsior	L	10
	Fairfield	L	12
	Futura Bold	I	10
	Futura Medium	I	12
	Garamont	M	11
	Goudy Light	M	11
	Granjon	L	12

Scale	Type Face	Make	Size
8	Ideal News	I	10
	Ionic #5	L	9
	Janson	L	11
	Kennerley Oldstyle	M	12
	Kenntonian	I	12
	Memphis Extrabold	L	8
	Sans Serif Bold	M	12
	Sans Serif Medium	M	12
	Scotch	M	11
	Scotch #2	L	11
	Spartan Light	L	12
	Spartan Medium	L	12
	20th Century Medium	M	12
	Vogue	I	12
	Vogue Extrabold	I	10
	Regal #1	I	10
9	Benedictine	L	10
	Benedictine Book	L	10
	Binny Oldstyle	M	10
	Bodoni	L	10
	Bodoni	I	10
	Bodoni Book	M	12
	Bookman	L	10
	Bookface	I	10
	Cairo	I	10
	Cairo Bold	I	10
	Century Expanded	M	10
	Century Oldstyle	M	10
	Cheltenham	L	12
	Cheltonian	I	12
	Cheltenham Wide	L	10
	Cheltonian Wide	I	10
	Deepdene	M	12
	Electra	L	11
	Egmont	I	12
	Excelsior	L	9

Scale	Type Face	Make	Size
9	Fairfield	L	11
	Futura Bold Cond.	I	12
	Futura Book	I	12
	Futura Demibold	I	10
	Futura Light	I	12
	Garamond	L	11
	Garamond	I	12
	Garamond	M	12
	Garamond	M	12
	Janson	M	11
	Medieval	I	10
	Memphis Bold	L	10
	Memphis Light	L	10
	Memphis Medium	L	10
	Memphis Medium Cond.	L	12
	Metroblack	L	10
	Metrolite	L	10
	Rex	I	10
	Sans Serif Light	M	12
	Scotch	L	11
	Scotch	I	11
	Spartan Heavy	L	10
	Textype	L	10
	Waverley	I	10
10	Baskerville	L	10
	Baskerville	I	11
	Beton Medium	I	10
	Bodoni	M	10
	Bodoni Book	M	11
	Bookman Oldface	M	10
	Cairo Medium	I	10
	Caledonia	L	10
	Caslon Oldstyle	M	10
	Caslon #2	L	10
	Caslon #3	L	10
	Caslon 137	L	10

Scale	Type Face	Make	Size
10	Caslon Oldstyle	M	10
	Century Expanded	L	9
	Century Expanded	I	9
	Century Schoolbook	M	9
	Cheltenham Wide	M	10
	Garamond	I	11
	Goudy Light	M	10
	Goudy Oldstyle	M	10
	Ideal News	I	9
	Ionic #5	L	8
	Janson	L	10
	Jenson	L	10
	Jenson	M	10
	Kennerley Oldstyle	M	11
	Regal #1	I	9
	Regal #2a	I	8
	Regal #2	I	6
	Scotch	M	10
	Scotch #2	L	10
	Stymie Light	M	10
	Stymie Medium	M	10
	20th Century Bold	M	10
	20th Century Light	M	12
	Weiss Roman	I	12
11	Baskerville	I	10
	Baskerville	M	10
	Bodoni Book	L	10
	Bodoni Book	I	10
	Caslon Oldface	L	11
	Caslon #3	L	9
	Century Expanded	M	9
	Cheltenham	L	11
	Cloister	L	12
	Cloister Wide	L	10
	Egmont Bold	I	10
	Electra	L	10

Scale	Type Face	Make	Size
11	Egmont Medium	I	10
	Excelsior	L	8
	Fairfield	L	10
	Garamond	M	11
	Garamont	M	10
	Granjon	L	11
	Granjon	M	11
	Janson	M	10
	Regal #2	I	8
	Scotch	L	10
	Scotch	I	10
	Stymie Extrabold	M	8
	Textype	L	9
	Waverley	I	9
12	Benedictine	L	9
	Benedictine Book	L	9
	Bodoni Book	M	10
	Bookman	L	9
	Bookface	I	9
	Caledonia	L	9
	Caslon	L	10
	Caslon	M	10
	Century Expanded	L	8
	Century Expanded	I	8
	Century Oldstyle	M	9
	Century School-book	M	8
	Excelsior	L	7
	Futura Medium	I	10
	Garamond	L	10
	Garamond	M	10
	Ideal News	I	8
	Janson	L	9
	Kenntonian	I	10
	Medieval	I	9
	Memphis Bold	L	9
	Memphis Light	L	9

10 Characters to the inch

12 Characters to the inch

Figures and divisions show pica measure into which typewritten characters will fit

Scale	Type Face	Make	Size
12	Memphis Medium	L	9
	Metromedium	L	10
	Regal #1	I	8
	Regal #2	I	7
	Regal #2A	I	7
	Sans Serif Bold	M	10
	Sans Serif Light	M	10
	Sans Serif Medium	M	10
	Stymie Bold	M	8
	Vogue Bold	I	10
13	Baskerville	L	9
	Beton Bold	I	9
	Beton Medium	I	9
	Binny Oldstyle	M	9
	Bodoni	M	9
	Bodoni Book	L	9
	Bookface	I	8
	Bookman Oldface.	M	9
	Cairo Bold Cond.	I	10
	Cairo Extrabold Cond.	I	10
	Cairo Heavy	I	8
	Cairo Medium Cond.	I	10
	Caslon	L	9
	Caslon Oldstyle	M	9
	Caslon 137	L	9
	Cheltenham	I	10
	Cheltonian	I	10
	Cheltonian Wide	L	8
	Cheltonian Wide	I	8
	Cloister	L	11
	Electra	L	9
	Egmont	I	10
	Fairfield	L	9
	Garamond	I	10
	Garamont	M	9
	Goudy Light	M	9

Figures and divisions show pica measure into which typewritten characters will fit

10 Characters to the inch

12 Characters to the inch

Scale	Type Face	Make	Size
13	Granjon	L	10
	Granjon	M	10
	Ideal News	I	7
	Ionic #5	L	7
	Kennerley Oldstyle	M	10
	Memphis Bold Cond.	L	10
	Memphis Med. Cond.	L	10
	Regal #1	I	7
	Rex	I	8
	Sans Serif Exbld.	M	8
	Scotch	M	9
	Scotch #2	L	9
	Spartan Light	L	10
	Spartan Medium	L	10
	Stymie Bold	M	8
	20th Century Medium	M	10
	Textype	L	8
	Vogue	I	10
	Vogue Exbld. Cond.	I	12
	Weiss Roman	I	11
14	Baskerville	I	8
	Baskerville	I	9
	Baskerville	M	9
	Cairo	I	8
	Cairo Bold	I	8
	Caslon Oldface	L	10
	Caslon Oldstyle	M	9
	Century Expanded	M	8
	Deepdene	M	10
	Futura Bold Cond.	I	10
	Futura Book	I	10
	Futura Light	I	10
	Garamond	M	9
	Janson	L	8
	Janson	M	9
	Jenson	L	8

Scale	Type Face	Make	Size
14	Scotch	L	8
	Spartan Black	L	8
	20th Century Light	M	10
	Textype	L	7
	Vogue Bold Cond.	I	12
	Vogue Extrabold	I	8
15	Benedictine	L	8
	Benedictine Book	L	8
	Binny Oldstyle	M	8
	Bodoni	L	8
	Bodoni	I	8
	Bodoni	M	8
	Bodoni Book	M	9
	Bookman	L	8
	Bookman Oldface	M	8
	Cairo Medium	I	8
	Caledonia	L	8
	Caslon	L	8
	Caslon	I	8
	Caslon Oldface	L	9
	Caslon #3	L	8
	Caslon #3	I	8
	Century Expanded	L	7
	Century Expanded	I	7
	Century Oldstyle	M	8
	Cheltenham	L	9
	Cheltenham Wide	M	8
	Cloister	L	10
	Cloister	I	10
	Cloister Wide	L	8
	Excelsior	L	6
	Futura Bold	I	8
	Futura Medium Cond.	I	12
	Garamond	L	9
	Garamond	I	9
	Goudy Light	M	8

Scale	Type Face	Make	Size
15	Granjon	L	9
	Jenson	M	8
	Kennerley Oldstyle	M	9
	Medieval	I	8
	Metroblack	L	8
	Metrolite	L	8
	Scotch	I	8
16	Baskerville	L	8
	Baskerville	M	8
	Electra	L	8
	Erbar Light Cond.	L	12
	Erbar Bold Cond.	L	12
	Fairfield	L	8
	Garamond	M	8
	Goudy Oldstyle	M	8
	Granjon	M	9
	Ideal News	I	6
	Ionic #5	L	6
	Janson	M	8
	Kenntonian	I	8
	Memphis Bold	M	8
	Memphis Light	L	8
	Memphis Medium	L	8
	Regal #1	I	6
	Rex	I	7
	Stymie Light	M	8
	Stymie Medium	M	8
	Weiss Roman	I	10
17	Binny Oldstyle	M	7
	Bodoni	M	7
	Bodoni Book	L	8
	Bodoni Book	I	8
	Bodoni Book	M	8
	Bookman	L	7
	Bookman Oldface	L	7
	Caslon Oldstyle	M	8

Scale	Type Face	Make	Size
17	Caslon #2	L	8
	Caslon 137	L	8
	Caslon Oldstyle	M	8
	Century Expanded	M	7
	Century Oldstyle	M	7
	Cheltenham Wide	L	6
	Cheltonian Wide	I	6
	Garamond	I	8
	Goudy Light	M	7
	Sans Serif Bold	M	8
	Sans Serif Light	M	8
	Sans Serif Medium	M	8
	Scotch	M	8
	Scotch #2	L	8
	Spartan Black	L	6
	Stymie Extrabold	M	6
	Textype	L	6
18	Beton Bold	I	8
	Beton Medium	I	8
	Bookface	I	7
	Cairo Bold Cond.	I	8
	Caslon #3	L	7
	Futura Demibold	I	8
	Garamont	M	8
	Granjon	L	8
	Rex	I	6
	Spartan Heavy	L	8
	Stymie Bold	M	6
	20th Century Bold	M	8
	Weiss Roman	I	9
19	Baskerville	L	7
	Benedictine	L	7
	Benedictine Book	L	7
	Bodoni	L	7
	Cairo	I	6
	Cairo Bold	I	6

Scale	Type Face	Make	Size
19	Cairo Heavy	I	6
	Cairo Medium	I	6
	Century Expanded	L	6
	Century Expanded	I	6
	Cheltenham	L	8
	Cheltonian	I	8
	Cloister	L	8
	Futura Medium	I	8
	Garamond	L	8
	Granjon	M	8
	Memphis Bold	L	6
	Memphis Light	L	6
	Memphis Medium	L	6
	Memphis Med. Cond.	L	8
	Metromedium	L	8
	Sans Serif Exbld.	M	6
	Scotch	L	6
	Stymie Bold	M	6
	Vogue	I	8
	Vogue Bold	I	8
20	Baskerville	M	7
	Bookface	l	6
	Bookman Oldface	M	6
	Caslon	L	7
	Caslon Oldface	L	8
	Caslon Oldstyle	M	7
	Century Schoolbook	M	6
	Deepdene	M	6
	Egmont	I	8
	Egmont Medium	I	8
	Erbar Bold Cond.	L	10
	Erbar Light Cond.	L	10
	Futura Bold	I	6
	Garamond	M	7
	Kennerley Oldstyle	M	8
	Metroblack	L	6

Scale	Type Face	Make	Size
20	Metrolite	L	6
	Spartan Light	L	8
	Spartan Medium	L	8
	20th Century Exbld.	M	6
	20th Century Medium	M	8
21	Baskerville	L	6
	Bodoni Book	L	7
	Bodoni Book	M	7
	Bookman	L	6
	Caledonia	L	6
	Caslon 137	L	7
	Cloister	I	8
	Cloister Wide	L	6
	Fairfield	L	6
	Futura Light	I	8
	Futura Medium Cond.	I	10
	Spartan Heavy	L	6
	Spartan Medium	L	6
	Vogue	I	6
	Vogue Extrabold	I	6
22	Binny Oldstyle	M	6
	Bodoni	M	6
	Caslon	I	6
	Caslon #3	L	6
	Caslon #3	I	6
	Century Expanded	M	6
	Century Oldstyle	M	6
	Cheltonian	I	7
	Cheltenham Wide	M	6
	Futura Bold Cond.	I	8
	Futura Book	I	8
	Goudy	M	6
	Jenson	M	6
	Weiss Roman	I	8
23	Baskerville	I	6
	Garamond	I	6
	Garamond	M	6
	Goudy Oldstyle	M	6
	Metromedium	L	6
	Stymie Light	M	6

Scale	Type Face	Make	Size
23	Stymie Medium	M	6
	20th Century Bold	M	6
	Vogue Bold	I	6
24	Baskerville	M	6
	Benedictine	L	6
	Benedictine Book	L	6
	Futura Demibold	I	6
	Medieval	I	6
25	Bodoni	L	6
	Bodoni	I	6
	Caslon Oldstyle	M	6
	Caslon #2	L	6
	Caslon Oldstyle	M	6
	Erbar Bold	L	8
	Erbar Light	L	8
	Kenntonian	I	6
	Scotch	M	6
26	Bodoni Book	L	6
	Bodoni Book	I	6
	Bodoni Book	M	6
	Cloister	L	6
	Futura Medium	I	6
	Garamond	L	6
	Sans Serif Bold	M	6
	Sans Serif Light	M	6
	Sans Serif Medium	M	6
27	Caslon Old Face	L	6
	Cloister	I	6
	Deepdene	M	6
	Futura Book	I	6
	Vogue Bold Cond.	I	8
28	Futura Bold Cond.	I	6
	Futura Light	I	6
	Futura Medium Cond.	I	8
	Garamont	M	6
	Granjon	L	6
	Kennerley Oldstyle	M	6
	20th Century Light	M	6
	20th Century Medium	M	6

SELF-TEST

This self-test will serve as a review of this chapter. The questions are either true or false, multiple choice, or for thought and discussion. The numbers following each question refer to the page number on which the correct answer can be found.

1. A layout is the same as a dummy, except that it consists of one page. (71)
2. Thumbnail sketches allow the layout man an opportunity for the best choice of his ideas. (71)
3. Layouts indicate how the job will look when completed. (71)
4. The comprehensive layout is made in a size other than that of the completed job. (74)
5. Type matter of the finished layout is indicated by ruled lines. (74)
6. The work of competent layout men on the same copy usually follows the same typographical design. (74)
7. Which layout do you like on page 75? Why?
8. Which layout do you like on page 77? Why?
9. Harmony refers to equivalent elements. (76)
10. Balance refers to the pleasing relation between type faces. (76)
11. Proportion refers to relationship between elements. (76)
12. Name the nine methods often used in minor display. (76)
13. Name a type face appropriate for a coal dealer ad. (78)
14. Name a type face appropriate for a hairdresser ad. (78)
15. Name a type face appropriate for a builder ad. (78)
16. Type measurements are always given in inches. (89)
17. Soft papers make type appear lighter than hard papers. (91)
18. Hard papers make type faces appear bolder than soft papers. (91)
19. Gravure type is screened, therefore it is thickened. (97)
20. Fine-lined type is good for the gravure process. (97)
21. How many lines of 6-point type, solid, can you set in 24 picas? (98)
22. How many lines of 8-point type, solid, can you set in 28 picas? (98)

23. How many lines of 9-point type, solid, can you set in 40 picas? (98)
24. How many lines of 10-point type, solid, can you set in 30 picas? (99)
25. How many lines of 11-point type, solid, can you set in 30 picas? (99)
26. How many lines of 12-point type, solid, can you set in 15 picas? (99)
27. How many lines of 10-point type, 2 point-leaded, can you set in 40 picas? (99)
28. How many lines of 9-point type, 3-point leaded, can you set in 29 picas? (99)
29. Reverse plates are those in which the white and the black copy is reversed? (100)
30. Typewriters have the following number of characters to the inch: (103)

    a. 8   c. 10   e. 12
    b. 9   d. 11   f. 13

31. What copyfitting scale would be used for 10-point Baskerville by Intertype? (106)
32. What copyfitting scale would be used for 8-point Caslon by Monotype? (106)
33. What copyfitting scale would be used for 12-point Century Schoolbook by Monotype? (106)
34. What copyfitting scale would be used for 7-point Ideal News by Intertype? (107)
35. What copyfitting scale would be used for 10-point Bodoni Book by American? (109)
36. What copyfitting scale would be used for 12-point Stymie Bold by American? (110)
37. Futura Bold in 12-point sets the same as 12-point Ideal News. (111)
38. Monotype Scotch in 11-point sets the same as 8-point Memphis Extrabold. (115)

39. Linotype Bodoni Book in 11-point sets the same as 9-point Century Expanded by Monotype. (117)
40. Intertype Bookface in 6-point sets the same as 10-point Linotype Erbar Bold Condensed. (124)
41. All 10-point sizes of Baskerville set the same by any one of the three manufacturers of machine-set type. (106)
42. It is necessary to mark the kind of type by manufacturs on layouts if accuracy is to be had in copyfitting. (90)
43. Name three methods of producing rules (lines) for offset-lithography. (93)
44. How is cold type affixed to art work? (93)
45. What term designates copy in its final form for offset-lithography? (93)
46. What are screens, stipples and the like called? (95)
47. Explain how airbrush work can be eliminated. (95)
48. What is meant by stock art? (92, 93)
49. Explain how letterpress work is used in offset. (93)
50. Explain how registration of color is prepared for offset. (96)

PROJECTS

1. Make a collection of cutout examples of type faces used appropriately in newspapers and magazines. (78)
2. Make a collection of cutout examples of hand-lettering used appropriately in newspapers and magazines. (80)
3. Make thumbnail sketches, using copy shown on page 82, in centered and squared line layout.
4. Make thumbnail sketches, using copy shown on page 82, in slanted and curved line layout.
5. Make thumbnail sketches, using copy shown on page 84, in centered line layout.
6. Make thumbnail sketches, using copy shown on page 84, in flush left and flush right layout.
7. Make thumbnail sketches, using copy shown on page 86, in squared and flush left layout.
8. Make thumbnail sketches, using copy shown on page 86, in rule ornament layout.

9. Make thumbnail sketches, using copy shown on page 88, in illustrated layout. Either draw illustrations by hand or use cutout illustrations in the layout.

10. Make thumbnail sketches, using copy shown on page 88, in type trick layout.

11. Make a collection of good and bad examples of gravured type, cut from the Sunday newspaper supplements. (97)

12. Practice copyfitting typewritten copy in various sizes and kinds of type, using the scales provided. (105-125)

13. Fancy yourself in the printing business. You need a complete assortment of printed matter as follows:

    a. Business cards

    b. Letterheads 8½ x 11 inches

    c. Statements

    d. Envelopes No. 6¾ and No. 10 sizes

    e. Billheads

Make layouts for the above in rough, comprehensive, and finished form. If type is set, provide proofs cut to correct size. Redesign the copy of printed matter on hand, in rough, comprehensive, and finished layouts.

14. Make a collection of printed matter of your own choice, and practice redesigning each piece.

THE FOUR KINDS OF TYPE COMPOSITION

An Intertype or Linotype Slug

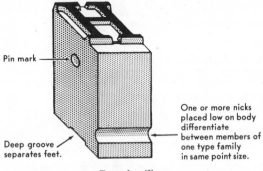

Pin mark

Deep groove separates feet.

One or more nicks placed low on body differentiate between members of one type family in same point size.

Foundry Type

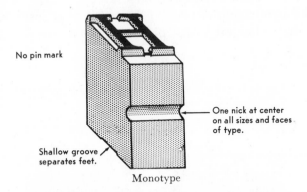

No pin mark

Shallow groove separates feet.

One nick at center on all sizes and faces of type.

Monotype

Ludlow

CHAPTER 4

How to Set "Hot" Type

Four Ways in Which "Hot" Type Is Set

Hand Composition. Type is still composed into lines by hand from foundry type, very similarly to the manner in which Gutenberg and his followers set type 500 years ago. However, rarely do we find great amounts of copy so composed. We do see a large amount of copy set by hand in headlines and other display matter, and a like amount of copy for commercial work in printing, as letterheads, envelopes, calling cards, advertisements, etc.

Intertype and Linotype. These two line- or slug-casting machines compose entire lines in one piece of metal, as against the hand-setting of foundry type letter-by-letter. Almost all composition of our newspapers is so composed in type, even to the headlines up to and including 60-point sizes. The Monotype is similar to the Linotype and Intertype.

Intertypes and Linotypes allow fast composition from the time the copy reaches the operator's hands until the slugs emerge from the machine. Slugs are easy to handle, compared with single types, and can be picked up the same way that a bunch of sticks of the same size can be handled.

Monotype. Monotypes cast two kinds of type: (1) for placing in type cases to be composed by hand, like foundry type and (2) straight paragraph matter in single letters, already spaced and justified, to be made up into pages or units of advertising and commercial printing jobs. Several machines are used; a keyboard punches a roll of paper, which is later fed into a casting machine for blocks of copy composition. Another machine casts large type up to 72-point size, and still another makes spacing material to fill out large blanks in a form.

Ludlow Typograph. This device allows the hand composition of brass matrices, which are placed in a caster. The resultant slug lines are made up into forms similarly to that of the other processes of type composition. This machine is used mostly for large faces of type such as headings, and for commercial printing work. Not much small type is so composed for straight paragraph matter.

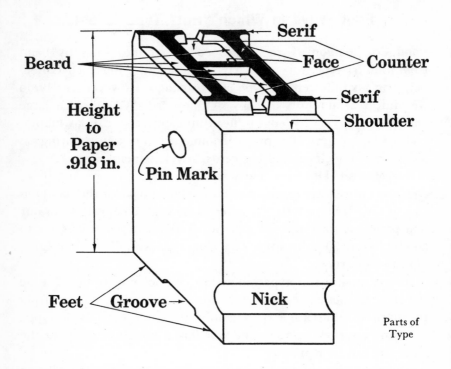

Parts of Type

Type Used in Hand Composition

A piece of foundry type is a strip of metal about an inch in height (exactly .918 of an inch) with a character cast in relief on one end, called the *face* of the type. Hand-set foundry types are cast in an alloy of lead, tin, antimony, and copper; they are accurate to 1/10,000 of an inch in all dimensions. The greater percentage of type metal is lead. Antimony is added to give hardness and fluidity. Tin allows a lower working temperature and makes the metal tougher. Foundry types are cast at 850° F.

Parts of Type. The various parts of a type are shown on the opposite page, and are explained below.

Face: the letter or character cast in relief at the top.

Counter: the sunken part within and around the face.

Serifs: the cross-lines at the ends of the main strokes.

Shoulder: the top of the type below the face, toward the nick.

Beard: the beveled part below the face and above the body.

Pin mark: the small round mark on the side of the type, made by the device that removes the type from the mold.

Nicks: the sunken sections across the body of the type which act as a guide to the compositor when placing the type in the composing stick. The number of nicks and their positions on the body also differentiate between faces of type in many instances.

Feet: the two projections on which the type stands, separated by the *groove.*

Kern: any part of the face that extends over the side of the type body, often found on letters f and j.

Point System. Types are made according to the typefounder's own system of measurement, by *points.* A point is about $\frac{1}{72}$ of an inch, and exactly .0138 for foundry type and .014 in Intertype and Linotype. The linear system of inches and fractions of inches is too cumbersome to measure type.

A *nonpareil* is 6 points.
A *pica* is 12 points.
An inch is 6 picas.

The above measurements are applied to all phases of type composition and should be used by all who work with printing.

The *line gauge* or *pica rule* is used by printers as well as those who plan printing. It is usually designed with inches on one side and picas and 6-point divisions on the opposite side. Some rules have *agate* lines, meaning $5\frac{1}{2}$-point divisions on one side. Newspaper advertisements are measured in agate lines.

Type Families. Each member of a type family has the same general characteristics of design, except that it may be light, bold, extra-bold, medium, etc. The Vogue family is shown below.

ABCDEFGHIJKLMNOPQRSTUVWXYZ
abcdefghijklmnopqrstuvwxyz fi fl ff ffi ffl $1234567890
Light

ABCDEFGHIJKLMNOPQRSTUVWXYZ
abcdefghijklmnopqrstuvwxyz fi fl ff ffi ffl $1234567890
Light Oblique

ABCDEFGHIJKLMNOPQRSTUVWXYZ
abcdefghijklmnopqrstuvwxyz fi fl ff ffi ffl $1234567890
Bold

ABCDEFGHIJKLMNOPQRSTUVWXYZ
abcdefghijklmnopqrstuvwxyz fi fl ff ffi ffl $1234567890
Bold Oblique

ABCDEFGHIJKLMNOPQRSTUVWXYZ
abcdefghijklmnopqrstuvwxyz fi fl ff ffi ffl $123456
Extra Bold

ABCDEFGHIJKLMNOPQRSTUVWXYZ
abcdefghijklmnopqrstuvwxyz fi fl ff ffi ffl $123456
Extra Bold Oblique

ABCDEFGHIJKLMNOPQRSTUVWXYZ
abcdefghijklmnopqrstuvwxyz fi fl ff ffi ffl $1234567890
Bold Condensed

ABCDEFGHIJKLMNOPQRSTUVWXYZ
abcdefghijklmnopqrstuvwxyz fi fl ff ffi ffl $1234567890
Extra Bold Condensed

The Vogue Family

Type Fonts. A font of type is an assortment of caps, lowercase, figures, fractions, and marks of punctuation called *points*. Small caps are often included in a separate font, in foundry type. Shown on this page is a font of Weiss Roman.

ABCDEFGHIJKLMNOPQRSTUVWXYZ

abcdefghijklmnopqrstuvwxyz$1234567890

fi fl ff ffi ffl Æ Œ æ œ tb & £ † ‡ — . , - ; ' : ' ! ? [( )]

ABCDEFGHIJKLMNOPQRSTUVWXYZ & Æ Œ

% @ * | § ‖ ¶ ⅛ ¼ ⅜ ½ ⅝ ¾ ⅞

Fonts of matrices on the Monotype, Linotype, and Intertype include both the light roman and italic, or roman and bold face. The same faces in a foundry font would be separate.

ABCDEFGHIJKLMNOPQRSTUVWXYZ

abcdefghijklmnopqrstuvwxyz$1234567890

fi fl ff ffi ffl Æ Œ æ œ tb & £ † ‡ — . , - ; ' : ' ! ? [( )]

Ta Te Ti To Tr Tu Tw Ty Va Ve Vo Wa We Wo Ya Ye Yo YA

FA PA TA VA WA F. P. T. V. W. Y.

Ta Te Ti To Tr Tu Tw Ty Va Ve Vo Wa We Wo Ya Ye Yo YA

f f. f, f- fa fe fo fr fs ft fu fy ff. ff, ff- ffa ffe ffo ffr ffs ffu ffy

Special characters called *logotypes* and *ligatures* are often provided with a font of Intertype and Linotype matrices. Some are shown above, and illustrate how a good fit between letters is secured with their use. Weiss Roman, shown here, is made as a foundry type by Bauer and in matrices by Intertype.

Type Sizes. Type sizes, based on the point system of measurement, are usually made in 6, 8, 10, 12, 14, 18, 24, 30, 36, 42, 48,

6 point

ABCDEFGHIJKLMNOPQRSTUVWXYZ
abcdefghijklmnopqrstuvwxyz

8 point

ABCDEFGHIJKLMNOPQRSTUVWXYZ
abcdefghijklmnopqrstuvwxyz

10 point

ABCDEFGHIJKLMNOPQRSTUV
abcdefghijklmnopqrstuvwxyz

12 point

ABCDEFGHIJKLMNOPQRS
abcdefghijklmnopqrstuvwxyz

14 point

ABCDEFGHIJKLMNOP
abcdefghijklmnopqrstuvw

18 point

ABCDEFGHIJKLM
abcdefghijklmnopq

24 point

ABCDEFGHIJ
abcdefghijklmn

30 point

ABCDEFG
abcdefghijk

36 point

ABCDEF
abcdefg

48 point

ABCD
abcdef

60 point

ABC

Sizes in Vogue Bold Series

60, and 72 points. However, other sizes are made in certain types
for special uses: 4, 5, 5½, 6, 6½, 7, 7½, 9, 10½, 11, 16, 28,
34, 54, 84, 96, 120 and 144 points. A type "series" refers to the
many sizes available in any one type family. The Vogue Bold
Series is shown on the opposite page. Type made in wood for
poster printing and where extremely large sizes are needed is sized
by the *line*. A line is 12 points; hence a piece of "12-line wood
type" would be 12 picas tall.

Type Storage. Type is kept in *cases,* which are shallow drawers.
Each case is divided into many compartments, and each character
of a type font is kept in one of them. Because type looks much the
same when it is difficult to see the face, it is necessary for the typesetter to take care when placing the types back into their respective
compartments, or *boxes.* If he does not take care, and puts type
in the wrong boxes, errors will occur in setting type from the
case, and will of necessity have to be corrected.

The most popular type case used by compositors is the *California Job Case.* See Fig. 4–1. Other cases, now largely out of date

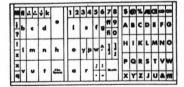

Fig. 4-1. *Left:* California Job Case   *Right:* New York Job Case

but in use in some printing plants, are the *News Cases* shown in
Fig. 4–2, and the *New York Job Case* shown in Fig. 4–1.

Type cases are seldom marked where types may be found. Those
learning to set type are therefore obliged to learn the positions of
the boxes in the case.

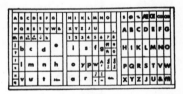

Fig. 4-2. A Pair of News Cases

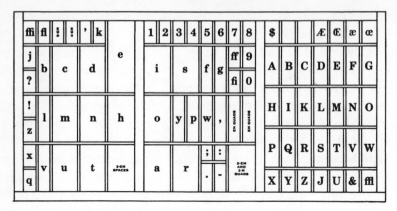

Fig. 4-3. Lay of California Job Case

SPACING MATERIAL

Because all of the types of a job do not print, low spacing material is provided to place in the parts of a type form that are not supposed to print. This includes the space between lines, between words, and at the ends of paragraphs.

Leads and Slugs. These thin strips of type metal are usually cut to pica and half pica lengths, for spacing in the form. They are stored in *lead* or *slug cases*. Leads are either one, two, or three points in thickness. Slugs are either six or twelve points thick.

Spaces and Quads. This low spacing material is made in the various type point sizes, and is used to provide the blank space between words, at the ends of paragraphs, and for indentions.

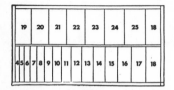

Fig. 4-4. Lead and Slug Case

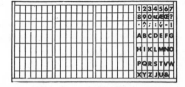

Fig. 4-5. Quadruple Case

All spaces and quads are based on the *em* which is the square of the type body of any size of type. Thus, a six-point em is six points square, a ten-point em is ten points square; a 24-point em is 24 points square, etc. See Fig. 4–6 on the opposite page.

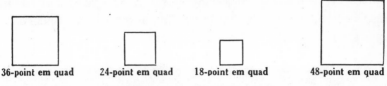

Fig. 4-6. Different Sizes of Em Quads

Spaces are the thinnest blanks used in setting type, up to one-third of the em in size. A three-to-the-em space is one-third the size of the em quad, and is usually referred to as a *three-em space*. The four-em space is one-fourth of the em quad, and the five-em space is one-fifth of the em quad. See Fig. 4–7.

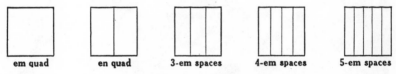

Fig. 4-7. Spaces and En and Em Quads

Quads are provided as follows: the en quad is one-half the width of the em quad. The two-em quad is twice the size of the em quad, and the three-em quad is three times the size of the em quad. This is in width only, as illustrated in Fig. 4–8, below. Type fonts 30 points in size usually do not have quads larger than the em quad.

Fig. 4-8. Comparative Sizes of Spaces and Quads in 12 Point

Reglet. This spacing material is of the same size and dimensions as slugs, but is made of wood instead of type metal. Reglet is used for locking type forms for the press, and is generally not used within a type form as spacing material.

Furniture. Furniture is made of both wood and metal. Metal furniture is used for large blank spaces within a type form, as well as for locking up forms for the press. Wood furniture, not so accurate as metal furniture, is used only for locking forms.

Furniture is made in pica widths of 2, 3, 4, 5, 6, 8, and 10, and lengths of 10, 15, 20, 25, 30, 35, 40, 50, and 60 picas. Special and larger sizes are available for special uses.

Fig. 4-9. Setting Type

Hairline
Half Point
One Point
Two Point
Three Point
Four Point
Six Point
Eight Point
Ten Point
Twelve Point
Eighteen Point
Twenty-Four Point

Fig. 4-10. Some Sizes of Rule

Borders. Straight lines and decorated units and strips of type metal are cast by Elrod, Ludlow, Intertype, Linotype, Monotype, and are also available from the foundry type makers. The machine-made borders are cast in strips, which are cut apart, mitered for corners, and used for borders in printing work. The foundry borders are made in individual units, or in strip form. See the various borders on the opposite page.

Rule. For the purpose of printing straight lines of various thicknesses, type founders provide brass or type metal *rule.* See the point sizes in Fig. 4–10. Intertypes and Linotypes, as well as Monotypes, make rule of a given point size on wider bodies. Hence a one-point rule could be on a six-point body. Brass rule is usable on both top and bottom.

TYPICAL DESIGNS IN BORDERS

6 Pt. 94

12 Pt. 525

179¼   6 Pt. 179   179½

6 Pt. 43

6 Pt. 70

6 Pt. 155

6 Pt. 41

12 Pt. 2514

6 Pt. 151

12 Pt. 2511

12 Pt. 2513

12 Pt. 2515

6 Pt. 95

6 Pt. 152

6 Pt. 505

6 Pt. 505a

6 Pt. 505a s.c.

6 Pt. 505c s.c.

6 Pt. 505 rev.

5 Pt. 506

6 Pt. 508

6 Pt. 508a s.c.

6 Pt. 508a

6 Pt. 509

6 Pt. 510

6 Pt. 510a

6 Pt. 510a s.c.

6 Pt. 513

6 Pt. 511

8 Pt. 511a

6 Pt. 291

2130a   12 Pt.   2130b

2131a   12 Pt.   2131b

2132a   12 Pt.   2132b

789a   12 Pt.   789b

12 Pt. 780

781   12 Pt.   782

12 Pt. 783

784   12 Pt.   785

12 Pt. 786

12 Pt. 786a

12 Pt. 579

12 Pt. 574

12 Pt. 572

Tools of the Composing Room

Composing Sticks. This receptacle is used for composing type by hand. The stick is adjustable in pica and half-pica graduations in various ways determined by the kind of stick used. Composing sticks must not be sprung by driving type into them. Should one line be made too tight, the remaining lines composed will be loose. See Fig. 4–11 for an illustration of a Rouse stick.

Fig. 4-11. Composing Stick   Fig. 4-12. Planer

Type Cabinets. Type cases are stored in type cabinets, which hold as many as 48 cases in which families of type are stored.

Quoins. Quoins are mechanical wedges used to lock forms in chases before they go to the printing presses. Some quoins, like the *Challenge,* consist of two parts (see Fig. 4–14), others like the *Wickersham* (see Fig. 4–13) are of one piece, which contain an eccentric cam which widens the quoin when operated by the key.

Fig. 4-13. Wickersham Quoin   Fig. 4-14. Challenge Quoin
         and Key   and Key

Planers. A planer is a block of hardwood used to knock all parts of a form to its *feet* so that a level printing surface can print properly. Planers should be tapped *lightly* with the mallet or quoin key—never struck violently, which might injure the type faces in the form. See Fig. 4–12 on the opposite page. Planers should never be placed with their bottoms on the imposing table because the planing surface may pick up small pieces of dirt or chips of metal which might be driven into the type faces or plates of a form.

Lead and Slug Cutters. These cut leads, slugs, borders, and type metal rule to even picas and half-picas. Brass rule should never be cut on these machines. See Fig. 4–15.

Fig. 4-15. Lead and Slug Cutter

Imposing Tables. These are either steel or marble-topped tables on which type forms are *locked up* for the presses. The surfaces of imposing tables must never be scarred or dented through misuse of tools, because the surface must be accurately flat for good work.

Chases. Steel frames in which type is locked for the presses are *chases*. Accurate when new, chases must never be sprung out of shape by too much pressure when forms are locked. The quoins need only enough pressure to hold the form in place.

Tweezers. Used only by experienced typesetters who have the training necessary for the use of the tool, tweezers in inexperienced hands injure the faces of valuable printing types, and hence are seldom given to beginners to use.

Type Brushes. These are used to clean forms and plates with fluids such as nonleaded gasoline. Before cleaning with a brush, the form must always be wiped off first with a cloth saturated in the fluid. This prevents ink being washed down between the type and slug lines.

Proof Presses. These hand or electrically operated printing presses are used for making the first print of a type form, so that errors can be found and corrected before the job goes to the presses. See Fig. 4–16. Some proof presses are hand-inked with the use of the *brayer,* or roller, which can be seen on the proof press pictured. Others have automatic inking rollers.

Fig. 4-16. Proof Press   Fig. 4-17. Rotary Miterer

Miterers. Hand miterers, shown in Fig. 4–18, allow the angle-cutting of borders and rule to make joints for boxes and borders. The Vertical Miterer shown in Fig. 4–17 cuts 45° angles only at a speed far greater than can be done by hand.

Fig. 4-18. Hand Miterer

Fig. 4-19. Power Saw

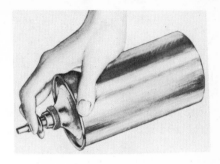

Fig. 4-20. *Above:* Benzine Can
Below: Numbering Machine

Saws. Composing room saws not only cut but also trim leads and slugs, borders and rule. Care must be taken to see that the material clamps are used, and that the work is not held by the fingers, which might be injured. Saws have gauges which may be set to half points as well as to picas and half-picas. See Fig. 4–19.

Solvent Cans. With safety valves, solvent cans are operated as shown in Fig. 4–20 (above). They usually contain white (non-leaded) gasoline, which is used on cloth for washing type forms to remove the ink. Gasoline or any other solvent must never be poured onto a type form, but onto the cloth, to keep ink from running down between the lines of type.

Numbering Machines. When locked up in a type form, these devices number each sheet on the printing press. Made in many models, numbering machines operate either forward or backward, depending upon the model. Such tools are delicate, and should be cleaned well, and kept in a bath of oil and kerosene when not in use. See Fig. 4–20 (below).

Other Devices not mentioned here help the compositor.

How to Set Type by Hand

When setting type by hand, the typesetter or compositor holds the composing stick in the left hand, with the thumb over the last piece of type set, in the manner shown in Fig. 4–21. Before setting a line he usually sets a lead or a slug the length of the line into the stick, and sets the first line of type against the lead.

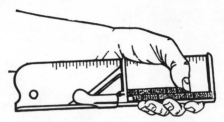

Fig. 4-21. How to Hold Composing Stick

Type is set from *left* to *right,* with the nick of the type up. This makes the type upside down, which reverse is necessary to get the correct printing on the paper.

Justification means making each line of type the correct length. A line is justified when it can stand alone in the stick—even when the stick and type is turned upside down!

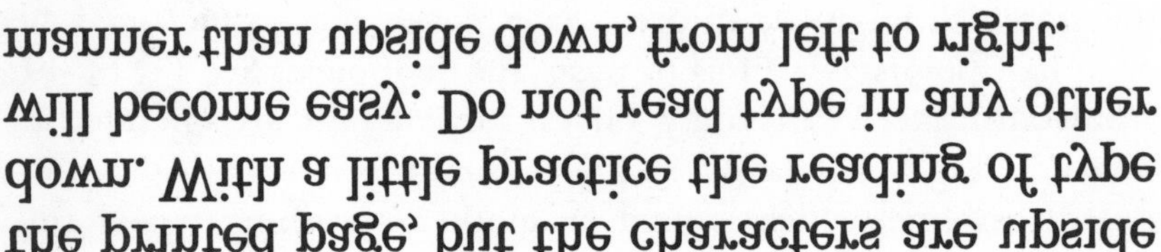

ɯɐuuǝɹ ʇɥɐu ndsıpǝ poʍu' ɟɹoɯ ʃǝɟʇ ʇo ɹıɓɥʇ˙

ʍıʃʃ pǝɔoɯǝ ǝɐsʎ˙ Ɒo uoʇ ɹɐǝp ʎbǝ ıu ɐuʎ oʇɥǝɹ

poʍu' ʍıʇɥ ɐ ʃıʇʇʃǝ bɹɐɔʇıɔǝ ʇɥǝ ɹǝɐpıuɓ oʇ ʎbǝ

ʇɥǝ bɹıuʇǝp bɐɓǝ' pnʇ ʇɥǝ ɔɥɐɹɐɔʇǝɹ ɐɹǝ ndsıpǝ

Ʇʎbǝ ıs ɹǝɐp ɟɹoɯ ʃǝɟʇ ʇo ɹıɓɥʇ ɐs ɐɹǝ ʇɥǝ ʃıuǝs ou

Type is read from left to right as are the lines on the printed page, but the characters are upside down. With a little practice the reading of type will become easy. Do not read type in any other manner than upside down, from left to right.

Fig. 4-22. How Type Is Read. Type Is Above; Print Below

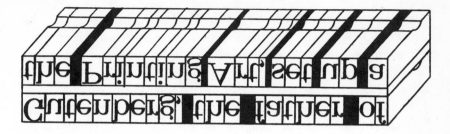

Gutenberg, the father of the Printing Art, set up a

Fig. 4-23. How Spacing Is Done between Words

Spacing means placing the correct space, or combinations of spaces in a line of type to make the space between words *appear* to be even, as shown in Fig. 4–23, above. Certain letters appear to be farther apart than others because of their design. These are round letters like the o, p, d, A, O, and others. Some appear to be closer together, like the l and h, H and L, and other combinations.

How to Space between Words. When setting type, start by placing a three-em space between words. When the type fills the measure, and a part of a word still remains to be set in the line, the spacing between words must be *reduced*.

How to Reduce Space between Words.

1. Substitute as many four-em spaces for the three-em spaces as are necessary to gain the required space.

2. If the four-em spaces are still too large to get in the last few letters of the last word on the line, substitute as many five-em spaces for the four-em spaces as are necessary to gain the space.

Place the widest spaces between words which have ending characters and beginning characters that appear to be closer together because of their design: dh, for example.

Place the thinnest spaces between words which have space at their sides because of their design: vo, wa, for example. Note the spacing in the lines shown in Fig. 4–23, above.

How to Increase Space between Words. In the event that the last word almost fills the line, and there remains insufficient space left to accommodate the next word, it is necessary to substitute *thicker* spaces or combinations of spaces originally set between words. The space between words must then be *increased*.

1. Substitute en quads for the three-em spaces originally placed between words as are necessary to fill the line. If the en quads do not increase the length of the line sufficiently,

2. Substitute a three-em space plus a four-em space *combined*, in as many places as are necessary to fill the line. In this combination of spaces does not tighten the line,

3. Substitute two three-em spaces *combined* as are necessary to tighten the line. If the line is still loose,

4. Substitute a three-em space and an en quad between as many words as are necessary to tighten the line.

See Fig. 4–24 for comparative widths of spaces and combinations of spaces.

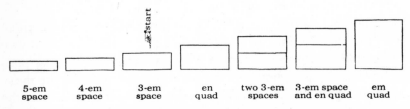

| 5-em space | 4-em space | 3-em space | en quad | two 3-em spaces | 3-em space and en quad | em quad |

Fig. 4-24. Comparative Widths of Spaces

Spacing between Sentences. Use the regular space between sentences that is used between words of the sentence. The period at the end of the first sentence gives the illusion of more space.

Dividing Words. Take no chances on the correct division of words. Use the dictionary in *all* cases of word division!

How to "Quad Out." When quadding out at the ends of short lines of paragraph endings, place the smallest spaces against the period at the end of the last sentence, and the largest at the end of the line. No thin spaces will then fall off when type is handled.

How to Distinguish between Puzzling Letters. Although quite confusing at first, the differences between certain type characters can be determined simply by following these rules:

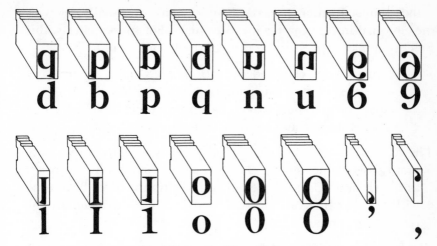

Fig. 4-25. Puzzling Type Characters

To distinguish between the b, d, p, and q, hold the type *nick up* and look at the face of the type. Note that all of these characters have a straight stem and a round loop. Holding the type nick up, imagine that the straight stem is pointed in the *opposite direction*. Visualize what character the type would be if this were so. Your correct visualization will be the correct answer. See Fig. 4-25, above, and practice this procedure in differentiating between the puzzling characters shown.

The n and the u are easily identified by looking at them *nick up:* If the letter looks like an n, it is a u. If the face looks like a u, it is an n. The same is true of the 6 and 9.

The lowercase letter l, the cap I, and the figure 1 can be distinguished one from the other by examining their designs of face. The lowercase l is thinner than the others, and at the top has one serif; the cap I has serifs at both ends of the letter; the figure 1 is wider, usually as wide as all other figures in the type font.

The lowercase o, cap O, and zero are not difficult to tell one from the other if it is remembered that the lowercase o is small on the body of the type, the zero is quite narrow, and the cap O is largest and usually round.

The comma has its face on the same side as the nick of the type. The apostrophe has its face farthest away from the nick.

Indentions. Regular paragraph indentions are usually set with the em quad in type matter up to 26 picas. For special effects, this indention may vary with the plan of the layout man.

> Squared and centered indentions are composed in type as shown in this paragraph. This style is often used to set type matter apart from other text, to give it display and more prominence.

The hanging indention style of straight matter composition, commonly used in newspaper classified advertisements, is composed as shown here. Usually one em of indention is used, beginning with the first line full measure, and indenting throughout the rest of the composition.

The half-diamond form of indention is used in some composition to give special effects to the reading matter as a part of the design. The first line is set to the full measure, and each succeeding line is indented equally at each end, being centered on the full measure.

Poetry indentions usually have rhyming lines indented equally, and blank verse usually has no indention. When quotation marks are used, they should be placed outside of the alignment, as shown below.

> "For 'tis the beauty of the soul,
> Not that of form or face,
> That makes a lovely character
> And gives it spiritual grace."

How to Letterspace. The setting of thin spaces between lower-case letters is not generally considered good form. Letterspacing of caps is common to give them a more pleasing appearance. Certain cap characters appear to be spaced widely apart because of the design of the letter combinations; for example:

AWAY FROM VALUE   AWAY FROM VALUE

In the line at the left (bottom of the opposite page), the first word *appears* to have more space between the letters than do the other words. Also, there appears to be more space between the V and A of the second word. *Corrective spacing* of the group of words at the right, with thin spaces, makes the type look much better.

How to Set Leaders. In order to carry the reader's eye properly across a line of type, particularly in tables, *leaders* are used. Leaders appear to be a series of spaced periods, but are set in hand composition in en, em, two-em, and three-em pieces of type. Some leaders have dots, others have hyphens; often leaders have one dot to the en, but may have two dots to the en. An example of leader work is shown below. Leaders are usually kept in special leader boxes, illustrated in Fig. 4–26. Dotted or straight rules are often used in place of leaders.

Old Name	Point Size
Pearl	5
Nonpareil	6
Minion	7
Brevier	8
Bourgeois	9
Long Primer	10
Small Pica	11
Pica	12

Fig. 4-26. *Left:* A Leader Box. *Right:* A Quarter-Sized Rule Case

A brass and type metal rule case is shown in Fig. 4–26. Rules are aligned with type by use of leads and slugs.

How to Set Figures. Most all fonts of type, either foundry or machine, have figures cast on the same width, which is usually the en of the type body. Figures should always be aligned at the *right,* as shown in the leader example above.

Roman numerals, set in either small caps or caps, are also aligned at the right, as shown below:

BIG STARTING LETTERS, called *initial* letters, are used to decorate the pages of books and magazines as well as certain kinds of commercial printing. Initial letters may be used in the same type family, as shown here in 60-point Baskerville with 11-point Baskerville as text, or in a contrasting type face, provided the two do not clash in their design. Type faces used as initial letters must be of a size that aligns well at the bottom as well as at the top of the lines covered by initial letter. The initial is usually followed by small caps, as shown here, or in caps, as shown below.

LARGE letters may be used in an *initial up* treatment, shown here. This initial is set in 30-point Baskerville to align with the bottom of the first line of type.

ALTHOUGH difficult because the type must be *cut in,* certain letters such as the A must be so composed as to bring the first line close to the initial. Were the cap Baskerville letter A not cut in as shown here, the letter A would look like a separate word, and cause confusion to the reader. The spacing around an initial letter should always be equal.

How to Remove Type from the Composing Stick. Printers' *pi* is mixed and jumbled type. Pi is difficult to distribute back into the cases, and extreme care must be taken to prevent this tedious

Fig. 4-27. How to Remove Type from the Composing Stick

Fig. 4-28. How to Hold Type for Removal to the Form

and difficult task. When type is taken from the stick, the safe method is to lay the stick flat on the galley, and *slide* the type out of the stick. Grasp the type in the stick between the thumb and first finger of each hand. Press the sides of the second finger of each hand hard against the ends of the type lines, as shown in Figs. 4–28 and 4–29. With practice, handling type lines becomes easy.

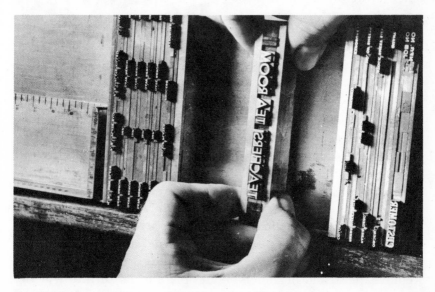

Fig. 4-29. How to Hold Type When Placing It in a Form

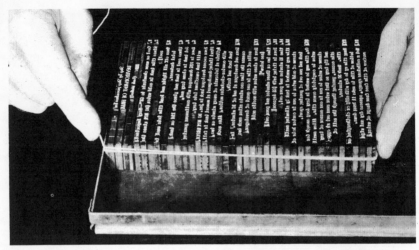

Fig. 4-30. *Above:* How to Tie Up a Form. *Below:* Tucking the String

How to Tie Up a Form. Secure a piece of string that will make at least seven layers around the type form. The length will of course depend upon the size of the form. Beginning at the upper left-hand corner of the type form, wind the string clockwise, catching the first layer by subsequent windings. Keep the string parallel and smooth as possible. *Do not tie a knot.* See Fig. 4–30, above. Push a loop under the windings of the string, and draw it tightly against a corner of the form. Some printers end the string in a particular place so that it can always be easily found when the string is to be removed. Tuck in the end as shown here with a lead or rule, leaving a short end protruding.

How to Make Corrections. When corrections are to be made in type, the first step is to place the type form on a galley, with the head (or top) of the form at the top or closed end of the galley. Remove the string. Beginners should place metal furniture at the sides of the form not held by the sides of the galley to hold type.

It is best to work on a *bank,* or inclined surface. Holding the type as pointed out previously, remove the line to be corrected; then place it in the composing stick. Make the corrections and re-space and justify the line, and replace it in the form.

If the correction will take more than one line, the type will have to be *over-run* into succeeding lines. To do this sensibly, place all succeeding lines in order along a long galley, and pick the type up, word by word, and replace it in the composing stick.

How to Distribute Type. Distribution is the term given to plac-ing all saved foundry materials back into the cases from which they were set, so that they can be used again. There is no distribution, as such, with machine-set type or slugs, except perhaps spacing material. Type ready for distribution is called *dead* matter. *Live* matter is type not yet printed. *Standing* matter is type held over for another printing and stored away in galleys.

Fig. 4-31. How to Hold Type for Distribution

The distribution of type is learned by doing, and, although a tricky job at first, it soon becomes an easy task. When distributing small amounts, the beginner does best if he selects a few lines at a time, and holds them as shown in Fig. 4–31 on the preceding page. Holding the type in a position that prevents any short top line from falling, *nick up* in *all* cases, pick up the last few letters from the right end of the line. *Read the word* from which these letters were taken. Holding the letters between the thumb and the first finger of the right hand, place the types back into their respective boxes in the type case. Distribution is often called *throwing-in*. Beginners should not take this literally, because a thrown type may become a battered type, and not usable for future work.

How to Keep from Mixing Type Cases. Mixed type cases mean errors in future work. Mixed type cases also mean missing type that should be in a case but lost in another. To do the job right, note these rules:

1. Always compare the face of the type to be distributed with the type in the case you have selected.

2. Always compare the nicks of the type in a like manner.

3. Always compare the sizes of the type by holding one against the other for a good comparison.

4. Always read every word distributed; not letter by letter.

5. Always find dropped pieces of type.

When distributing large display faces, place all lines of the same type face and size together in a galley, and then follow the procedure set forth above.

How to Pull a Proof

After a type form is tied securely on a galley, a *proof* is printed to see if any errors have been made. This is done on a *proof press*. Sometimes the proof is taken with the type in a galley, and sometimes the type form is slid from the galley to the press "bed."

The usual proof press does not have automatic inking, and without it the form must be inked by hand with a brayer, an inking roller. Run the brayer over the ink plate several times, and place it on the type form, running it back and forth to make sure that all areas of the form have been inked. See Fig. 4–32.

Fig. 4-32. How to Ink a Form with a Brayer

Hold a piece of paper by opposite corners and lay it carefully over the type form. Do not move the paper once it has touched the form, or it will get smeared. Operate the proof press so that the roller will pass over the paper and form. Strip the paper from the form as illustrated in Fig. 4–33, on the next page.

Beginners usually use too much ink when taking proofs. It is best to use too little rather than too much ink on proofs. If a suction sound is heard as the brayer is passed over the inking plate, too much ink is being used, and should be *sheeted off* by holding paper on the plate and running the brayer over the top of the paper.

How to Pull a Stone Proof. For pulling proofs of forms too large for the proof press, ink the type on the imposing table. Moisten a sheet of paper large enough for the proof with a sponge and water. Holding the paper by opposite corners, lay it carefully over the form with the dampened side up. Lay a *proof planer* (a felt-bottomed planer) on the form and tap it lightly with a mallet or quoin key. Plane the entire form, and see that no areas are left unplaned. Then strip paper from form as shown in Fig. 4–33.

Fig. 4-33. How to Strip Printed Proof from Type Form

How to Wash the Type Form. It is extremely important to wash ink from a type form after proofing. Pour a little gasoline or other ink solvent on a rag, and rub the ink from the form. If gasoline is poured over the form, it will carry ink down between the lines.

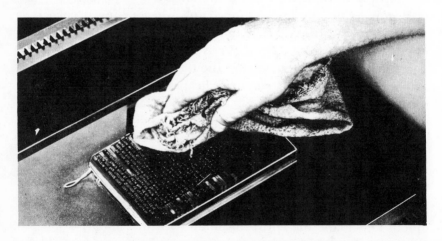

Fig. 4-34. How to Wash the Type Form After Proofing

How Lines Are Cast on the Linecasting Machines

Intertype and Linotype machines cast *slugs* of type in which all the letters are made on one piece for each line. These two machines are similar in appearance, and do identical work. They are the fastest machines in time for setting type from copy to completed slugs.

Fig. 4-35. A Late Model Mergenthaler Linotype, The Elektron, Delivers Lines of Newspaper Copy from Punched Tape

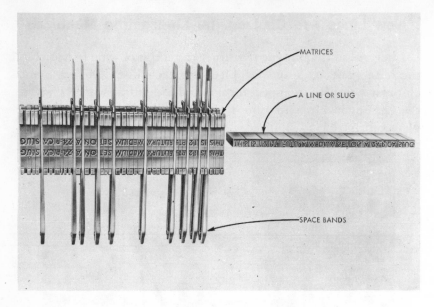

Fig. 4-36. Matrices, Spacebands, and Cast Slug

Most of the straight composition done today is cast on the Linotype and Intertype machines. Many of the larger display sizes of type are also set on these machines, especially on newspapers. The machines use molten metal and cast new slugs for each job of printing. Type can be composed on these machines at four to ten times the speed possible by hand. Slugs are much more easily handled in assembling type matter in make-up than are individual types or type composed on the Monotype machines.

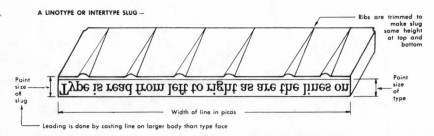

Fig. 4-37. Linotype or Intertype Slug

Fig. 4-38. Linecasting Machine Keyboard

Both the Linotype and Intertype machines use the principle of the circulating *matrix,* which is a small brass object having one or two characters stamped into one side, and having "distributor teeth" at the top. As explained on the following pages, the operator manipulates the keyboard (see above) of the machine, and matrices are assembled in a line. When the line is completed, the matrices are returned automatically to the *magazine* whence they came, and a slug line of "type" is ejected from the casting mechanism of the machine. Instead of selecting a space as used in hand composition of foundry type, the Intertype and Linotype operator merely strikes the *spaceband* key. A wedge-shaped device falls into the line to be cast, as between words. When the line is sent into the machine, the spaceband adjusts the spacing between words so that all spaces are equal in width.

As most matrices carry two letters, it is possible for the operator to get two faces of type from the same magazine. On *mixer* models, he can get four or more faces on some models of machines.

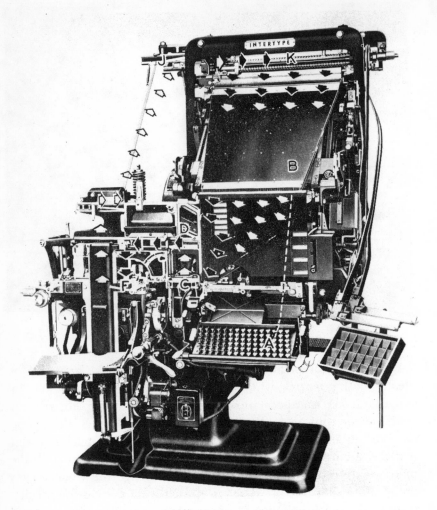

Fig. 4-39. How Matrices Are Assembled

The illustration above shows the principle of the circulating matrix used on Intertype and Linotype machines. As the operator touches the keys at A, matrices fall from the magazine B. The matrices and spacebands are assembled at point C. When a line is completed, the operator raises it to point D, where the machine takes over all of the work mechanically. The slug line is cast at

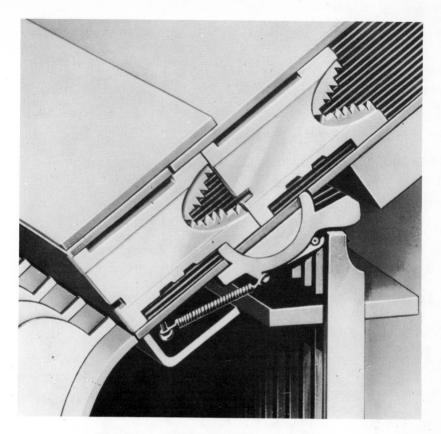

Fig. 4-40. How Matrices Are Released on Intertypes

point F, and the matrices and spacebands are raised as indicated by the arrows. At point J, the matrices enter a distributing mechanism, and fall into their respective channels in the magazine B at point K. These operations are shown in more detail on the following pages. The spacebands are returned automatically to a storage box under point D. A spaceband is shown below.

Fig. 4-41. Spaceband

The magazine in which the matrices are stored.

The escapements which release the matrices as the operator depresses the key buttons.

Keyboard cam mechanisms.

Fig. 4-42. How Matrices Are Released

The Intertype and Linotype keyboards are power-driven, and only the slightest pressure is needed to release matrices. When the operator presses a key, a cam drops onto a rubber roll, which gives the upward thrust that actuates the escapement mechanism.

Matrices stored in the magazine in parallel rows.

Matrices being carried to assembling elevator by conveyor belt

Assembling mechanism

Fig. 4-43. How Matrices Are Assembled

Matrices are stored in the magazine, 8. As the matrices fall, they drop through the partitions, 9, and are then carried by a conveyor belt to point 11, above, which is the assembling mechanism. A *star wheel* at point 10 stacks them in order as they are keyboarded.

At this point the operator may cause certain matrices to be above the others in the line by merely pulling a lever. When this is done, the *auxiliary* position of the matrix is used, which is either the italic, small cap, or bold face of the roman type used.

Spacebands falling to assembling elevator.

Assembling mechanism.

Fig. 4-44. How Spacebands Are Released

When the operator taps the spaceband key either on the left or right of the main keyboard, the spacebands are released from the spaceband box shown at point 12 above, and fall to point 13, at the correct spot between words made up of matrices.

When spacebands are driven up in the casting mechanism, the line is spaced out to fill the full measure of the line. Spacebands may be either thin or fat, to suit the size and design of type.

Fig. 4-45. Automatic Action Takes Place

When the Linotype or Intertype operator presses a lever, either at the right or left below the keyboard, the line of matrices is taken over automatically by the machine.

The matrices and spacebands move from point D, above, to point E, and then straight down to point F, which is the casting position. While the line is coming into position, the mold, which was at position 15, is brought into position to receive the matrices at point F. Now the line is locked tightly against the mold.

The illustration below shows a rear view of matrices and space-bands in position against the mold. The top of the mold has been broken away to show how the punched letters on the matrices close up one side of the aperture made by the matrices and the mold. The mold body is below, the mold cap on top; and liners, which are changed for type size and width of line, are at each end.

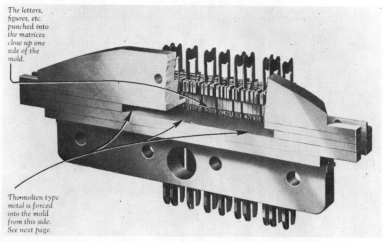

The letters, figures, etc. punched into the matrices close up one side of the mold.

The molten type metal is forced into the mold from this side. See next page.

Fig. 4-46. Rear View of Mold and Matrices

Note that the spacebands are forced upward, making the line of matrices and spacebands fill the measure, which is adjustable on Linotypes and Intertypes up to 30 picas on most models, and up to 42 picas on others. Measures start at four picas by half picas.

Figure 4–48, on the opposite page, shows the detailed arrange-ment of the metal pot, plunger, well, and throat of the casting mechanism. Linotype and Intertype metal is composed of an alloy of lead, tin, and antimony, and is kept at a temperature from 535° F. to 550° F. in either gas-fired or electrically-heated pots.

Fig. 4-47. Large Line Cast on "Recessed" Mold

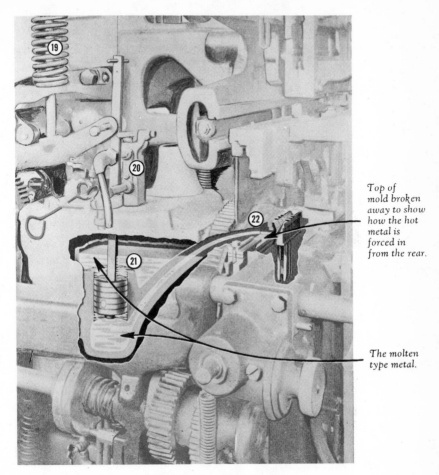

Top of mold broken away to show how the hot metal is forced in from the rear.

The molten type metal.

Fig. 4-48. How Lines Are Cast

The throat (22) and mouthpiece (22) are also kept at the correct temperature.

The type metal in the pot shown at 21 above is in a liquid state, and is forced by the plunger in the well up through the throat (22) against the matrices making up the right side of the mold that forms the line. Power is given to the plunger from the strong spring (19). A thermostat (20) keeps the metal within a few degrees of the needed temperature.

Fig. 4-49. Matrices and Spacebands Are Returned

After the line is cast, it is ejected onto a *galley*, which is a flat tray at the left of the operator. The slug is trimmed on the bottom and sides to the correct size. During this time, the machine is proceeding to distribute the spacebands and matrices whence they came, as shown above. An elevator takes the matrices and spacebands to point of the arrow at 32 above, where they are transferred to the right at 33. Here the spacebands are separated from the matrices, and fall into the box at point L.

A second elevator drops from the top of the machine to point 33, where the matrices are engaged by their teeth and lifted (see point 34) to the distributor box at point J.

The illustration below shows how the matrices are returned to the channels of the magazine. The distributor box feeds the matrices singly to the distributor screws, which carry them along on a distributor bar. Each different matrix has its own combination of teeth, which slide in the distributor bar at K, which extends along the top of the magazine. The distributor bar has teeth which correspond in reverse to the combinations on the teeth of the matrices. When the teeth of the matrices meet the right combination of the bar, they drop into the magazine. This allows the matrices to be used over and over again.

On mixer models of the Intertype and Linotype, matrices can be keyboarded from two adjacent magazines (some machines have as many as four main and four side magazines) and a special arrangement allows continuous distribution.

Both the Intertype and Linotype are available in various models (Intertype designated by letters of the alphabet, as C, F, and G; and Linotype by numerals, as 5, 33, and 35) each adapted to certain kinds of slug composition.

Fig. 4-50. How Matrices Are Returned to Magazine

Special equipment is available, such as quadding and centering and justified indention devices. See Fig. 4–51. With the *quadder* the operator does not keyboard any blank spaces; he merely moves a lever, and the line is automatically cast centered, flush left, or flush right. He can adjust the mechanism also to indent certain lines of copy at both ends, as shown.

Linotypes and Intertypes cast lines in sizes ranging from four point to condensed 60 point. As pointed out previously, the lines may be cast up to 30 picas wide on some machines, and 42 picas wide on others. When longer lines are needed, it is possible to *butt* the slugs; that is, use more than one for each line.

Intertypes and Linotypes can be equipped with a number of different molds from one to six. These molds can be changed to different sizes of type as well as for length of line.

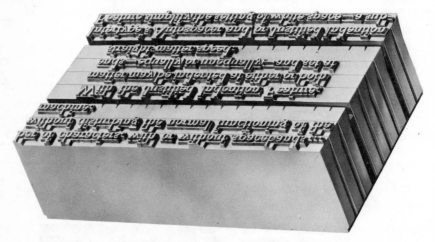

Fig. 4-51. Product of Intertype and Linotype

The Teletypesetter. Tape-operated linecasting machines have enabled press associations and newspaper chains to send news and features by wire, and the syndicates to deliver their tapes by mail. Using tapes punched locally, the system has been able to treble manual production, and centralized tape punching has allowed national magazines to produce identical slugs in printing offices all over the country. It is easier to store tapes than type metal for re-runs since 200 lbs. of tape can be stored in six cubic feet, as contrasted to 42 tons of type-metal occupying 150 cubic feet.

Tapes are produced on perforators and fed to linecasting machines, featuring special keyboards, where 12 lines are cast each minute. (See Fig. 4-52.) One machine operator can look after as many as four Linotypes or Intertypes by himself.

Fig. 4-52A. Teletypesetter Perforator

Fig. 4-52B. Perforated Tape Activates Keyboard

Recently introduced electronic computers can increase production 40% to 60%. The computers receive Teletypesetter tape in unjustified form without word divisions. The several computers can:

1. "Read" unjustified punched paper tape.
2. Hyphenate (divide words) correctly.
3. Justify the type lines (with no loose or tight lines).
4. Make a new tape to operate linecasting machines.

In addition the computer can handle the entire operation, including the elimination of corrections in hot metal or on film. It can handle galleys or pages for adding corrections, divide the galleys into pages, and strip film into individual pages.

Speeds are phenomenal: one make of computer can process more than 4,000 lines of newspaper text in one hour.

Fig. 4-53. Overhang Slug Composition for Difficult Setups

The New Improved
SOAP For Hard Water **2** Large Cakes **31**c

Fig. 4-54. Print of Slugs Pictured in Fig. 4-53

Overhang Slug Composition. Pictured at the top of this page is an example of *overhang slug composition,* quite popular in advertising composition, especially for grocery advertisements in newspapers. When composed by hand this kind of typesetting is quite difficult and painstaking work. However, when cast on slug-casting machines, much time is saved and an added advantage is gained: that of *justification,* or making each line the same width necessary to lock up the type for platemaking or printing on the press. Set by machine, the job consists of only three pieces. Set by hand, the same job requires at least 56 individual pieces of type. See Figs. 4–53 and 4–54.

How Type Is Cast on the Monotype

The Monotype system of composition consists of several machines, each of which does a particular job for type composition:

The Keyboard, illustrated in Fig. 4–55, operated by compressed air, perforates a paper ribbon with a series of small holes as the operator "types" the copy on a standard typewriter arrangement of keys. As the holes are punched, the widths of the letters are recorded on a justifying scale. The ribbon moves forward as other keys are struck, and the thickness of each letter is totaled. A bell notifies the operator when a line is almost filled. Noting the recorded total widths of all letters, the operator touches two keys; this takes care of the line spacing automatically when the ribbon runs through the composition caster later. The speed of the keyboard is limited only by the speed of the operator.

The widths of the letters, or the *set size,* bear a fixed relation to the em of the type size being composed. The basic letter capital M is divided into 18 equal parts, and these units are used in determining the width of the other characters in the font of type. The paper strip on which the holes are punched, referred to as the *controller ribbon,* is run through the caster backwards so that the spacing material size already noted on the ribbon for the line is set in order. Ribbons may be held for future recastings.

The Monotype system, with keyboard and caster along with additional equipment, can manufacture single-letter type composition up to 60 picas wide, deliver leads, slugs, and decorative and plain line borders in thickness from 1½ to 12 points in long strips or cut to pica size, and individual types for the cases in sizes up to 36 point. Both high and low spacing material can be cast on the Monotype caster. High spacing material is best for duplicate platemaking, and low spacing is best for printing from the type.

Fig. 4-55. Monotype Keyboard

Fig. 4-56. Monotype Composition Caster

The Composition Caster, illustrated in Fig. 4–56, manufactures, sets, and justifies lines of type in *single* letters, in contrast with the Intertype and Linotype machines which cast slug lines in *one* piece. Sizes range from 5 through 12 point, and some machines are equipped for casting 18 point. Three faces can be cast with each *matrix case* (see Fig. 4–57); for example, light roman, bold roman, and light italic. For special work other faces are added.

Fig. 4-57. Monotype Matrix Case

Spacing may be slightly varied between letters on the Monotype Composition Caster. Space between lines is accomplished by casting the face on a larger point body. *Corrections are made by hand.*

Fig. 4-58. *Left:* Flat Monotype Matrix. *Right:* Cellular Matrices

Cellular matrices, shown in Fig. 4–58, fill the Monotype matrix case (272 to 324 characters available). *Flat matrices* are used for casting single letters.

Tabular matter, or a series of independently justified units, such as mathematics or technical material, on one line, is best done on the Monotype, as several sections may be justified without regard to the other sections in the same line. Vertical rules and cross rules may be added by splitting these justified columns. Lines may be cast up to 60 picas in width, and with a special attachment, lines 90 picas wide may be cast.

In the Monotype Composition Caster, the ribbon, previously punched on the Monotype Keyboard, passes over a tracker similar to that of an automatic piano. Compressed air is forced through the holes in the ribbon and actuates the matrix case (Fig. 4–57). The matrix case stops momentarily over the mold, and a letter is cast. Small types may be cast at a speed of 150 characters per minute. Justification is made possible by an automatically shifting wedge, which is directed by the last four holes of each line punched in the controller ribbon by the operator.

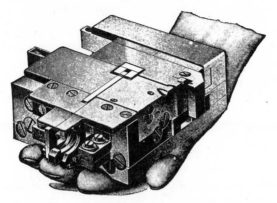

Fig. 4-59. Monotype Mold

Monotype Type and Rule Caster. Single letters, to be placed in cases and composed as foundry type, are made on this Monotype. Cellular and flat matrices are used, which are placed in a holder and put into the machine over the mold, which is interchangeable for various sizes from 5 to 36 point. An extra attachment allows "material" (leads and slugs) to be made.

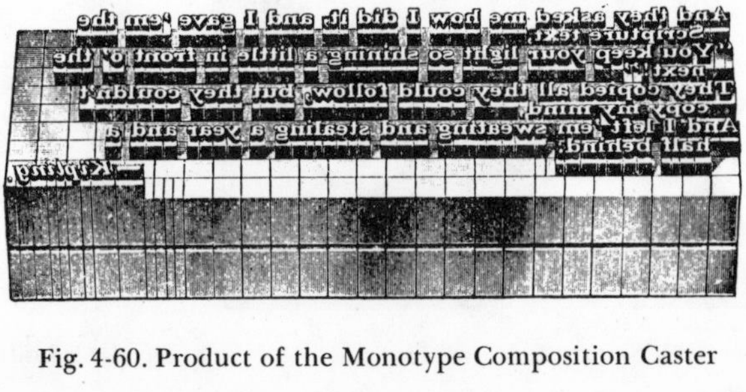

Fig. 4-60. Product of the Monotype Composition Caster

Monotype Material Maker. This machine makes *material;* that is, leads, slugs, line, and fancy borders. Such material is made so cheaply that it is not usually distributed back into the type cases after use. All of a form, type, and spacing material is melted over again into pigs of metal, which are again fed into the machine. Material is made on the Material Maker in sizes from 1 to 12 points in thickness, and either cut to size on the caster or in strips about 24 inches long, to be cut on composing room saws.

The Giant Monotype Caster. This machine casts both type and furniture in sizes from 14 through 72 point. Borders may also be cast.

The Monotype-Thompson Typecaster. This machine is a type-founding machine which casts single letters from matrices from 5 through 48 point. Special attachments allow casting single types from matrices used on machines other than the Monotypes.

How Lines Are Cast on the Ludlow Typograph

The Ludlow Typograph can be learned easily by any competent compositor within a short time, because of the extreme simplicity of its operation. The compositor picks up several matrices at one time, the number depending upon their size. Figure 4–61 shows a compositor assembling Ludlow matrices, and Fig. 4–62 two of the many sizes of matrices. Figure 4–63, on the opposite page, illustrates the Ludlow caster and two matrix cabinets. Justification and spacing on the Ludlow is quick and simple, and accomplished more easily than with type composed from cases.

Fig. 4-61. Setting Ludlow Matrices   Fig. 4-62. Ludlow Matrices

Fig. 4-63. Ludlow Typograph Caster and Matrix Cabinets

After the Ludlow compositor has assembled and spaced his matrices, he places the stick in the caster, pushes a lever, and the line is cast on either a 21-pica or 22½-pica slug, with either a 6- or

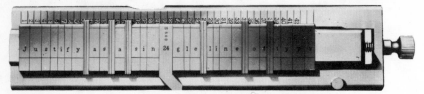

Fig. 4-64. Ludlow Matrices in Regular Ludlow Stick

12-point body. Larger types extend beyond these point limits. Lines longer than 21 or 22½ picas are cast in two or more sections of these lengths, which are cut to size on composing saws. Measures up to 112½ picas are possible with single justification.

Fig. 4-65. Casting Side of Ludlow Matrices

Ludlow matrices are available in many series and families of type faces, from 4 to 96 point, and lining type faces from 6 to 24 point. Type sizes from 120 to 240 points are cast lengthwise of the slug. Italic faces are cast from matrices which have a 17° slant, as shown in Fig. 4–67, on the opposite page. This casting allows kerns (parts of the face that overhang the body on foundry and Monotype) that are unbreakable, and a close setting of characters. See Figs. 4–64 to 4–67, which illustrate Ludlow matrices set in sticks. The Ludlow system is used mostly for job and display composition.

Fig. 4-66. Print of a Line Cast from the Matrices in Fig. 4-65.

The *Ludlow Supersurfacer* is a machine which cuts a small amount of metal from the face of the slug, which makes a smooth surface for printing large types on smooth papers.

An advantage of the Ludlow is that the compositor never runs out of type. Another is that he can compose, space, and justify lines quickly and easily. He may also recast many lines.

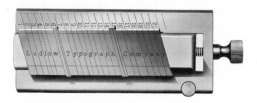

Fig. 4-67. Ludlow Italic Matrices in Special Italic Stick

Self-quadding and self-centering composing sticks are available on the Ludlow to help speed composition of slug lines.

The Elrod is a companion machine to the Ludlow. It casts leads, slugs, and furniture in strips from 1-point to 36-point thicknesses for underpinning the **T**-shaped slugs and spacing; also line borders.

Safety Hints

Work in the composing room is not necessarily hazardous to either limb or health. Although a variety of machines are operated, the printing industry as a whole ranked third from bottom in the number of accidents and is one of the lowest of 31 major industries. Printing shows a good accident record. Handling objects, not machines, causes the greatest number of accidents in the graphic arts.

There are no "occupational diseases," as such, in the graphic arts. In fact, the life span of printers has been raised from 44 to 65 years. Rumor has said that lead poisoning is a printing hazard. This is false. Lead poisoning is confined only to those who remove dross from metal pots. Long and continuous employment in the graphic arts does not interfere with reasonably good health.

The following table should be studied by all who expect to work in the composing rooms, in school or in industry, to keep healthy and to prevent accidents.

Hazard	Preventive
Clothing	Loose clothing may be caught in moving parts. Remove neckties, and roll up sleeves and trousers.
Composing machines	Place metal pigs carefully into metal pots to prevent splashes. Keep away from belts, gears, and any moving parts. See that automatic stops function properly so that metal "squirts" are prevented.
Dim lights	See that work is done under adequate lighting to prevent eyestrain.
Fire	Use matches away from gasoline and other inflammable liquids.
Lead	Refrain from creating lead dust by not splashing pigs in metal pots. Eat outside of the shop area. Keep hands clean. Do not place type in the mouth.
Lifting and carrying	Get aid when lifting or carrying heavy forms and chases. Always lift with the leg muscles, not with the muscles of the abdomen. Bend the *knees,* not the *body,* when lifting.
Littered floors	Keep floors clean to prevent tripping.
Miterers	Keep fingers away from cutting parts.
Oiling machines	Lubricate machinery when it is *not* running.
Oily floors	Keep floors wiped to prevent slipping.
Play	Refrain from playing and wrestling in the shop. Play no practical jokes on fellow workmen.
Plates	Printing plates often have sharp or beveled edges. Use care in handling.
Saw trimmers	Use the workholders and saw blade guards at *all* times.
Slug cutters	Keep fingers away from moving parts.

Hazard	Preventive
Watching operators	Refrain from standing near operators; your presence may make them nervous, and cause accidents.
Talk	Refrain from talking to machine operators.
Type	Do not force thin spaces into lines being set in composing sticks; the spaces may be driven into the fingers.
Type cases	Close all types cases, even when leaving them for only a moment. Another person may bump against the case, or trip over a case left open at the bottom of a type cabinet.

SELF-TEST

This self-test will serve as a review of this chapter. The questions are either true or false, multiple choice, or for thought and discussion. The numbers following each question refer to the page number on which the correct answer can be found.

1. Foundry type and monotype are identical except that foundry type carries a pin mark. (130)
2. Most type for newspapers is cast in slugs on the Linotype or Intertype. (131)
3. Type height is .918 of an inch. (132)
4. Foundry type is made of four ingredients: (132)

   a. Zinc   c. Lead   e. Antimony
   b. Copper   d. Tin   f. Aluminum

5. A shoulder is the top of the type below the face. (133)
6. The beard is formed by the feet of a type. (133)
7. A kern is a part of the face that extends over the side of the body of a type. (133)
8. Nicks act as guides for the compositor. (133)
9. A point is about $\frac{1}{72}$ of an inch. (133)
10. Twenty-six picas equals four inches. (133)

11. A nonpareil equals six points. (133)
12. Six inches equals about 36 picas. (133)
13. Agate lines are equal to six points. (133)
14. A type family is an assortment of letters in the case. (134)
15. Ligatures and logotypes are made to allow close fitting between certain characters. (135)
16. Type sizes usually run in 8, 10, 14, 18, 24, 30, 36, 42, 48, 60, and 72 point. (136)
17. Wood type is measured in picas or lines. (137)
18. The most popular type case is the *Yankee*. (137)
19. Which of the following caps do *not* run in alphabetical order in the type cases: (137, 138)

    a. K   c. J   e. Q
    b. U   d. H   f. W

20. Leads and slugs are used between letters in the line. (138)
21. The em quad is the square of the type body of any size. (138)
22. Four en quads equal a two-em quad. (139)
23. Fifteen five-em spaces equal to two two-em quads. (139)
24. Three three-em spaces equal a two-en quad. (139)
25. Metal furniture is used within a type form. (139)
26. Wood furniture is used mostly for locking up. (139)
27. A one-point face rule is often cast on a six-point body. (140)
28. Borders are made in both type units and strips. (140)
29. A composing stick is adjustable to any linear measurement. (142)
30. Quoins are used to lock forms in the press. (142)
31. Cases are placed on imposing tables to compose type. (143)
32. A chase is a device for setting type. (143)
33. A brayer is an inking roller. (144)
34. A miterer cuts angles on border and rule. (144)
35. The composing stick is held in the right hand. (146)
36. Type is set from right to left, nick up. (146)
37. Justification is the correct placing of space between words. (146)
38. The first step to reduce space between words is to substitute an en quad for the three-em space. (147)

39. When quadding out, the smallest spaces are used at the ends of the lines. (148)

40. Distinguish each letter or character pictured below: (149)

a.   b.   c.   d.   e.   f.   g.   h.

41. The apostrophe has its face on the same side as the nick. (149)

42. Hanging indentions are usually used for classified advertisements in newspapers. (150)

43. Letterspacing of lowercase is considered good form. (150)

44. Corrective letterspacing makes caps look better. (150)

45. Leaders are a series of dots cast on quads. (151)

46. Figures and roman numerals should be aligned at the right. (151)

47. Initial letters should align at both the top and bottom. (152)

48. Pi is mixed and jumbled type. (152)

49. Knots are used when tying type forms with string. (154)

50. Explain differences between live, dead, and standing type. (155)

51. Type for distribution is always read nick up. (156)

52. What are the five rules for distributing type to keep from mixing the type cases? (156)

53. Stone proofs are pulled on the proof press. (157)

54. Gasoline is poured on the type form when cleaning it. (158)

55. Intertypes and Linotypes do identical work. (159)

56. Intertype and Linotype matrices have from two to three characters stamped into them. (161)

57. Spacing between words on Linotypes and Intertypes is done automatically with the use of spacebands. (161)

58. Intertypes and Linotypes usually cast two kinds of letters with the use of the auxiliary rail. (165)

59. Liners determine line widths on Linotypes and Intertypes. (168)

60. Slug-casting machines have metal heated to 850 degrees. (168)
61. From one to eight molds are available on Intertypes and Lino-types. (172)
62. Slug casting machines equipped with Teletypesetters need no keyboard operators. (172)
63. Overhanging slug composition allows the casting of many sizes on the same point size body. (174)
64. Lines of copy are keyboarded on the Monotype caster. (174)
65. The Monotype casts individual letters, spaced and justified. (174)
66. One letter is contained on monotype matrices. (174)
67. The monotype type-and-rule caster makes type from 6-point through 72-point. (177)
68. Ludlow matrices are hand assembled. (178)
69. No matter what the size type, Ludlow lines are cast on the same point size of body. (180)
70. Nicks vary in number on Monotype-cast characters. (130)
71. Ludlow slugs are cast on a **T**-shaped slug. (130)
72. Hand composition is similar to what it was 500 years ago. (131)
73. Three inches is about 18 picas. (133)
74. Twelve 12-point lines make twelve picas. (133)
75. Twenty-six picas equal $45\frac{5}{16}$ inches. (133)
76. A font of type or matrices is an assortment of sizes. (135)
77. Two 18-point em quads equal one 36-point em quad. (139)
78. A 12-point three-em quad is equal in dimension to a 36-point three-em space. (139)
79. Four 24-point em quads equal one 48-point em quad. (135)
80. Reglet is made in the same sizes as slugs of metal. (139)
81. The tighter that type is composed in the stick the better. (142)
82. Composing room saws may cut to half-point graduations. (145)
83. Numbering machines are used to number each sheet when printed on the press. (145)
84. List the steps in reducing space between words. (147)
85. List the steps in increasing space between words. (148)
86. Printing is not a hazardous occupation. (181)
87. Most accidents occur when handling objects, and not on print-ing machines. (181)

88. Lifting should be done with the legs, and not with the body. (182)

89. Why is it bad practice to watch and talk to workmen when they are operating machines? (183)

90. What two safety devices are important on saw-trimmers? (182)

PROJECTS

1. Draw a picture of a California job type case (or fill in any available prints of a case) and designate where letters are stored in the case.

2. Using 6-point type borders and a piece of 10x15 pica furniture, make up a border panel 11x16 picas.

3. Using 12-point type borders and a piece of 10x20 pica furniture, make up a border panel 12x22 picas.

4. Set in type the bottom half of illustration 4–22 on page 146.

5. Set in type "How to Reduce Space between Words" on page 147.

6. Set in type "How to Increase Space between Words" on page 148.

7. Set in type the squared indention paragraph on page 150.

8. Set in type the hanging indention shown on page 150.

9. Set in type the half-diamond indention shown on page 150.

10. Set in type the poetry indention shown on page 150.

11. Set in type the illustration showing the use of leaders on page 151.

12. Set in type the illustration showing the use of roman numerals on page 151. Use cap letters for roman numerals.

13. Using any size initial letter, set the first paragraph appearing on page 152.

14. Using any size initial letter, set the second paragraph appearing on page 152. This is the "up" initial style.

15. Set the paragraphs referring to "How to Keep from Mixing Type Cases' appearing on page 156.

16. Set the type for all layouts made as assigned in Chapter 3.

ORIGINAL

VARIATIONS

PERSPECTIVE

VARIATIONS

CURVE

SCREENS

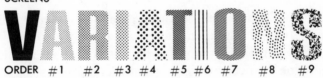

ORDER   #1   #2   #3   #4   #5   #6   #7   #8   #9

REVERSE

OUTLINE AND DROP SHADOW

VARIATIONS

The examples above are a few of the almost limitless possibilities of cold type
Courtesy of Warwick Typographers, Inc.

CHAPTER 5

How to Set Cold Type

THE UBIQUITOUS TERM "COLD TYPE" embraces any method of reproducing type matter without direct benefit of molten metal (as from linecasting, Monotype or Ludlow machines or from hand-set type—now generally referred to as "hot type"). Cold type devices may be classified as follows:

1. Hand-assembled paper or plastic alphabets.
2. Keyboarded text-on-paper machines.
3. Keyboarded Phototypesetting.
4. Photo lettered display.

Generally speaking, cold type table-top devices produce text matter less expensively than hot type methods do, particularly in unjustified right-hand margins (excluding the Justowriter and IBM Selectric which justify lines with one keyboarding) and in tabular composition. On most machines, the operator training period is relatively short.

Hand-Assembled Paper or Plastic Alphabets

More than a dozen manufacturers provide paper or plastic alphabets, mostly to users who operate small offset printing plants. The use of this material eliminates the need for securing reproduction proofs from letterpress printers. Further, these shops enjoy the control over production of artwork and copy. Type sizes run from 10 point to 144 point, in hundreds of designs, depending upon the manufacturer. Several systems are explained below.

Fototype features pads of letters printed on cards which are assembled in a special composing stick. Completed lines are held together with Scotch tape. See Fig. 5–1 on following page.

Fig. 5-1. Fototype Pads of Letters, Cases, and Composing Stick

Prestype, Letraset, and **Transfer Type** employ a dry transfer method. Letters are positioned on the artwork and the top of the plastic sheet is rubbed with a blunt tool, which transfers the pigment to the paper. See Fig. 5–2.

Prestotype is printed on paper wider than the characters, and the paper is overlapped in composition.

Artype (see Fig. 5–3), **Trans-Art, Craftype, Formatt,** and **Cello-Tak** consist of letters printed on clear acetate with pressure-sensitive backing protected with a backing sheet. Letters are cut out with a stylus or blade, aligned on the artwork, and then rubbed to make them adhere.

Fig. 5-2. Dry Transfer Cold Type (Letraset)   *Left:* The Character Is Placed over Correct Position on the Artwork and Rubbed then   *Right:* Then Pulled Away

1   2   3   4

Fig. 5-3. Artype Letters Printed on Pressure-Sensitive Acetate Applied to Artwork
First, the protective backing is removed and the acetate is laid loosely on the backing, then (1) the letter is cut out with a stylus (2) the letter is picked up with a stylus (3) next the letter is aligned on the artwork on a previously drawn line (4) the letter is rubbed to make it adhere.

Redi-Kut characters are printed on pressure-sensitive clear acetate and are pre-cut for easy removal.

Archbold and other sources provide alphabets printed on regular paper which are cut out and pasted to artwork with rubber cement.

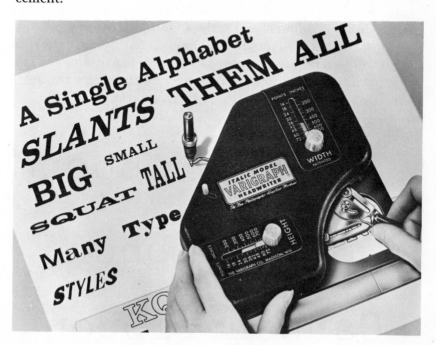

Fig. 5-4. The Varigraph Headwriter

The Vari-graph Headwriter is a non-photographic cold type device used for preparing display lines from 14 point to 72 point in size. One matrix alphabet, with letters cut intaglio, guides a pen which produces the characters on paper in various sizes. Letters may be italic, roman, or backslanted according to needs. Letters may be condensed or expanded by the proper adjustments on the device. Lines may be produced in curved or circular form by using an attachment from any of the matrix alphabets. See Fig. 5–4.

Other lettering devices include the Leroy, Wrico and Senso lettering guides, which are used with pens to create display letters on copy or plates.

Keyboarded Text-on-Paper Machines (Strike-on)

Although any regular typewriter can be used for cold type text matter, the trend is to use machines which simulate hot type characters. The normal typewriter characters have only one width; that is, the lowercase *i* is the same width as the capital *W*. Proportional spacing typewriters, however, have their individual letters designed to vary from three increments to five or more. This variation more closely approximates hot type characters, which are normally produced from one to eighteen increments.

Cotton ribbon

Silk ribbon

Carbon ribbon

Fig. 5-5. Results in Three Different Typewriter Ribbons

Figure 5–5 illustrates three different kinds of typewriter ribbons: cotton, silk, and paper carbon. The carbon ribbon is the best of the three, as illustrated, because it makes the dense black and even print which is necessary for photographic reproduction.

Most typewriters may be specially equipped with a paper carbon-ribbon attachment. A substitute for this, although difficult to use, is a piece of carbon paper that can be typed through with the ribbon removed from the machine.

VariTyper. This machine is made in several models featuring changeable type faces in sizes from 6 to 12 points, both proportionally-spaced and not proportionally-spaced. Justification is automatic on second keyboarding. Some models rule lines in various sizes for forms work. See a few of the hundreds of typefaces available below. Also see Fig. 5–6.

12 pt. Alexandria Medium (880-12A)

ABCDEFGHIJKLMNOPQRSTUVWXYZ&
abcdefghijklmnopqrstuvwxyz abcdefghijk

10 pt. Alexandria Light (650-10B)

ABCDEFGHIJKLMNOPQRSTUVWXYZ& AB
abcdefghijklmnopqrstuvwxyz abcdefghijklmn

10 pt. Bell Gothic Light (FL950-10B)

ABCDEFGHIJKLMNOPQRSTUVWXYZ& AB
abcdefghijklmnopqrstuvwxyz abcdefghijklmn

10 pt. Bell Gothic Bold (FL980-10B)

ABCDEFGHIJKLMNOPQRSTUVWXYZ& ABC
abcdefghijklmnopqrstuvwxyz abcdefghijklmn

10 pt. Gothic Bold Condensed (FL970-10B)

ABCDEFGHIJKLMNOPQRSTUVWXYZ& ABC
abcdefghijklmnopqrstuvwxyz abcdefghijklmn

Justowriter. This is a cold type composing machine (with a standard typewriter keyboard), and is capable of automatic justification. It includes a *recorder unit* in which copy is produced on a perforated tape, as well as a typed sheet which is used for checking purposes. The perforated tape is placed in a second unit, the *reproducer,* which types and justifies copy for reproduction at a

Fig. 5-6. The most sophisticated VariTyper Model 1010 features a very light touch on the keyboard. Spacing between words is entirely automatic with a second keyboarding for justification. Two type fonts can be on the machine at any time to be manually changed. Paper advance and carriage return are automatic, and centering of lines is accomplished without calculations by the operator. Type fonts may contain rule characters to make straight lines for office forms.

Fig. 5-7. The Justowriter

speed of 100 words per minute. Type styles are not interchangeable. However, a machine may come equipped with any one of several type styles. See Fig. 5–7.

I.B.M. Electric Executive Typewriter. This is another machine frequently used for cold type composition. Although a number of type faces are available in sizes ranging from 8 to 12 point, only one type face is available on any one typewriter. The machine provides for both proportional and differential spacing, which is accomplished manually. See Figs. 5–8 and 5–9.

The effect of beautiful book printing is obtained by proportional spacing which allows each character the proper amount of space according to its width.

Fig. 5-8. IBM Executive Typewriter Cold Composition

Fig. 5-9. One Model of the IBM Proportional Spacing Typewriter

IBM Selectric Typewriter. *The IBM Selectric Typewriter* features changeable typefaces on a sphere-shaped element which moves from left to right across the paper which remains stationary. There is no conventional carriage. Figure 5–10 illustrates the IBM spherical element which contains the usual characters. Arrows indicate how the element moves to place the letter impressions on the paper. The element can be quickly substituted for other elements containing different type styles. Figure 5–11 shows a few of the type faces available for the Selectric in fonts from 7 points through 12 points.

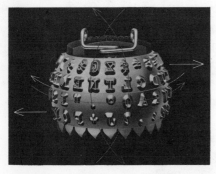

12 pt. Pyramid Medium
11 pt. Univers Bold
11 pt. Univers Medium
10 pt. Press Roman Italic
10 pt. Pyramid Medium
10 pt. Aldine Roman Italic
8 pt. Pyramid Medium
8 pt. Pyramid Italic
8 pt. Aldine Roman Medium
8 pt. Bodoni Book Medium
8 pt. Aldine Roman Italic

Fig. 5-10. This single sphere-shaped element of the IBM Selectric contains all the usual typewriter characters

Fig. 5-11. A few samples of the many type faces and sizes available for the IBM Selectric typewriter

3	4	5	6	7	8	9
i ;	I (	J	P y	B	A Y	M
j '	f)	a	S *	C	D w	W
l '	r !	c	b †	E	G ¾	m
. -	s /	e	d $	F	H ½	
,	t	g	h +	L	K &	
	:	v	k =	T	N %	
		z	n]	Z	O @	
		?	o		Q ¼	
		[	p		R –	

Fig. 5-12. The IBM Selectric Composer typewriter. Margins are automatically justified on second typing

Fig. 5-13. IBM type is designed in a nine-unit system that permits seven different letter widths

The IBM Selectric Composer, Fig. 5–12, allows automatic justification of the right-hand margin with a retyping. Characters for these IBM machines are proportionately spaced as shown in Fig. 5–13. The spherical element contains 88 characters which approximates the character fitting of hot type. Leading between lines is dialed from 5 to 20 points.

Fig. 5-14. The IBM Magnetic Tape Selectric Composer. Recording units are shown in the background with the typewriters used to type rough copy which is stored on magnetic tape. On the left in the foreground is the tape reader, and on the right is the control console which produces camera ready copy from the tape.

The IBM Magnetic Tape "Selectric" Composer, Fig. 5–14, is a more sophisticated series of devices including one or more recorders on which copy is typed without regard to justification. The copy is first stored on magnetic tape which holds about 4000 words. A "tape reader" reads the magnetic tape at 20 characters per second. The operator sets up the control console (Fig. 5–14) and the Composer reads the tape automatically to produce camera ready copy at speeds up to 14 characters per second with automatic justification.

How to Correct Typewritten Copy

Because of the sensitivity of camera and film, erasures are not made on typewritten copy for reproduction. As the stenographer types her lines of copy on the final reproduction proof, she ignores errors she has made until she finishes the line worked upon. Then, *in the margin,* she types the corrected word. Letters are usually not so typed, because they are difficult to paste in place over the error.

In proofreading, to see if other errors have been made, corrections are typed also in the margin, or on another sheet of the same paper used for the original typing. The corrections are then cut out carefully, and "floated" into place over the error with rubber cement. This is shown in Fig. 5–15.

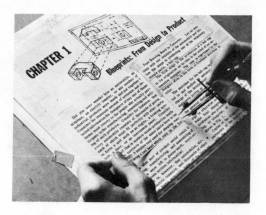

Fig. 5-15. How to Correct Typewritten Copy

Typewriter Accessories

The Justigage consists of a movable pointer and a fixed gauge. The typewriter carriage is placed at the desired margin, and the pointer is aligned at the zero position. The operator can determine, with this system, the number of half spaces needed to justify the right-hand margin.

The Marginator can be installed on most electric typewriters to justify the right-hand margin. The scale is laid over the first

Fig. 5-16. The Marginator *(Arrow)* on an IBM Executive Typewriter, Model C

Fig. 5-17. The Optype

typing, enabling the operator to read the exact setting of the lines to justify on the second typing, when letter and word spaces are evenly widened or condensed. See Fig. 5–16.

The Optype. To eliminate retyping to align the right-hand margin on typewriters, the Optype device can be used on any typed manuscript. Short lines can be stretched and long lines condensed with the use of a lens. The operator views each line in a viewer, then turns the knob to adjust the length of the line. Lines are photographed in the device. Lines and words can also be italicized. See Fig. 5–17.

The Typit adapts electric typewriters to use special characters not normally on the machine. When special characters or symbols are needed, the operator places a special character in position, strikes a key, removes the Typit and resumes typing.

The Doublebold attachment for electric typewriters allows the operator to double-strike any characters to make them appear bolder than the regular type face of the machine.

Keyboarded Photo-Typesetting

The Fotosetter. The Intertype Fotosetter looks like the hot-metal machine and uses circulating matrices. See Fig. 5–18. In place

Fig. 5-18. Fotosetter and Keyboard

of the metal pot on the hot-metal machine, Fotosetter has a camera. The matrices have one or two characters in the form of a negative. A turret of lenses allows justified lines from 3 to 72 point to be photographed. Four magazines are contained on the Fotosetter. Including all designs and sizes there are 8,208 characters available to the operator. Lines can be composed in widths up to 51 picas. Roll film is developed in a darkroom. The Intertype Fotomatic, with one magazine, can be operated by Teletypesetter tape. These machines are out of production.

The Linofilm Phototypesetting Machine. Among the latest cold type devices for type composition is the Mergenthaler Linofilm device. The machine provides type images from 4 to 108 points in measures up to 96 picas at a speed of 15 newspaper column lines per minute. A typewriter in the keyboard unit makes perforations in a tape, which is then fed into the photographic unit (Fig. 5–19 through Fig. 5–22). Justification is automatic with space distribution between words. Change from one point size to another is affected by pushbutton control. Leading between lines is from zero to 18 points and is spaced by the keyboard.

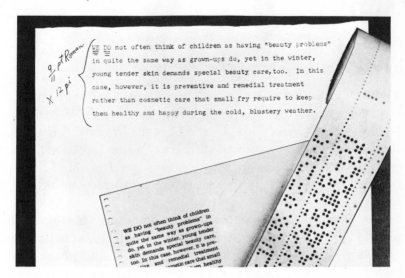

Fig. 5-19. The Linofilm Copy, Tape, and Film

Fig. 5-20. The Linofilm Turret

Fig. 5-21. The Linofilm Keyboard Unit

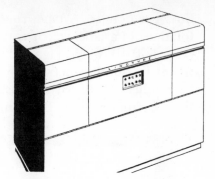

Fig. 5-22. The Photographic Unit

Eighteen grids (fonts) are carried on the turret and they give 1,584 characters. A keyboard error is killed by erasing the entire line from the tape. Corrections can also be made by correcting the tape itself. The corrector unit will shear away a line from the film and weld the corrected line in its place, at a speed of three lines per minute. Actuated by perforated tape, the turret can change its fonts in a few seconds.

The Photon Photographic-Type Composing Machine. The photon device for cold type composition handles straight matter as well as display from a typewriter keyboard, and places images on film at speeds up to three times that of conventional slugcasting machines. The operator selects line lengths up to 42 picas in 100th-inch increments. Leading between lines is adjustable to a tenth of a point. Any of 16 type families in 12 sizes (5 through 36 point) can be keyboarded, and any can be mixed. Copy is readily seen as typed, and the words and spaces are stored in the machine until the line is composed. The machine then photographs a character at a time at the speed of eight per second. Corrections are easily made on the keyboard. Accessory devices allow the composition of an entire advertisement. Type families and styles may be changed as wanted, and a single matrix disc makes selection of 192 fonts possible. Film is processed through dark room procedures for use in any of the printing processes. Centering, or flushing left and right, are entirely automatic and multiple justifications are accomplished with ease.

Figure 5–23 shows the parts of the Photon Consol in greater

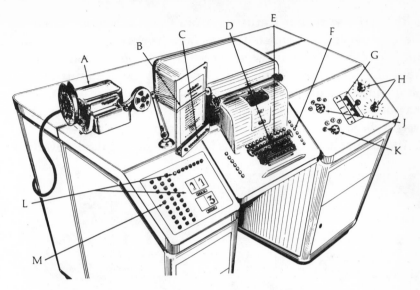

Fig. 5-23. Parts of the Photon Consol

A. Motorized Tape Punch
B. Copy Holder
C. Justification Range Indicators
D. Typewriter Keyboard
E. Tabs, Spaces, and Leaders
F. Justifying and Quadding

G. Typeface Selector
H. Indention Selectors
J. Magazine Selectors
K. Punch Selector
L. Letterspacing Controls
M. Line Length Controls

Fig. 5-24. The Photon Matrix Disc
Holds 16 Different Type Faces

detail. The parts are keyed by letter and identified below the illustration. Figure 5–24 shows the Photon matrix disc which contains sixteen different type faces.

The ATF Typesetter features two units, a keyboard (similar to the Justowriter) on which the operator prepares a coded tape, and a photographic unit which decodes the tape and sets justified lines on film in sizes from 5 to 14 point. With two fonts on the photographic unit, two faces may be set on the same line. Tapes may be saved for future settings. Fonts of 176 characters are lightweight discs. Each font holds two type designs. See Fig. 5–25.

The Monophoto cold type machine has the standard keyboard

Fig. 5-25. The ATF Typesetter Keyboard and Photographic Unit

Fig. 5-26. Monophoto Master Negative Case and Ribbon

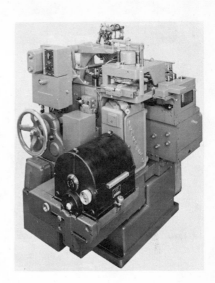

Fig. 5-27. The Monophoto

used for the hot-metal Monotype. The keyboard produces a ribbon which activates the Monophoto photographic machine, providing lines up to 60 picas wide on film from 6 point through 24 point. One, two, or three master negative cases are used for various work. The maximum composition area is 60 picas wide by 24 inches long. Each matrix case contains 255 characters. Two or more columns can be set side-by-side even when keyboarded as one column. Film from the machine is processed in a darkroom. See Figs. 5–26 and 5–27.

The Monoblique Computer Input 300-key keyboard produces 6, 7, or 8-level punched tape as computer input. It is electric, not pneumatic.

The Alphatype uses magnetic tape in its operation. The three-unit system consists of an electric typewriter connected with a recorder, and an exposure device. As the operator keyboards the copy, each character width and space is recorded on magnetic tape. The tape is then fed into the exposure unit which produces type in justified lines on film in sizes from 6 to 18 point. Fonts are provided for each size of type. All sizes align with each other and are readily mixed. See Fig. 5–28.

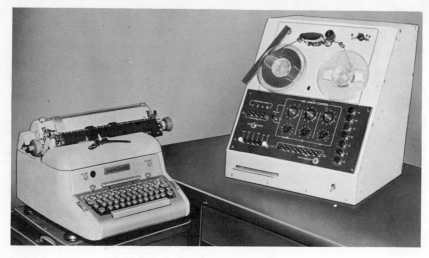

Fig. 5-28. The Alphatype

The Megatype sets cold type from 6 to 200 point sizes in justified lines. Make-up of lines is eliminated in the process. Type is exposed in position following a layout. As lines are typed, an electronic unit records the width of each character in a memory storage unit. The line is then justified by various controls. Master fonts are on four grids, and each font contains 126 characters—or a total of 504 ready for exposure. See Fig. 5–29.

Fig. 5-29. The Megatype

Hadego Photocompositor. The ATF Hadego Photocompositor (See Fig. 5–30) photographs lines of composition from white letters on black backgrounds, similarly to the assembly and casting of Ludlow Typograph matrices. Any fractional part of a point size can be photographed, like 49½ point, for exact fittings to a layout or dummy. Used in in the lighted room, the operator assembles letters in a composing "stick" from a case, places the stick in the machine, adjusts for exact size, and photographs the line of composition. Enlargements and reductions of one font of letters are made through simple adjustments. One model reproduces images from 4 to 34 point from a 20 point font, and from 10 to 82 point from a 48 point size. Another model reproduces images from 20 to 115 point from the 48 point font. A complete layout can be composed in any size up to 11 x 14 inches in mixed type faces in a variety of sizes of type and a multiplicity of lines without stripping negatives. Lines are automatically centered, and enlargements and reductions are quickly determined on a circular computer.

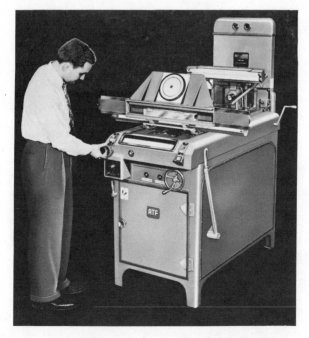

Fig. 5-30. The ATF Hadego Photo-Compositor

Photolettered Display

Many and varied devices have been introduced to provide display lines and occasional small sizes of type. Explanations of representative photolettering machines follow.

The Photo-Typositor is a projection cold type machine which permits enlarging and reducing to 175 different point sizes from a single font of type, from 9 point to 144 point. Each font contains material for 2,800 variations. The type may be resized, condensed, expanded, italicized, back-slanted, reproportioned, overlapped, exaggerated, distorted, angled, shadowed, or stepped. The strip film is developed in the machine. No darkroom or camera is needed. See 5–31.

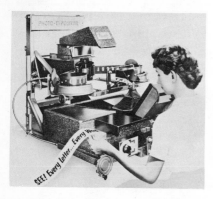

Fig. 5-31. The Photo-Typositor

Fig. 5-33. The Morisawa

Fig. 5-32. The Headliner

Fig. 5-34. The Filmotype

The Headliner features fonts similar in appearance to a phonograph record, and which contain images of characters. A dial is turned for each character and a button is pushed to make any exposures up to 72 point. See Fig. 5–32.

The Morisawa allows 5 to 18 point or 12 to 72 point type from a "letterplate," which contains characters in negative form. The spacing of words and letters is automatic. Type can be set at angles from 10 to 30 degrees, and can be expanded, condensed or distorted. Type sizes are varied with interchangeable lenses. The area for setting is 10 by 12 inches. Film is processed in a darkroom. See Fig. 5–33.

The Filmotype uses fonts, including connecting scripts, in cylindrical form from 12 to 144 points. Wheels are turned, a lever actuates the exposure, the work is developed. See Fig. 5–34.

The Typro has a built in darkroom; sizes from 6 to 144 point. It can compose lines above, below, or over others; it can space art lettering automatically, overprint and screen shadows. (Fig. 5–35.)

The Strip Printer is used to produce lines of type in various sizes on paper or 35 mm. film. A film font is moved to the desired letter, and is photographed by pressing a lever. Development is made in a darkroom. See Fig. 5–36.

Fig. 5-35. The Typro   Fig. 5-36. The Strip Printer

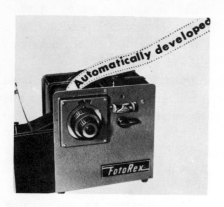

Fig. 5-37. The Fotorex

Fig. 5-38. The Protype

Fig. 5-39. Kameratype Characters

Fig. 5-40. Fototype

The Fotorex uses fonts of type on film to make lines of type from 6 to 84 point. A dial is turned to the degree indicated on the film font which insures proper spacing. See Fig. 5–37.

The Protype. On this machine, the exposure is made letter-by-letter from film type fonts in sizes from 6 to 90 point. An entire job may be composed on paper 17 inches wide. No darkroom is needed. See Fig. 5–38.

The Kameratype. White characters are assembled by hand in this system letter-by-letter. They are then placed before a camera to secure the negative in reduced or enlarged form. See Fig. 5–39.

The Fototype Compositor. This system projects 100 type sizes from 10 to 96 point. A typewriter keyboard activates the machine and produces "hard copy" for proofreading. Horizontal spacing and film speed is automatic. The carousels containing the fonts have 70 type positions plus 30 additional spaces for extra characters. (Fig. 5–40).

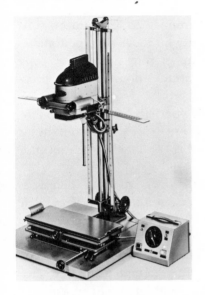

Fig. 5-41. The Starlettograph

Fig. 5-42. The Pasco System of Cold Type

The Starlettograph is a projection system of producing varied cold type composition. Sizes from strip film range from 1/25″ to 4″. Regular display or other composition can be achieved. In addition, different type sizes can be set into one another; individual letters can be placed in any position; vertical and rotary setting is possible. Type may be right-reading and inverted, set up-side down, screened or partially screened, and negative and positive combined. See Fig. 5–41.

The Pasco method involves black letters which are magnetically attracted to a grid featuring a non-photographic grid pattern used in positioning. Letters are set in position from "type" cases and then photographed. See Fig. 5–42.

The Staromat allows the operator to view the developed image of one letter while setting the next. Images appear in black seconds after exposure. Sizes range from a quarter-inch to five inches. Letters can be staggered, tightly spaced, set in circles and the like.

The UD Phototypesetter Model 106 features automatic spacing between characters on two-inch film or paper processed in the machine.

The Alphagraph makes single lines from 18 to 72 point on rolls of film. Characters are selected manually on movable type fonts.

The Form-o-Type System is made up of four devices for copy preparation, text composition, forms composition, and film processing—which take the place of manual work.

The AM 725 Phototypesetter (VariTyper) is operated by 6-, 7-, or 8-channel tape to provide 6 to 18 point from a disc containing three fonts of 112 characters each. Speed is 12 characters per second, or about 20 justified newspaper lines.

The Fairchild PhotoTextSetter 2000 is operated from Teletypesetter tape and produces up to 18 lines per minute in ten sizes from 5 to 18 point. Model 8000 produces 80 lines per minute and has 4608 characters available.

The JusTape unit by Compugraphic automatically converts unjustified six-level perforated tape to perforated tape justified to any line measure for any type face at about 6,000 standard newspaper lines per hour. Basically, it does not provide for hyphenated line endings. It ends lines between words and justifies using spacebands and fixed spacing or letterspacing. A program allows the elimination of spacebands by using only fixed spaces. JusTape eliminates the need for making end-of-line decisions in the keyboard operation, as well as shift and unshift functions. See Figure 5–43.

The Compugraphic Model CG 7200 is a keyboard operated display phototypesetting device offering four type faces in sizes from 14 to 72 point, with no strip font changes. Keyboard kerning eliminates cutting time in production. See Figure 5–44.

Three other Compugraphic phototypesetting text matter units provide for a variety of needs, mainly on newspaper production. The CG 4962 provides type from 5 to 12 point in lengths up to 33 picas. Thirty-five to 40 lines a minute are produced from a two-frame, six-level computor generated tape. It can be set to operate with two duplexed pairs of 90-character fonts. See Figure 5–45.

Model CG 4961 is a high-speed mixer photosetter and operates from unjustified or justified six-level tape, justified wire service tape, or direct keyboard input at 25 to 30 lines per minute. The machine's four faces can be changed in less than a minute. See Figure 5–46.

Fig. 5-43. Justape Jr.

Fig. 5-44. CG 7200 Photo Typesetting Machine

Fig. 5-45. CG 4962 Font Strip

Fig. 5-46. 4961 Photo Typesetting Machine

Model CG 2961 produces text from unjustified or justified six-level tape at 25 to 30 lines per minute, 8½ point 11 picas. Its automatic hyphenation capability eliminates operator hyphenation decisions. Type size range is 5 to 12 point. The unit can process the combined output of from three to five operators punching unjustified tape.

The Astrocomp accepts copy through a typewriter keyboard which provides hard copy and a magnetic tape as input for computerized photocomposing machines. Information goes first to a temporary core storage of a miniature computer, which permits instant corrections of any keyboard errors.

Comp/Set by Fairchild can set two different kinds of type composition at the same time, reading unjustified tape at speeds to 400 characters per second. Comp/Set can punch justified, hyphenated tape at 24,000 lines per hour to operate linecasters and photo-textsetters.

Justotext is a phototypesetting machine activated by tape produced on the Justowriter keyboard. Two 90-character fonts can be used to produce roman and italic or light and bold type faces. It will produce about 30 11-pica lines of eight point per minute.

The ATF Photocomp 20, operating from tape, sets 20 standard news lines a minute. Type images are made through an oscillating disc. Sizes from 5 to 18 point are produced.

The Ludlow Swiftape produces justified punched tape for automated typecasters. A computer takes care of instructional codes usually done by the operator.

The PDP Typesetting Systems handles newslines as well as advertisements, accepting unjustified and unhyphenated tape which are automatically justified and hyphenated.

The Addressograph Multigraph Phototypesetter, producing from 6 to 18 point type on film, is actuated by prepared justified tape at 20 newspaper lines per minute. Three 112-character type fonts can be used at one time.

The Unisetter produces camera-ready copy for offset by direct signals sent by wire services to newspapers. It is entirely electronic—it has no moving parts. A kindred machine is the Offsetter.

"Third Generation" Phototypesetters

These systems are under test and experimentation to bring incredible speed in photosetting. They include:

The Linotron. In this Mergenthaler system letter images are continually projected onto a cathode tube from which the device selects each wanted character in microseconds (a microsecond is a millionth of a second). The images are converted to video signals and are reproduced on a cathode ray tube, and then to film. Type is produced from 250 to 1,000 characters per second. Tape operates the system. See Fig. 5–47.

The RCA Videocomp is all-electronic, and sets type on film from 5 to 24 point. A scanner breaks characters into groups of thousands of "bits", which are stored in an electronic memory system. Letters are called for from the memory and "written" on a cathode (TV) tube. Six hundred characters per second can be produced, or a newspaper page in two minutes. Input is tape. See Fig. 5–48.

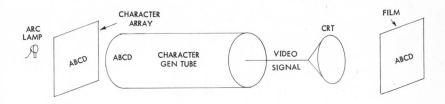

Fig. 5-47. Linotron

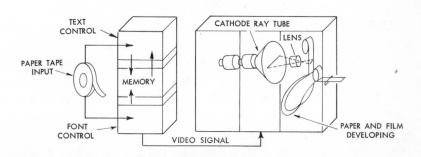

Fig. 5-48. RCA Videocomp

The Fototronic by Harris-Intertype produces a full page at a time in a two-unit CRT set-up. The first unit stores up to 40 type fonts (4,000 characters) in a digital memory system generated by magnetic tape. Pages are composed in a second print-out unit, in from 4 to 24 point sizes, which can be condensed, expanded or slanted by electronics. Speed is over 1,000 characters per second in the 7 point size.

The IBM 2680 CRT is activated by an IBM 360 computer. Justification and hyphenation is automatic. Type ranges from 4 through 18 point. Pages 8x10 inches in 8 point can be produced at about 10 per minute; a phone directory page in about 8 seconds.

Reading Machines

Because punched tape is usually required to operate the hot or cold typesetting machine, and because this operation is performed by hand at about 50 words per minute, there is a need for faster preparation of tape. One way is to have a computer "justify" the line and divide the words by logic or with a built-in dictionary. Then the keyboard operator sets "idiot" tape.

Machines exist which will "read" typewritten and even long-hand manuscript and convert this copy to tape which will operate the phototypesetting machines. ("Readers" are now in use in several postoffices to read Zip Codes.)

A Sylvania device will read up to 2,500 characters per second. Characters are scanned vertically and horizontally a half dozen to over two dozen times—at amazing speed.

Word Division by Computer

Although computers used to process tape to operate photographic and hot metal composing machines can process "idiot" tape (tape not directing line endings, justification and word division) can be made almost perfect, the cost is tremendous. The preparation of "idiot" tape is highly desirable because the keyboard operator can increase production from 40% to 60%. Hence, the percentage of correct word divisions will vary according to the financial ability of individual printing plants. Some newspapers apparently ignore word divisions perhaps on the theory that usage, not the dictionary, will establish style in the future. Most readers do not know if a word is correctly divided, and if they do, they don't care. The expense of perfection in word division is often thought not to be worth the cost.

A hyphenation program of relatively low efficiency can reduce the frequency of "bad" lines by 75%.

One hyphenation program for computers is based on letter sequences or "logic." For example:

Use a hyphen after x, as ex-ample, ex-plain, etc. But not anx-ious.

Use a hyphen ahead of j and q, as sub-ject, ac-quaint, etc. But not anti-que, pro-ject (noun).

Use a hyphen ahead of ly at the end of a word, unless the preceding letter is a b, as probab-ly.

Use a hyphen ahead of ty at the end of a word, unless preceded by an h.

Use a hyphen ahead of tion when they are at the end of a word or within a word, teen, tain, and main.

Use a hyphen between double consonants, m-m, p-p, etc. But l and s would create many wrong divisions, as pas-sing.

Use a hyphen ahead of ment, mend, dent, etc.

Use a hyphen following col, com, con, cor, cos.

Use a hyphen ahead of ing at the end of a word, but not when preceded by d, t, h.

Use a hyphen following pro, in, im, il, ig, as protect, etc.

Use a hyphen ahead of day, as Mon-day.

Newspapers usually accept the division of such one syllable words as seem-ed and snow-ed. Commercial and book printers do not usually accept this. It should be remembered that many more words must be divided in short column measures, the usual 11 pica column on newspapers.

SELF-TEST

1. Explain how the Fotosetter operates. (200)
2. How does the Linofilm function? (200–202)
3. The Photon sets lines three times as fast as linecasting machines. (202–203)

4. Photon operators may select from 16 fonts of type on the machine. (202–203)
5. The ATF Typesetter is operated from tape. (204)
6. The Monophoto keyboard serves a dual purpose. (204)
7. The Alphatype is tape operated. (205)
9. The Hadego is keyboard operated. (207)
10. The Photo Typositor enlarges or reduces from one font. (208)
11. The Morisawa sets type from 5 to 72 point. (209)
12. The Headliner operator dials letters. (209)
13. The Filmotype fonts consist of discs. (209)
14. Films taken from the Typro are darkroom processed. (209)
15. The Strip Printer is a projection machine. (209)
16. The Fotorex sets type from 6 to 84 point. (210)
17. Protype negatives are processed in the darkroom. (210)
18. The Kameratype uses circulating matrices. (210)
19. The Starlettograph uses film fonts for each type size. (211)
20. Pasco letters are hand assembled. (211)
21. The IBM Selectric justifies lines in a second operation directed by magnetic tape. (196)
22. The VariTyper has automatic line justification in a retyping operation. (193)
23. What do the following composers have in common? Linotron, Videocomp, Fototronic and IBM 2680. (216)
24. How many newspaper lines will the Justape produce in an hour? (212)
25. How many type faces does the Compographic Model CG 7200 offer? (212)
26. What type of keyboard produces the tape that activates the Justotext? (214)
27. What is a kindred machine to the Unisetter? (214)
28. Name four "Third Generation" phototypesetters. (215–216)
29. Divide (hyphenate) the following words according to the hyphenation program on page 217:

a. expound	e. crafty	i. colon
b. object	f. missing	j. venting
c. really	g. amendment	k. caring
d. probably	h. corset	l. Wednesday

CHAPTER 6

How to Prepare Manuscript
and Proofread

How to Prepare Copy

EDITING should be done on the manuscript *before* the manuscript is set in type. The compositor, setting type by hand or by machine, has no authority to change the writer's copy. Furthermore, he does not have the time under pressure of work to note changes in style. *Style* refers to the manner in which words are arranged and spelled. The word catalog should not be spelled "catalog" in one sentence and "catalogue" in another, for example. Style also refers to the compounding of words, the use of figures or figures spelled out, the use of italic and bold-face types; and the use of commas, semicolons, colons, and other points used in punctuation. Style sets *uniformity* of copy.

The printer has no right to change the writer's manner of expressing himself, taking out copy, or rewriting sentences. Manuscript copy preparation does include, however, the following: correcting any misspelled words, wrong punctuation, wrong compounding of words, errors in grammar, and other *obvious* errors.

The hand or machine compositor does not usually make such changes. They are sometimes made by the "front office" in printing plants trying to give the best service to their customers.

Author's Alterations. When the printer makes an error, and does not follow the customer's copy correctly, he corrects the work without charge to the customer. However, when the customer submits copy, and makes corrections on the proof that *change the original copy,* he must pay for the additional charge of type composition. These changes from copy are referred to as *author's alterations.* To save cost and time it is best that errors be eliminated from the manuscript, or copy, before it is set in type.

The Best Physical Form of Manuscript. The following rules will aid those in the preparation of copy for the printer:

1. Use original sheets of *typewritten* copy. Carbon copies are often difficult to read.

2. Doublespace the copy, and leave a good margin all around. One inch or more margin is better than narrow margins.

3. Number all pages.

4. Use *one* side of the paper. It is confusing to the printer to use both sides of a sheet of paper.

5. Follow one style of spelling, punctuation, etc., as explained.

How to Mark Specifications. All instructions to the printers, whether furnished by the consumer or by the layout man, should be explicit and complete. These instructions should contain:

1. The kind of type; name, manufacturer, size, and leading between lines. An example of this might be: Baskerville, 11 point, Intertype, set on a 13-point slug.

2. The width to set the type, in picas; *never in inches.*

3. The paragraph indentions in ems, or ems and half-ems.

4. For display composition, designate whether centered, flush left or flush right.

5. Use printers' marks which designate italic, bold-face, small caps, caps, etc., as explained below:

a) A word or line underscored once means set in *italic light.*

b) Two underscores mean set in SMALL CAPS.

c) Three underscores mean to set in CAPS.

d) A wavy underscore means set in **bold face.**

e) A straight line and a wavy line mean set in ***bold italic.***

f) Three straight lines and one wavy line: set in **BOLD CAPS.**

g) Circled figures mean to spell out the figure: five.

h) A circled abbreviated word means to spell out the abbreviation.

i) A diagonal line crossing out a cap character means to set the character in loweracse.

j) The paragraph mark (¶) is used to tell the printer to start a new paragraph where indicated.

k) A line drawn from the last word of a paragraph to the first word of the next paragraph means to *run in* the type.

How to Proofread

In the beginning of printing, little attention was devoted to correcting the errors made by typesetters. According to one historian, the *First Folio Shakespeare,* an early book, contained about 20,000 mistakes. The first men hired to correct errors, or to proofread, were scholars. Two of these men were Samuel Johnson and William Julius Mickle; later, writers like Dickens, Browning, and Victor Hugo participated in the work.

Today, proofreading is done either in the shop, in the business office of the printing company, or perhaps even by the customer. The proofreader holds the proof, and a copyholder reads aloud to him from the copy. *Horsing* is a term applied to type that has had no proofreading with benefit of a copyholder. *Railroading* refers to no proofreading at all, but sending type to press hoping for the best.

Duties of a Proofreader. The following procedure is common to proofreaders on the job:

1. Check the size of type marked on the copy with the proof of the type set.
2. Check the width of the column.
3. Check the kind of type.
4. Check the leading between lines.
5. Check the spelling of all words and word divisions.
6. See that style is uniform.
7. Correct obvious errors in grammar.
8. Make queries to the author: in cases where a name might be spelled "Smith" in one place and "Smythe" in another, and where a firm might be referred to as "Jones & Company" in one place and "Jones Company" in another. (Good copy preparation would prevent this being done.)

Duties of the Copyholder. Taking instructions from the proofreader is the first duty of the copyholder. To speak both *distinctly* and to read copy *accurately* is necessary. The copyholder also calls out the marks of punctuation, capitalization, paragraphs, and any other information necessary to the proofreader.

Proofreading should be done in a quiet place. Reading proof amid the clatter of machines often results in errors missed.

A *revise* is a second proof, which is checked against the first proof to insure that corrections have been made. The *first revise* is so designated, as are any other proofs, as *second revise, third revise,* and so on, until the job is corrected properly.

Reference Books for Proofreaders. The first need of a reference book for proofreaders is a good, unabridged dictionary. Spelling and word divisions can be found in it quickly. The next is a good book on English grammar and usage. Other needs, depending upon the particular work in the shop, would include the local telephone directory, the city directory, the street directory, the *World Almanac,* the Bible, a good atlas and a good encyclopedia.

Proofreaders' Marks. The illustration at the bottom of this page, Fig. 6–1, demonstrates how certain proofreading signs and symbols indicate corrections to the compositor. Some proofreaders draw lines from the errors to the marks in the margin. It is imperative that all who mark proofs for the printer use these signs and symbols in order to coincide with the procedures in use in all composing rooms. Other and individual marks may not be understood by the printers, and in any event will cause some confusion and delay the work.

Each proofreader's mark is illustrated and explained in detail on the following pages.

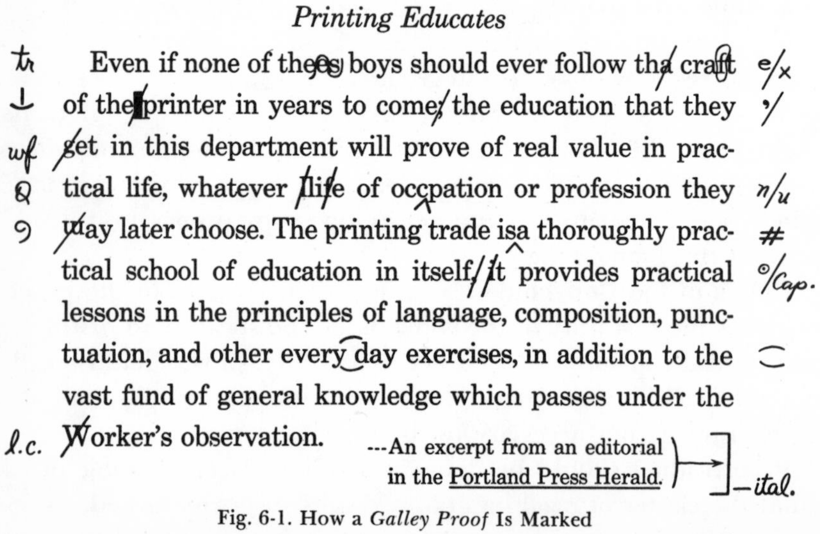

Printing Educates

tr   Even if none of these boys should ever follow the craft   e/x
⊥   of the printer in years to come the education that they   ⅋/
wf   get in this department will prove of real value in prac-
Ⓠ   tical life, whatever life of occpation or profession they   n/u
9   may later choose. The printing trade isa thoroughly prac-   #
     tical school of education in itself//It provides practical   %/Cap.
     lessons in the principles of language, composition, punc-
     tuation, and other every day exercises, in addition to the   ⊂
     vast fund of general knowledge which passes under the
l.c.   Worker's observation.   ---An excerpt from an editorial in the Portland Press Herald.   —ital.

Fig. 6-1. How a *Galley Proof* Is Marked

Take out or delete.

stet ...   Let it stand. Used when type is corrected or marked out of the proof, and then ordered returned as it was originally.

/   This is a *stop,* used in marginal marks. See Fig. 6–1.

First and closing quotation marks, in order.

Period. Usually placed in a circle.

Comma. Note inverted v (caret) above the mark.

Hyphen. Note *two* short lines.

Semicolon. Note stop.

Colon. Note circle.

Apostrophe. Note caret (see comma above).

Interrogation mark.

Exclamation mark.

Em quad.

En dash.

Em dash.

Two-em dash.

Push down space or spacing material.

#	Insert a space.
less #	Use less space.
eg. # ∧∨	Equalize the spacing in a line. Check marks are placed between words.
∧	Insert (copy written in margin) at this place.
⌐	Move up. Points or picas often indicated.
∟	Move down. Points or picas often indicated.
⊏	Move left. Points or picas often indicated.
⊐	Move right. Points or picas often indicated.
℮	Turn over, as a foundry letter upside down.
tr.	Transpose, as when letters or words are out of order.
(/)/	Parentheses, beginning and ending, in order.
[/]/	Brackets, beginning and ending, in order.
⊗	Broken type; reset in new type.
w.f.	Wrong font, as a bold character mixed with light face.
&	Ampersand, or "and" sign.
¶	Paragraph.
⌒	Close up, as a space wrongly placed in a word.
⌣	Use less space where indicated.

Set in caps. Often "caps" written in margin.

Set in small caps. "Small caps" often written in margin.

Set in light italics. "Ital." often written in margin.

l.c. Set in lowercase letters.

rom. Change to roman type.

(?) Query to author to verify copy encircled.

Set in bold face.

Superior characters; small letters above the alignment.

Inferior characters.

Straighten the type matter.

Asterisk, sometimes called "star."

out — see copy Reference to copy not set.

Ellipses; periods and spaces.

lig. Use ligatures, as fi, fl, ff, ffi, ffl.

Diphthong, or connecting characters.

(5) Encircled figures mean to spell out.

(five) Encircled letters mean to use figures.

Hanging indention style.

SELF-TEST

This self-test will serve as a review of this chapter. The questions are either true or false, multiple choice, or for thought and discussion. The numbers following each question refer to the page number on which the correct answer can be found.

1. Style sets a uniformity of copy. (219)
2. A machine compositor has the right to change copy when the expressions are not to his liking. (219)
3. What is meant by a "set style"? (219)
4. The printer's customer pays for his changes in copy after the type is composed. (219)
5. "Author's alterations" refer to errors made by the printer. (219)
6. Both sides of copy paper are used. (220)
7. Name the five rules for the physical form of manuscripts. (220)
8. Widths of lines are only designated in picas. (220)
9. One underscore means set in italic. (220)
10. Two underscores mean set in bold face. (220)
11. Three underscores mean set in small caps. (220)
12. List eight duties of the proofreader. (221)
13. List the duties of the copyholder. (221)
14. A revise is the first printer's proof. (222)
15. Copy each proofreader's mark and tell what it indicates. (223)

CHAPTER 7

How to Lock Up and Impose Pages

The Lockup Procedure

Lockup for the press is a step between the okaying of a *page proof* and the *makeready* (setting up the press) preparatory to the actual printing of the job. Lockup is necessary to hold the type form in position while it is being printed on the press.

Tools Used for Lockup. Type forms are locked up on an imposing table, which consists of a steel-topped table of good working height. Older imposing surfaces used marble-topped tables, hence the term "stone" is often used in connection with the lockup procedure. A *stone hand* is one who does the lockup and imposition in a printing plant.

Forms are locked in chases, which are steel frames (see Fig. 7–3). The wedges that hold the form in the chase are called quoins, and they are pictured on page 142. A planer is used to knock all parts of the type form to the same level (see Fig. 4–12, page 142). Wooden or fibre mallets are used to tap the top of the planers when planing down a type form. Furniture and reglet are used to hold the type form in position in the chase (see page 139). *Patent base,* explained on page 230, is used when wood or metal furniture is not wanted.

The Lockup Procedure. When a job of letterpress printing is ready for the printing press, it is shoved from a galley to the imposing table, and a chase is laid over it. When hand fed platen presses are used, the form is positioned slightly above the center of the chase. The position of the printing on the paper will also have a bearing on this position. For example, on cylinder presses, this position will be fixed by the *gripper* side of the chase.

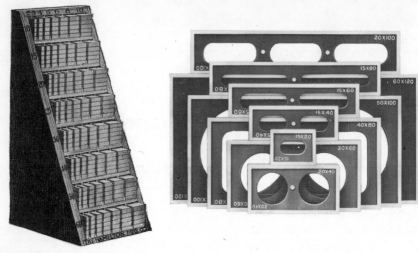

Fig. 7-1. Wood Furniture in a Furniture Rack

Fig. 7-2. A Few Sizes of Metal Furniture

As illustrated in picture 1, in Fig. 7–3 on the opposite page, furniture is placed at the bottom of the form to fill the space between the form and the bottom of the chase. For a good, square lockup, the form is usually made up to furniture lengths: 10, 15, 20, 25, 30, 35, 40, 45, 50, or 60 picas. This is usually done, if off one of these measures, with either steel or wood furniture in the smaller sizes, and slugs.

Picture 2 shows the second step, placing furniture at the left of the form. The furniture is staggered in size to insure a rigid lockup.

Picture 3 illustrates the third step of placing the top furniture in place with a quoin. Reglet is usually placed on each side of the quoin to protect the furniture from any impression the quoin might make against the soft wood surface.

Picture 4 shows the furniture and quoins and reglet placed in position at the right of the form.

The quoins are now tightened with the fingers (not the quoin key). This slight tightening is necessary before the full pressure of the quoins are made on the form, and before the form is planed.

Now the planer is placed on the form, after being wiped off on the bottom with the palm of the hand to remove any dirt or particles of metal which might be in the planing surface. The planer is then tapped *lightly* with quoin key (for small forms) or mallet.

Now the quoin key is applied to the quoins. Because of the leverage which transfers tremendous pressure, the quoin key should not be turned to tighten the quoins too much. Chases can be broken or sprung out of shape with the application of too much pressure.

To test the lockup to see if all elements of the form are held in place, and will not work loose on the press, one edge of the chase is lifted so that it rests on a piece of wood furniture. The form is now tested with a downward pressure of the fingers in *all* its parts. If all parts hold, and do not slip downward under pressure of the fingers, the form is ready for the press. If certain parts do move downward, the form must be unlocked, and corrections made in the justification of the loose lines.

Care should be taken to see that furniture is not binding against other furniture. Note that the quoins are always placed at the top and right side of the form in the chase. This is necessary to maintain *register* with the *guides* on the printing press, which are at the bottom and left with reference to the form on hand-fed platen printing presses. Quoins should point away from the quoins.

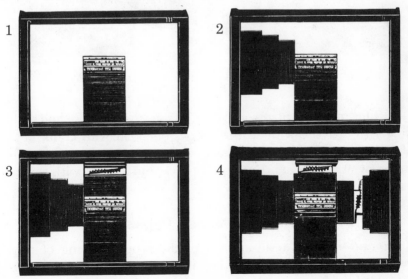

Fig. 7-3. Steps in Locking Up Type Form for the Press

Patent Base. For long press runs type forms are often *plated;* that is, duplicate printing plates are made from the forms called electrotypes. These electrotypes are sometimes nailed on wooden blocks to make them type high. However, wood base is notoriously bad because it is affected by humidity and temperature changes. Patent base is made of steel, and is adjustable to fit various sizes of chases. An interlocking block of patent base is illustrated in Fig.

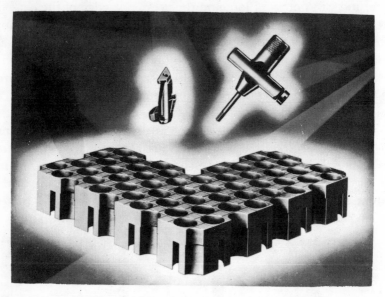

Fig. 7-4. Honeycomb Type Patent Base. *Upper Left,* the Hook. *Upper Right,* the Key

7–4. The printing plates are beveled on their edges, and held snugly to the base with register hooks operated with crank keys. Most books are plated and printed many pages at one time on the larger printing presses. Lockup is quick and simple with patent base and its accessories.

How to Impose Pages

Imposition is the term applied to the proper placing of page forms in a case, so that when the printing is done and the sheets are folded, each page is in order. Imposition also includes the work of finding the correct margins and *registering* the back-up sheets.

Work and turn forms are those on which all the pages on both sides of the sheet are imposed on one form. When the paper is turned and "backed up," or printed on the other side with the same form, each sheet printed makes two copies.

Sheetwise forms are those that are backed up with a different type form.

Each section of a book is known as a *signature*. A signature may be either of 4, 8, 16, or 32 pages. Large presses print as many as 64 pages sheetwise, which results in a 128-page signature.

Crossbars are often used in chases in order to simplify the locking up of many pages in the same form.

After a form is locked up and a sheet printed, it is usually checked for alignment on a *line-up table*.

Pamphlet and book pages are imposed according to the manner in which the printed job is to be folded. If folded by hand, a certain imposition may be used. This imposition may vary if the job is to be folded on a make of automatic folder known as the Baum, which may differ when folded on the make known as the Cleveland. The bookbinder is always consulted before imposition is made.

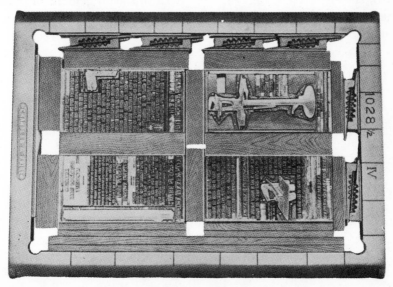

Fig. 7-5. Four Pages Imposed and Locked Up

How to Make an Imposition Dummy. Beginners in imposition should make up dummies to aid them in imposing pages for lockup. This is done by securing a sheet of the size to be used for the job, and folding it to the number of pages to be printed at one time.

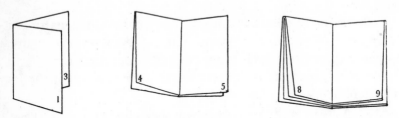

Fig. 7-6. Four-, 8- and 16-Page Dummies

Illustrated in Fig. 7–6 are three dummies: 4, 8, and 16 pages, reading from left to right. These dummies are used by the stone man to figure his margins and trim of the booklet, according to the specifications on the layout man's furnished dummy.

Four-Page Imposition. Four pages can be imposed in three different ways, as shown here. A square four imposition, work-and-turn, is illustrated in Fig. 7–7 below. In this arrangement of pages, the form is printed, and then the sheets are run through the press a second time and backed up so that pages appear in correct order.

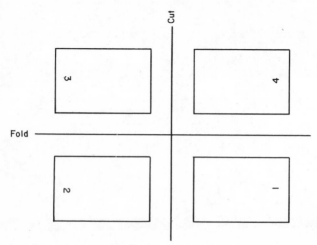

Fig. 7-7. Square Four-Page Imposition, Workand-Turn

The same four-page booklet can also be printed in two different forms, as shown in Fig. 7–8 below. This method uses two different lockups of two pages each.

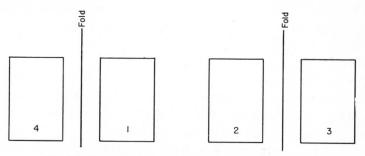

Fig. 7-8. Four-Page Imposition, Sheetwise in Two Forms

Still another method of imposing four pages is shown in Fig. 7–9. Here we have a long four-page imposition, which is printed on one side and then on the other so that the pages appear in order.

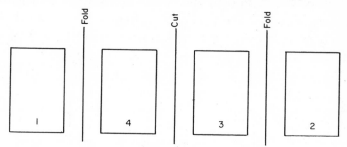

Fig. 7-9. Long Four-Page Imposition, Work-and-Turn, in One Form

The manner in which pages are imposed is decided by several important and different factors:

1. The size of the printing press.
2. The size of the completed book.
3. When the job is to be folded by hand.
4. When the job is to be folded by a certain make of folding machine.
5. How the booklet is to be bound.
6. How the booklet is to be gathered into signatures, which are the sections which will make up the completed booklet.

The examples here are imposed for hand folding.

Eight-Page Imposition. An illustration of an eight-page imposition to print sheetwise, that is, for two forms, is shown in Fig. 7–10. The same job could be printed work-and-turn, as in Fig. 7–11.

The same eight-page form could be imposed similarly to the four-page form shown in Fig. 7–9. With a long eight imposition, the sheet would take two parallel folds, either by hand or by machine.

Twelve-Page Imposition. Twelve pages can be imposed for work-and-turn forms. One part of the form has eight pages, and the other has four pages. The same job, sheetwise, could be imposed for three signatures of four pages each.

Sixteen-Page Imposition is quite common, especially in book work. These impositions are to be made work-and-turn or sheetwise, depending upon conditions in the printing plant.

Thirty-two-Page Imposition, also common where books are printed on large printing presses, can also be figured for the various kinds of work-and-turn and sheetwise forms. A 32-page form, run sheetwise, will make a 64-page signature when folded. Signatures as large as 128 pages are used, consisting of two 64-page sheetwise forms.

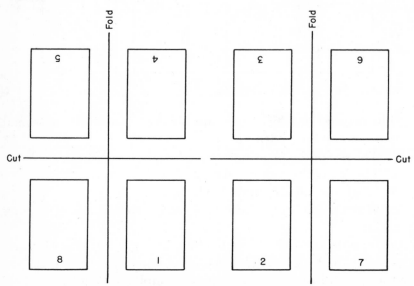

Fig. 7-10. Eight-Page Imposition, Sheetwise, in Two Forms

Allowance for Trim. Because a booklet must be trimmed at the top, right side, and bottom, an allowance must be made in the imposition for this trim, which is usually one-quarter of an inch.

Books Produced by Offset-Lithography. When books are produced by the offset-lithographic process, the same imposition is usually used. However, the man who imposes pages in offset work is called the *stripper*. Instead of working with type metal forms, chases, quoins and furniture, the stripper works with razor blade, goldenrod paper, **T**-square, ruler, and negative or positive film. He works over a "light table," which is glass-topped and has a light source underneath so that light shines through the negatives and positives.

The Stone Man. The man who works "at the stone," to use the language of the trade, is a very important man in the composing room. Very likely he is a "premium man," or one who makes over the scale of wages. In many cases he also acts as foreman of the shop, especially in the smaller composing rooms.

Upright and Oblong Books. *Upright* books are those which have the short dimension across the top. *Oblong* books are those which have the long dimension across the top.

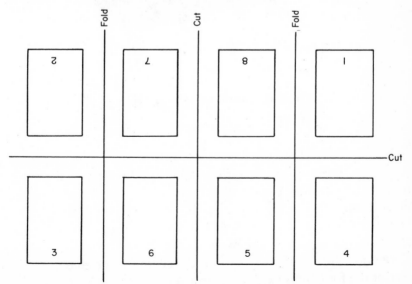

Fig. 7-11. Eight-Page Imposition, Work-and-Turn, in One Form

Line-up and Register Tables are used in up-to-date printing establishments to find the correct position of not only printing forms, but also elements within the form. A line-up table consists of a large glass-topped table, under which a light source is located. The light shines through a sheet of paper, which makes the print on its opposite side visible. Traveling pencils can make lines straight and true vertically and horizontally on a press sheet locked into position on the glass top of the line-up table. With this device it is a simple matter to adjust the pages of a form to within 1/72 of an inch tolerance. A line-up table is shown in Fig. 7–12.

Fig. 7-12. Line-Up and Register Table

SELF-TEST

This self-test will serve as a review of this chapter. The questions are true or false, or enumeration. The numbers following each question refer to the page number on which the correct answer can be found.

1. A stone hand is one who works at the imposing table. (227)
2. Chases are used to plane down forms. (227)
3. Cylinder forms are locked up in the center of the chase. (227)
4. List the four steps in locking up a form. (228)
5. A type form is locked tightly and then planed down. (228)

6. It necessitates great pressure to knock type to its feet when being planed down. (228–229)
7. Quoins should point away from quoins in the lockup. (229)
8. Beveled plates are often nailed to wood base. (230)
9. Imposition means the proper placing of more than one page in a chase. (230)
10. Work-and-turn forms are those on which all of the pages of a signature appear in the same chase. (231)
11. Sheetwise forms are those backed up with the same form. (231)
12. Imposition is the same, no matter what method of folding is specified. (231)
13. Four pages can be imposed in four different ways. (232)
14. Name six factors governing the imposition of pages. (233)
15. A line-up table allows position finding to within one point of space. (236)

PROJECTS

1. Lock up a simple type form in a platen press chase.
2. Make a dummy for a four-page imposition in three different ways.
3. Make a dummy for a six-page lockup.
4. Make a dummy for an eight-page lockup in three different ways.
5. Make a dummy for a 2-page imposition, work-and-turn.
6. Make a dummy for a 16-page lockup.
7. Make a dummy for a 32-page work-and-turn imposition.

CHAPTER 8

How to Understand Letterpress Printing Plates

Photoengravings

ILLUSTRATIONS in letterpress printing are made from *plates,* either the original plate made by the photoengraver, or duplicates of these originals. There are two kinds of photoengravings:

Line Engravings, which contain no screen, thereby giving no intermediate shades of gray *tone* except when treated with special screening media which are later explained. Copy for line photoengravings may be ink drawings, hand-lettering, proofs of type matter, and photographs or photostats made from them. Line photoengravings cannot be made from photographs having a *continuous tone;* that is, having no screen and varying gray shades of color.

Halftone Engravings, which produce the intermediate gray shades, or the "half tones" of the copy. This is made possible by printing with black ink in thousands of small "halftone" dots,

Fig. 8-1. This Is a Line Engraving

Fig. 8-2. This Is a Halftone Engraving

which are usually so small that the eye cannot see them. See Fig. 8–2 for an example of a halftone illustration, and compare it with Fig. 8–1 of the same subject, which illustrates a line engraving. Fig. 8–3, at the right, shows a coarse-screen halftone. Fig. 8–4, below, is blown up photographically to illustrate how the printing

Fig. 8-3

plate is made up of thousands of small halftone dots, which are usually so small that they cannot be noticed. Viewed from a distance of about twelve feet, the halftone dots which make up Fig. 8–4 cannot be distinguished, and the picture takes better form. A fine-screened halftone takes form at reading distance.

Magnesium plates have been developed in the photoengraving process. Research has brought about a greater use of magnesium plates and in a recent two year period their use appeared to have doubled. The lightness of the plates reduces mailing costs between advertisers and printers or newspapers. The lightness also allows increased rotary press speeds while reducing hazards. The magnesium plate has less centrifugal force than the heavier copper and zinc plates. Magnesium also etches faster than zinc, and tolerances in the plate can be held to 0.0005-inch. In addition, magnesium is

Fig. 8-4. A 4¼x Enlargement of Fig. 8-3, Showing Halftone Dots

less expensive than copper. The new metal allows screens from 55 to 150 to the inch. More stereotype matrices can be made from magnesium plates because of its hard surface. An additional use for magnesium is backing material for laminated electrotypes.

Copy for Photoengravings should be prepared with the requirements of the process in mind. Although improvements can be made in the plate by the photoengraver, there is extra expense. Remember: the better the original, the better the plate.

Pen-and-ink drawings on a good white grade of bristol paper stock make the best copy for line plates. Bluish tinges in ink and paper should be avoided. Lines should not be too close together and white spaces should be quite definite. Any necessary pencil outlines should be made in non-photographic light blue. Avoid any color in the drawing. Overlays can be made on mat-surfaced transparent plastic, and the photographing of extra colors for the plate may be included in the same focus by the photographer.

Make drawings twice the size of the completed plate. This will speed the work of the artist or draftsman, and slight defects in the drawing will be minimized in the plate.

Reproduction (etch) proofs of type matter should be made with great care. They should be clean and sharp and evenly inked on a slightly matt-surfaced white paper.

Photographs for making halftones should be glossy prints with a high contrast. Poor, faded photographs should be retouched with the aid of an airbrush. Great care should be taken in making photographs for reproduction on printed products and their backgrounds should always be considered. In many instances a white sheet placed behind the subject being photographed will improve the photograph.

How Line Photoengravings Are Made. The traditional process of making line photoengravings involves these steps:

Fig. 8-5

1. A negative of the copy is made on a camera to the desired reduction, enlargement, or the same size as the original (Fig. 8–5).

2. The negative, along with others, making a "flat," is placed face

Fig. 8-6

Fig. 8-7

down (for needed reversal) on a zinc or other metal plate which has a light-sensitive coating and both are placed in a photo-printing machine. A light source passes through the transparent parts of the negative, placing a coating of the image on the plate (Fig. 8–6).

3. The image is developed and fixed, making the image acid resistant.

4. The plate is etched slightly in a tank of corrosive acid, rinsed, dried, and brushed with a fine resinous powder called "Dragon's Blood" (Fig. 8–7).

5. The plate is heated to fuse the powder on the plate. The process of powdering and etching is repeated up to five times until the image is in sufficient relief for letterpress printing (Fig. 8–8).

6. The non-printing areas of the plate are routed deeper. The plate is usually affixed to a block to make it type high for printing.

How Halftone Photoengravings Are Made.

Fig. 8-8

Halftone photoengravings are made similarly to line plates, except that the negative is broken into many small dots by photographing the copy through a screen. The screen is made of two pieces of plate glass. Each piece of glass has parallel lines running diagonally across it. These two pieces of glass are cemented together so that the engraved opaque lines cross each other at right angles to form a mesh or a screen. (See Fig. 8–9.)

These screen rulings are of various sizes to satisfy the demands of the coarseness or fineness demanded by the paper used or the quality of the work being printed. Screens run 50, 55, 60, 65, 85, 100, 110, 120, 133, 150, 175 and 200 lines to the inch. Fifty to 100-line screens are called coarse, 110 to 200-line screens are

Fig. 8-9

Fig. 8-10. Cross-Section of an Etched Halftone

Fig. 8-11. Samples of Ben Day Screens Used in Line Engravings

called fine. Newsprint paper usually takes a screen from 50 to 85 lines; bond, ledger, and line papers, from 85-line to 100-line; machine finish book and sized and supercalendered papers from 100-line to 133-line; and coated (smooth) papers from 120-line to 150-line screens.

Depending upon the screen size, the depth of etch of halftone photoengravings is a minimum of .002- to .003-inch for the highlights, .001½- to .002½-inch for middletones, and .001- to .002-inch for shadows, as shown in Fig. 8–10.

Coarse-screen halftones are usually made on zinc, and fine-screened halftones on copper.

Combination Plates consist of both line and halftone, which adds sharpness to elements like lettering which might be fuzzy on the edges if screened. Two negatives are made and combined.

Ben Day is a process of applying screen tints and textures to plates before they are etched, or perhaps laid on a negative for a reverse

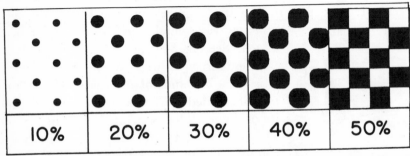

| Fig. 8-12 | Fig. 8-13 | Fig. 8-14 | Fig. 8-15 | Fig. 8-16 |

Halftone Screen Values, 10 Per Cent to 50 Per Cent, Greatly Enlarged effect. A total of 160 various screens are available in halftones, lines, grains, herringbones, stipples, and textures. Ben Day is often applied to line work, and a common example can be found in comic sections of newspapers. Other shading media are Bourges and Contax. See Fig. 8–11 for examples of Ben Day screens in common use for newspaper illustrations in advertisements.

Another shading medium which gives halftone effects through the less expensive line engravings is Craftint paper. The "Doubletone" drawing paper allows an artist to shade certain parts of his drawings by merely painting them with a special fluid, which brings Ben Day effects out of the drawing paper. See Fig. 8–17. Shading films are also available to place over white areas.

Fig. 8-17. Craftint Shading.

Costs of Photoengravings. Tables are furnished to buyers of photoengravings on which the costs of plates are based on *units*, which in turn are based on the number of square inches used. Odd-shaped plates cost more than are regular shapes.

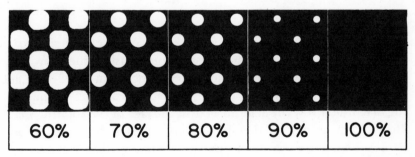

Fig. 8-18. Halftone Screen Values, 60 Per Cent to 100 Per Cent, Greatly Enlarged

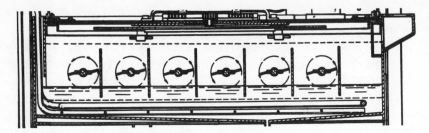

Fig. 8-19. Diagrammatic View of the Dow Etch Process

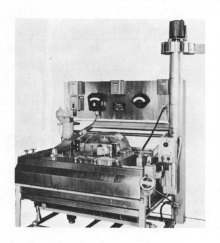

Fig. 8-20. A Dow Etch Machine

Fig. 8-21. Exposing a Dycril Plate

Powderless Etching. Many photoengravers are changing from traditional methods to powderless etching, using the Dow Etch Process, which requires one acid "bite" rather than powdering and etching up to five times. In the newer process, paddles in the etching machine throw the acid up against the face of the rotating plate. No etching occurs on the sides of the images, because the acid strikes these parts at a lesser angle. See Figs. 8–19 and 8–20.

Photopolymer Plates. A plastic plate, sensitive to ultra-violet light, is used in the Dycril process. The negative is placed in contact with the plate and exposed to light, which hardens the exposed areas of the film in about eight minutes. The plate is ready for the press after it is washed in a dilute solution of caustic soda, which washes away the unhardened parts. See Figs. 8–21 and 8–22.

The Kodak Relief Plate. The plate is a polymer form of the letterset (offset with no water) of the wrap-around type. It is only .025 inches thick, made up of a layer of emulsion, a white pigment, and a .013 inch layer of acetate and a steel plate .010 inches thick. The relief plate is .011 inches thick. After the plate is exposed (as in Dycril) the acetate is removed by immersion in an alkaline solution. Plates are still good after a half-million impressions on the press.

Electronic Platemakers. Halftones and often line plates may be produced without negatives and etching. The copy is placed on one cylinder and a plastic or metal plate on the other. An optical system "reads" the copy and directs a heated stylus to penetrate the plate about 640 times a second, producing the plate. These machines include the Scan-a-Graver, Scan-a-Sizer, Scan-a-Graver Cadet, Scan-a-Graver Dual, Scan-a-Graver Illustrator, Kleischograph, Photolathe, and Elgramma. See Fig. 8–23.

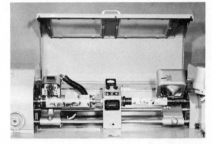

Fig. 8-22. A Dycril Washout Machine   Fig. 8-23. The Scan-a-Graver in Operation

How to Scale Artwork. It is often necessary to know the depth of a drawing or a photograph when it is marked for width when reduced in layout work. Original artwork is usually reduced to achieve the sharpness wanted in the final printing photoengraving. If copy is enlarged, sharpness is diminished.

Problem: Find the depth of an engraving when the artwork is 6x4 inches, and the type column is 13 picas.

Solution: 1. Find how many inches are contained in 13 picas. Consult the Comparison Scale for inches and picas on page 247. It will be noted that 13 picas are $2\frac{5}{32}$ inches.

2. Draw a rectangle six inches wide and four inches deep. See *A* in Fig. 8–24. The drawing may be made on transparent paper placed over the photograph or drawing.

3. Draw a diagonal line *B* from the upper left corner to the bottom right corner.

4. Lay a **T**-square over the drawing, and, by the use of a pica line gauge, find the point on the diagonal line which is exactly 13 picas from the right side of the rectangle. This is point *C* on the illustration below.

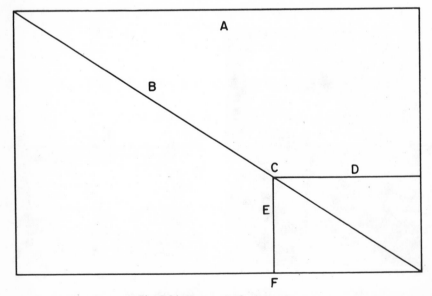

Fig. 8-24. How to Scale Artwork

5. Draw a line from point *C* to the right side of the rectangle, *D*.

6. Draw a line *E* from point *C* to the bottom of the rectangle.

7. Measure from point *C* to the bottom of the rectangle at point *F*.

8. The depth of the photoengraving, when reduced in width to 13 picas, will be 1⁷⁄₁₆ inches.

How to Mark Artwork for the Photoengraver.

1. Mount artwork and photographs on a stiff sheet of cardboard. Use an art paste or rubber cement to prevent curling and wrinkling. A cover of tissue and kraft wrapping paper is usually pasted to fold back, to prevent the work from getting dirty.

2. Mark the size screen wanted if a halftone. Mark "line" for a line engraving.

3. Note if the plate is to be on copper or on zinc. Zinc is used on copy up to 85- or 100-line screen, but not higher.

4. Place all marks, called "crop marks," for sizing the part of the work to be reproduced in the margins of the mounting. Never draw lines on the photograph.

5. Mark dimensions for either the height or the width on the margins, not on the art work itself.

6. Refrain from using paper clips on the artwork; the impression of the clip might mar the work and show on the negative.

7. Refrain from writing *too heavily* on the back of photographs. The camera may catch any indentations made.

8. Photographs and artwork should never be rolled. They might crack.

Fig. 8-25. Comparison Scale for Picas and Inches

Kinds of Halftone Plates. Possibilities in styles of halftone plates are endless. A few of the most used are:

1. Squared, where the screen is cropped (cut off).
2. Squared, with a "finishing line" of solid metal beyond the screen of the halftone.
3. Squared with a black-and-white finishing line cut by a tool, which prints clean when surrounded by white space.
4. Ovals and circles.
5. Silhouette, which follows the contours of the subject, without the screen squared.
6. Combination of halftone and line.
7. Vignette, which has re-etched edges that fade away into the white of the paper.
8. Phantom, where certain areas are subdued to give prominence to other more important areas.

Rubber Plates. Various types of rubber plates have largely taken the place of hand-cut linoleum blocks, a common amateur way to illustrate Christmas cards, short-run souvenir booklets, and kindred work. A thin rubber surface is mounted on a wood base to make it type high. The design is drawn or transferred in reverse on the rubber surface, and the nonprinting areas are cut away.

Tint Blocks, used to print solid backgrounds for photoengravings, may be made of rubber or plastic-topped wood bases. Screened tint blocks may also be furnished by the photoengraver.

Mounting Plates. Photoengravings may be mounted on wood bases, or the plates may be built up to a greater height, beveled at the edges, and used on steel patent base on the press.

How Colored Copy Reproduces. When colored copy, such as colored photographs, are reproduced in one color on "colorblind" plates and films, the colors in the copy reproduce as follows:

Red reproduces black.
Blue reproduces almost white.
White reproduces light gray, because of the over-all screen.
Gray reproduces light gray.
Purple reproduces medium gray.
Bright green reproduces dark gray.
Brown reproduces almost black.

Fig. 8-26. Yellow Plate

Fig. 8-27. Red Plate

Fig. 8-28. Blue Plate

Fig. 8-29. Black Plate

Fig. 8-30. Red and Yellow Plates

Fig. 8-31. Yellow and Blue Plates

Fig. 8-32. Red, Yellow, and Blue Plates

Fig. 8-33. All Color Plates

Courtesy of Photopress, Inc.

Process Color Printing. The beautiful colored pictures appearing in magazines and newspaper supplements, as well as in some books, are usually reproduced by the four-color process method. Advertising folders for many products, and comic sections in color, are also printed by this method by all printing processes.

Four-color process printing, although containing perhaps all colors of the rainbow, is usually reproduced by printing in yellow, red, and blue inks. A black plate is used to give more detail to the illustration. Transparent inks are used, which allow one to see all colors through the four overlapping coatings of ink on the white paper. For example, although green inks are not used, a green shade can be reproduced by a yellow and a blue plate, each placing their respective colors on the paper. The yellow and blue inks are placed on the paper in the form of halftone dots, which can be easily seen through a powerful magnifying glass. A light green would have larger yellow halftone dots than blue halftone dots, and a dark green would have larger blue halftone dots than yellow. Purples in the picture are reproduced by the combined plates of red and blue, and orange shades by red and yellow.

Halftone plates are made from negatives of each color, from which separate plates are made. The subject or colored photograph may be "shot" with a "one-shot color camera," in which the four negatives are made in the camera. Filters eliminate all colors from the negative except the color wanted. Processes are used also to reproduce color plates from copy having only one color—black.

Example of Four-Color Process Printing. The two preceding pages show "progressive proofs" and the final result of four-color process printing.

Figures 8–26 through 8–29 show the color plates for yellow, red, blue, and black. Fig. 8–30 shows the red and the yellow plates printed together in their respective colors. Fig. 8–31 shows the yellow and blue plates and Fig. 8-32 shows all color plates without the black plate. Fig. 8–33 illustrates all four plates. Note the green produced by the combination of the yellow and blue plates.

A usual sequence in printing colors is to print the yellow plate first, then the red plate, then the blue plate, and last the black. However, there are 24 possible sequences.

Duplicate Printing Plates

The two most used processes for duplicating printing plates in halftone and line, and type matter, are *electrotyping* and *stereotyping*. Electrotypes are used for duplicating an original form for the following reasons:

1. To allow the same form, as an advertisement, to be printed at the same time in different printing establishments.

2. To save original type setups and plates from wear.

3. To print two or more copies of the same type form at the same time on a large sheet. For example, as many as 16 electrotypes of the same office form can be printed at one time, which is called *ganging-up*. Large press runs are usually printed in this way.

Stereotypes are used largely by newspapers, and the process allows advertisers to send paper matrices of their ads to various newspapers about the country so that the same ad can be printed on the same day. Most daily newspaper pages are stereotyped, and half-cylindrical plates are cast from them so that they can be placed of the rotary presses.

How to Prepare Forms for Electrotyping. The lockup man uses a special chase for locking forms for electrotyping, although any type of chase will do. He surrounds each form locked in the chase with type high bearers, usually 12 points thick. The form should be a solid one, and not springy. High spacing material is used in the type matter, particularly in any open areas. All elements of the form should be type high, and worn types should not be used. Cuts should be reblocked if not type high, or if the base is warped. No rules having smaller bodies than two points should be used. Hairline rule should not be used, and quarter-point face should be substituted for it. Rules should also be beveled on both sides —not on one side only. Forms should be proofed after lockup to see if any type lines are off their feet, and to check any low or worn letters.

How Electrotypes Are Made. The older method in making an electrotype is in making the *case* for *molding*. Wax, the oldest mold used in electrotyping, requires a minimum of pressure from the type form. Lead molds require tremendous pressure which type matter cannot stand. Hence, *Tenaplate* and other special molding materials usually consist of a sheet of aluminum foil .006-inch thick. Another compound, vinylite, makes molds superior to any of these other molding materials.

Wax engraving still enjoys more use than is commonly realized, although not much publicity has lately been given to the process. It is a favored medium for high quality and intricate rulework, and also for map and music engraving. Special tools are required, however, for music engraving on wax.

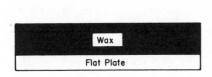

Fig. 8-34. The Case

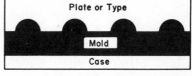

Fig. 8-35. Form Being Molded

Molding pressures are as great as 1,500 tons to make an impression of the type and plate forms in the mold.

After the mold is made, it is graphited in a machine which sprays graphite and water in a thin paste over the wax mold, which is necessary to make the mold a conductor of electricity.

Now the mold is placed in a deposition tank, shown in Fig. 8–36. A negative power source is fastened to the mold, and a positive power source is fastened to a pure copper bar. Both are suspended in the plating solution. The copper is deposited on the mold.

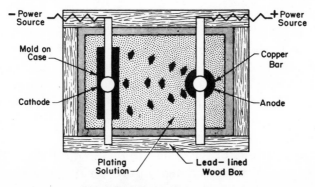

Fig. 8-36. Electroplating Process

The electrolytic process deposits a coating of copper on the mold from .006 to .008 of an inch thick. Nickel is substituted for copper to make *nickeltypes*. These duplicate plates are made for extremely long press runs because they wear longer than electrotypes, and are also used to offset the action of certain colored inks used in presswork. Copper electrotypes may also have a nickel or chromium surface placed on them to stand long press runs.

After the coating has been applied to the mold, it is removed from the mold by pouring boiling water over the copper shell, which destroys the wax mold.

The shell is laid face down, and strips of tinfoil are applied to the back, which act as a bond between the shell and the metal backing. The casting operation is performed when metal, consisting mostly of lead, is poured over the tinfoiled back of the copper shell. See Figs. 8–37 and 8–38.

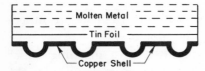

Fig. 8-37. Metal Is Fastened to Shell   Fig. 8-38. Completed Electrotype Plate
with Tinfoil

An automatic plate shaver shaves the plate down uniformly to an 11-point thickness, or about .152 of an inch. Parts of the plate below the printing surface are routed down to prevent smudging on the press. Any defects in the plate are corrected by a hand, and all elements are brought up to correct plate height.

Electros may be mounted on wood base, or the edges beveled for use on patent steel base. Electros to be used on rotary presses are curved to fit the impression cylinders.

Wax Engravings. A similar process to electrotyping is the manufacture of "wax engravings," used for some ruled forms, maps, and charts. The design is hand or machine-engraved, or photographed onto the wax case as a guide for engraving. Type matter may be stamped on the wax in correct position. Engravers' tools cut the design or lines of the design to the depth of the wax coating of the case. Wax engravings insure the joining cross-lines, particularly on ruled forms.

Stereotypes

Stereotypes are duplicate printing plates cast in metal from paper matrices. They are a coarser product than electrotypes, and are limited in the screens used for halftone illustrations. Screens are usually 85-line or less. Many daily newspapers are produced from curved stereotypes, cast from paper matrices rolled from pages made up flat by the usual composition processes.

Matrices are made as shown in Fig. 8–39. Dry matrices are usually used, although the wet matrices are sometimes used. A specially gummed backing felt is required for the *backing-up* process. The felt is placed on the matrix in areas where no type or plates appear, and where the casting metal may force the matrix out so that certain areas may be too high for correct printing. After backing the paper matrix, it is "scorched" (heated) in preparation for casting. A *tail piece* of kraft paper is then fastened to one end of the prepared matrix.

Fig. 8-39. The Matrix Press, Showing the Stereotype Matrix after Pressing

Stereotypes may be cast in shell or type high thicknesses. The shell casts are either mounted on wood bases or fastened to metal bases for further stereotyping or printing. Fig. 8–40 illustrates the casting process.

The molten stereotype metal cools fast, and the matrix and cast are removed from the casting box. The matrix is stripped from the cast, and can be used for making more stereotypes. The cast stereotype is planed to type height.

Figure 8–41 illustrates the work involved in cutting off the dead metal from the stereotype cast. The saw used is similar to those used in composing rooms.

Routing is pictured in Fig. 8–42. Any high parts of the stereotype are tooled away on the routing machine to prevent smudging on the printing press.

It is common practice for national advertisers to send matrices to weekly and daily newspapers so that their advertisements need not be set in type in the newspaper composing rooms.

Fig. 8-40. Casting a Stereotype from a Paper Matrix

Fig. 8-41. Cutting Off Dead Metal from a Stereotype Cast

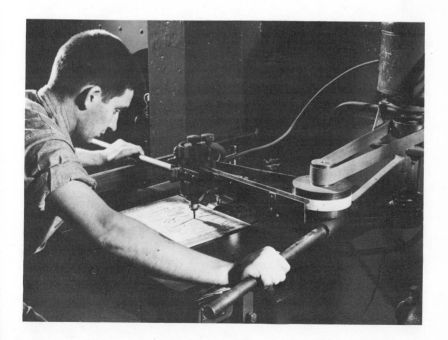

Fig. 8-42. Routing the Stereotype Cast

Rubber Duplicate Plates. Most printing seen on glassine, paper, and cellophane bags, such as bread wrappers and other bags, is done on rotary presses in aniline ink from rubber printing plates. Although not generally used on regular letterpress printing machines, rubber plates have good application to specialty printing which includes napkins, manifold office forms, cartons, matchbox covers, cloth bags, and kindred work.

A plastic mold is made from a form containing photoengravings and type matter, and the rubber plate is in turn vulcanized against this plastic matrix. The life of a rubber plate may run to a million printed impressions on aniline-ink presses, and between 200,000 and 400,000 with regular oil inks. Aniline inks dry quickly and do not attack rubber printing plates like they may other duplicates in metal form.

Molded Plastic Duplicate Plates. The foremost advantage of plastic duplicate printing plates is lightness in weight—one-eighth that of an electrotype—which saves considerable postage cost to advertisers who must ship plates to printers everywhere.

A plastic matrix is molded from the original, which may contain fine-lined halftones. Copies of the matrix are then manufactured in the same manner.

Hamilton Roll-Fed Letterpress Press

Letterflex is a newly-developed clear plastic plate used instead of stereotypes on newspaper rotary letterpress presses. Made from a negative, the plate has backing, bonding and photosensitive layers, totally about 0.025 inch, and has about 0.020 inch of relief. This new plate allows the use of cold type with the conventional letterpress process.

SELF-TEST

This self-test will serve as a review of this chapter. The questions are either true or false, or are asked to create thought and discussion. The numbers following each question refer to the page on which the correct answer can be found.

1. Line engravings reproduce no screen pattern in the intermediate shades of gray unless specially treated. (238–244)
2. Halftone engravings reproduce the intermediate shades of gray in the copy. (238)
3. Line plates are usually made on zinc. (241)
4. Halftones may be made on either zinc or copper. (242)
5. Etching powder prevents the acid from etching on a line or halftone engraving. (241)
6. Halftones are etched to a depth of .002- to .029-inch (242)
7. Six bites are taken by the acid in etching an engraving. (241)
8. A 100-line screen is considered coarse. (241)
9. A 110-line screen is considered fine. (241)
10. What is the name for an engraving consisting of both line and halftone? (242)
11. Ben Day screens can be applied to the plate or the drawing when making a line engraving. (243)
12. Screens can be placed on the original artwork through a chemical process which brings out over-all designs. (243)
13. Crop marks are placed on photographs to indicate the size wanted when ordering engravings. (247)
14. Fourteen picas equal two and three-sixteenths inches. (247)
15. Four and one-quarter inches equal 25½ picas. (247)
16. Photographic artwork is usually rolled. (247)
17. In what two ways are engravings mounted? (248)

18. Blue copy reproduces almost white in one-color engravings. (248)
19. White copy reproduces light gray in halftones. (248)
20. Opaque inks are used in four-color process printing. (251)
21. The four-color process inks are yellow, red, blue, and green. (251)
22. What is the usual sequence in printing four-color process printing plates? (251)
23. Name three major reasons for making duplicate plates. (252)
24. Stereotypes are used largely by commercial printers. (252)
25. One-point rule bodies should not be used on forms which are to be electrotyped. (252)
26. Most electrotype molds are made in wax. (252)
27. Electrotype molding pressures often exceed 1,000 tons. (253)
28. Copper and nickel is deposited through the use of electricity in the electrotyping process. (253)
29. The electrotype shell is from .006 inch to .008 inch in thickness. (254)
30. Electrotypes may be curved to fit rotary press cylinders. (254)
31. Electrotypes are made from wax matrices. (255)
32. Stereotype screened work is usually limited to sizes below 110-line for halftones. (255)
33. Stereotypes are cast in two thicknesses. (256)
34. National advertisers often send stereotype matrices rather than electrotypes or stereotypes to newspapers. (256)
35. Cellophane and glassine printing is usually done in aniline inks from rubber plates. (258)
36. Plastic plates are one-tenth the weight of electrotypes. (258)
37. The gray shades of a halftone are made possible by a multitude of tiny dots which appear gray to the eye. (238)
38. The Dycril process is the same as powderless etching. (244)
39. Photopolymer plates do not require a negative. (244)
40. No negative is used on the Scan-a-Graver. (245)
41. Discuss the procedures used on three different photoengraving processes other than in traditional photoengraving.
42. Letterflex plates are made from positives. (259)

CHAPTER 9

How to Do Offset-Lithographic Printing*

Platemaking

THE FIRST ITEM an offset-lithographer needs to work with is a negative or a positive of his type and illustrations. When lithographing by the *albumin process,* which is subsequently explained, he makes a negative from a paper proof of his type matter. If he prints by the *deep etch process,* he either makes a negative from a printed proof, and then makes a positive from the negative, or he uses a transparent cellophane proof as a positive film. A positive looks like the finished print; a negative has the white and black reversed. The same is true of all illustrations.

The offset-lithographer usually buys his proofs from a *trade composition house,* one which sets type only. He makes his own positives and negatives of all illustrations.

Many offset printers operate their own cold type departments for making both "body" type and larger display type, and by-pass the hot type composition houses entirely. See Chapter 5 on Cold Type.

Methods of Making Repro Proofs (Etch Proofs). The proofs of type made for offset-lithography are called *repro proofs* (etch proofs) because they are *reproduced* photographically. Several ways are used in which slug lines and individual types are handled to make repro proofs: by proving press, by cylinder press, and by platen press. Care must be taken to see that repro proofs are well printed. Low areas are built up so that the entire proof will be good enough to reproduce well when photographed.

---

*For more details, refer to Chapters 5, 6, 7, 8, 9, and 10 in *Graphic Arts Procedures— The Offset Processes.*

Transparent Proofs. Acetate or cellophane proofs are pulled to be used in the same manner that positive prints are used for illustrations. Transparent proofs are made in several different ways:

1. Printing on one side of the cellophane.

2. Printing on one side of the cellophane and dusting the freshly printed sheet with iron oxide or lampblack to make it a dense black. The dusting greatly improves the impression of the type matter.

3. Printing on one side of the cellophane by the letterpress process, and offsetting the same type impression from a rubber blanket on the reverse side. An impression is first printed on a rubber blanket covering the impression cylinder of the proof press. Then a sheet is printed so that the impression is made on both sides of the cellophane. Both sides may or may not be dusted with lampblack or iron oxide, depending upon the local printing plant procedures.

Conversion of Letterpress to Offset. Several procedures are used to convert hot type forms to negatives or positives which can be used in offset-lithography, gravure, and screen process printing:

Scotchprint. An impression is pulled on a dimensionally-stable plastic film with an ink-receptive surface. The film then becomes a translucent positive from which negatives can be made.

Type-to-Litho. Proofs are pulled from hot-type forms on an orange colored film. The image is then dried at 160 degrees for thirty seconds, and is ready to use as a negative to make offset plates.

DuPont Cronapress. Negatives are made on non-photographic film when small, bouncing steel balls impact against the printing surfaces of hot type forms. Other conversion processes include Silvertype, d-i, RIT Gard, Instant Negative and Converkal.

Verticon Camera. In this system, hot type plates are placed on a platen, bathed in a sweeping, oscillating light which produces the negative used in offset printing. See Fig. 9–1.

Brightype. This camera converts hot type forms to film photographically. The type form is sprayed with an opaque solution, burnished on the face with a rubber pad to give the face a reflective nature. Then the form is placed before a camera lens sur-

Fig. 9-1. The Lanston Verticon Camera

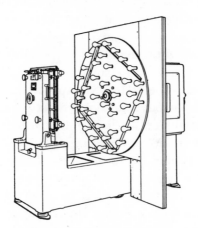

Fig. 9-2 The Brightype Camera

rounded by a battery of rotating lamps, which produces a negative. See Fig. 9–2.

Other conversion devices and processes include Converkal, Instant Negative, Silvertype, and Texoprint.

The Stripping Operation. After the negatives or positives of illustrations and type matter have been prepared in the camera room, the job must be *stripped* on a layout so that press plates may be made. The stripper is to the offset-lithographer what the makeup and lockup man is to the letterpress printer.

Both the stripper in offset-lithography and the makeup and lockup man in letterpress work from a layout or dummy. Where the letterpress makeup man arranges engravings and slug lines or type lines in a galley, the stripper in offset-lithography arranges the negatives or positives of film on a layout, usually referred to as a flat. The layout is the foundation on which the stripper builds.

The purpose of the layout or flat is to get the work, in either positive or negative form, square to the edges of the sheet to be printed, and in correct position in all elements of the form with relation to the printing plate.

Stripping Procedure for Negatives. The letterpress makeup man works *under* a light—but the offset-lithographer stripper works *over* a light, on a glass-topped table, so that he can see the negatives and positives. After an offset plate is made, changes cannot be made *on* the press as in letterpress printing. One cannot add space between lines, change the type faces, or move illustrations on an offset press. Any changes must be made on the layout prepared by the stripper. However, proofs can be made of the stripper's work by various means of contact photographic printing.

The stripper works on his light table with ruler, razor blades, straightedge, and triangles; he places the negatives in reverse on goldenrod-colored paper cut to the press plate size. The goldenrod paper supports the negatives and acts as a mask to the action of light. The negatives are placed in position with colored scotch tape, and the paper is cut away where the image shows in the negative.

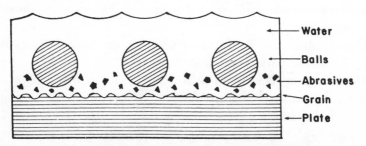

Fig. 9-3. Exaggerated Diagram of the Graining Operation

Stripping Procedure for Positives. As noted, negatives are used for making albumin plates, and positives are used for making deep-etch plates in offset-lithography. Both processes are subsequently explained.

Positives used for stripping flats for the deep-etch process are stripped on a piece of transparent acetate, a clear substance like glass, with transparent tape. Goldenrod paper is not used for stripping positive films in the deep-etch process.

Several different kinds of offset plates are in use, and include:

Aluminum	Plastic
Bi-Metal	Presensitized (ready for exposure)
Tri-Metal	Paper
Stanless Steel	Xerox
Zinc	

STEPS IN MAKING ZINC SURFACE-COATED (ALBUMIN) PLATE

The making of an offset-lithographic plate involves the following (See Fig. 9–3):

Step 1. The Plate Is Grained. Because the plates are smooth when new, they must be *grained* to give them the slightly roughened surface which will hold the water and ink used on the press.

Graining Machines are large shallow boxes which swing in an arc of about three inches and at a rate of about 150 to 250 revolutions per minute. Steel, glass, wood, or porcelain marbles press abrasives in the form of aluminum oxide or carborundum into the plate under water. Plates are grained for the following purposes:

1. The grain provides an anchorage for the light-hardened colloid or image that is to be printed on the plate from the negative or positive film.

2. The grain provides a fundation for the attraction of ink from the inking rollers of the press.

3. The fine hills and valleys of the grain give support for the press rollers and the rubber blanket of the offset press.

4. The hills and valleys in a grained plate provide reservoirs for moisture from the press-moistening rollers.

5. The images from old jobs are removed by graining so that the plate can be used again. The purchase of "presensitized" plates from suppliers often eliminates this operation.

Step 2. The Plate Is Counter-Etched and Washed. Counter-etching is done to remove any foreign elements such as dirt, and to remove any oxidation (rust) from the plate.

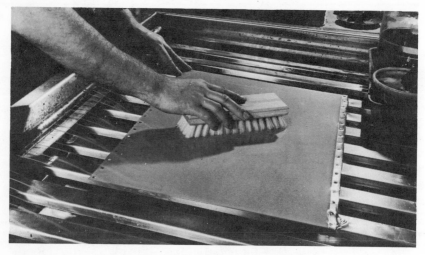

Fig. 9-4. Plate Is Washed in Running Water After Counter-Etching

In counter-etching, the plate is placed in a pan usually containing six ounces of acetic acid to one gallon of water. The plate is left in this solution for about ten seconds. The plate is then washed under running water, as shown in Fig. 9–4.

Step 3. The Plate Is Sensitized. The plate is now sensitized so that the image to be printed will adhere to the rubber blanket of the offset press after being inked, and from which it will be "off-set" to the paper as the press revolves. Plate sensitizers differ with lithographers, but one in use consists of:

2½ oz. egg albumin .   1½ oz. 28% solution ammonium
   1 oz. ammonium bichromate   23 oz. water

The plate coating machine used by the offset-lithographer for sensitizing the plate is called a *whirler*. This device consists of a

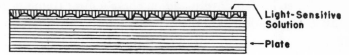

Fig. 9-5. Exaggerated Sketch of a Sensitized Plate

turntable within a cabinet or pan. The plate is placed on the turntable, grain up, and the sensitizing fluid is poured onto the middle of the plate as it spins. This insures an even coating. The plate is left on the whirler for drying, with the lid of the whirler closed. Drying is often helped with an electric air drier. This procedure is shown in Fig. 9–6, below. Some large whirlers are upright to conserve floor space. Most small whirlers are horizontal.

Step 4. The Plate Is Printed. When the offset plate has been sensitized, the stripper's flat is placed on the plate, and both together are placed in a *vacuum frame.* The negative and plate are pressed firmly together because air is drawn out of the vacuum frame from between a sheet of glass and a rubber mat. This insures the tight contact necessary for making a good plate. A strong light is turned on, which shines against the flat, and an image is made on the sensitized plate under the flat.

Fig. 9-6. Offset Plate Being Sensitized on a Whirler

When deep-etch plates are made on the vacuum frame, a negative print results This makes the exposed parts of the plate insoluble in water, and forms an image substance for the negative print.

Fig. 9-7. Stripper's Flat against the Plate in a Vacuum Frame

Deep-etch plates are slightly *intaglio;* that is, the image is slightly below the surface of the plate. A special developer, applied to the whole surface of the plate, dissolves the image or unexposed part of the light-hardened sensitive coating. The solution used in deep etch eats away parts of the grained surface, and forms slight recesses for the image areas. Developing ink is added to form an image base.

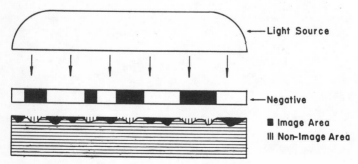

Fig. 9-8. How Light Shines through the Image in a Vacuum Frame

Step 5. The Plate Is Developed. After the plate has been exposed and printed in the vacuum frame in a matter of minutes, it is *developed* by rubbing developing ink over the grained side.

Fig. 9-9. Offset Plate Being Developed with Developing Ink

The plate is then washed under running water, and this removes the developing ink from the nonprinting areas. The plate is then gummed.

Fig. 9-10. Offset Plate Being Washed. Image Areas Retain the Ink

Presensitized Aluminum Plate. Presensitized plates are surface coated with a light sensitive solution by the manufacturer ready for exposure when removed from their original package. These plates are by far the most popular and most commonly used because many steps in making a plate are eliminated such as: washing, counter-etching, coating, etc.

Only four major steps may be necessary in the preparation of a presensitized plate and all steps are practically done the same way as other surface coated plates. These steps are: (1) Exposing, (2) Developing, (3) Washing, and (4) Gumming.

Each manufacturer of presensitized plates carries a complete line of their own prepared solutions for their plates. It is advisable to follow the instructions and use the solutions of each manufacturer. However, the following steps are general and accepted.

NOTE: When a plate is removed from its package, the package should be immediately resealed to protect the remaining plates within the package from light.

1. Remove a plate from its package and place on the plate exposure unit. Place the stripped-up flat containing the negative on the plate (face-up) aligning it across the top of the plate and down one side. Lower the glass cover and fasten. Turn on the vacuum and wait a minute or two so the vacuum seal between the plate and glass is complete before turning the plate directly facing the light. Turn the plate toward the light, turn on the light and expose for the desired length of time (Fig. 9-11).

Fig. 9-11. The negative and plate are placed in the vacuum frame for exposure

2. After exposure is complete, remove the plate and negative from the exposure unit and place the plate on a clean dry surface. Apply a small amount of process gum on the plate (Fig. 9–12) and wipe evenly over entire plate using a clean soft cellulose sponge or cloth. Remove excess gum leaving only a thin film on the plate. Before the gum dries, add a small amount of developer about the size of a half dollar on the plate (Fig. 9–13) and using a second clean sponge or cloth, rub the developer in a circular motion over the entire surface of the plate. Continue rubbing until a strong uniform image appears. If the developer tends to dry while applying, add a small amount of gum to keep the developer moist and workable.

Fig. 9-12. Applying Gum Arabic Solution on Plate

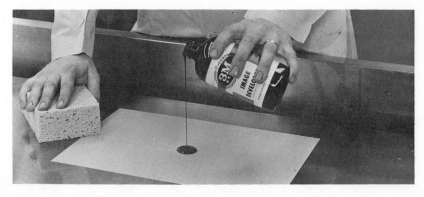

Fig. 9-13. Pouring Developing Ink on Small Plate

3. Regum the plate, polish dry with a clean soft cloth and the plate is ready for the press. See Fig. 9–14.

Depending upon the size of the plate a fourth step may be added, that is, after the developer is added to the plate, the plate is placed in a sink and luke-warm water is used to wash off the developer (Fig. 9–15). This becomes the third step, and the fourth step is then to remove the excess water off the plate and regum as stated in 3 above. Washing off the developer with water may be eliminated when using a plate up to size 14" x 20". Over this size washing with water is recommended.

Fig. 9-14. Final Application of Process Gum

Fig. 9-15. Washing off the Developer with Water

Copperized-Aluminum Deep Etch Plates. The copperized-aluminum deep etch process is made on a marble grained plate. The reason for this is to make the aluminum more hyrophillic and to make the image run longer because the surface area has been increased, allowing it to receive more water and enabling the image to have more adhering surface. The following eight steps are necessary to place an image on the plate:

1. *COUNTER-ETCHING:* this step cleans the plate of as much aluminum oxide, dirt or grease as it can, which really conditions or prepares the plate for the next step.
2. *COATING:* deep etch coating is whirled on the plate with a plate with a rotating table, which allows the coating to be placed on the plate with centrifugal force. After the plate is dried, the coating is light-sensitive.
3. *EXPOSURE:* the plate is placed under a positive film and exposed to light which selectively produces image areas.
4. *DEVELOPING:* deep etch developing solution is used to dissolve away all unexposed areas of the plate. In other words, these areas have been cleaned down to the bare aluminum.
5. *DEEP ETCHING:* aluminum deep etch solution is used to rid the image areas of any residual amounts of deep etch coating that might be left behind in the image areas, and it also etches down into the aluminum, leaving an image base which will be below the non-image areas.
6. *COPPERIZING:* copper base solution is used to chemically place a copper image on the aluminum. After copperizing, we have an image which is slightly raised above the non-image areas.
7. *LACQUERING:* deep etch vinyl lacquer is wiped down on the plate to insure ink receptivity of the image.
8. *INKING:* deep etch developing ink is wiped down on the plate to protect the lacquer when the stencil or non-image areas are removed with water. After the stencil has been removed, the plate has been completely processed.

PLACING IMAGE ON
COPPERIZED-ALUMINUM PLATE

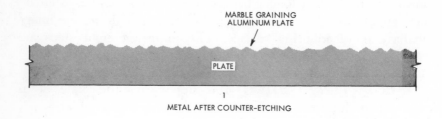

MARBLE GRAINING
ALUMINUM PLATE

PLATE

1

METAL AFTER COUNTER-ETCHING

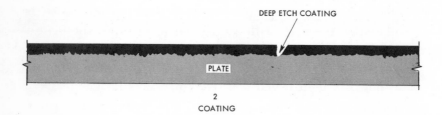

DEEP ETCH COATING

PLATE

2

COATING

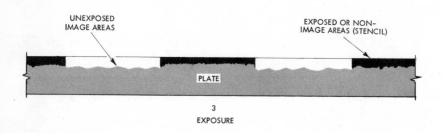

UNEXPOSED
IMAGE AREAS

EXPOSED OR NON-
IMAGE AREAS (STENCIL)

PLATE

3

EXPOSURE

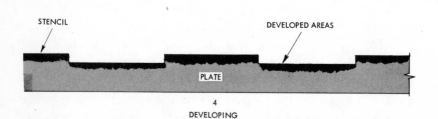

STENCIL

DEVELOPED AREAS

PLATE

4

DEVELOPING

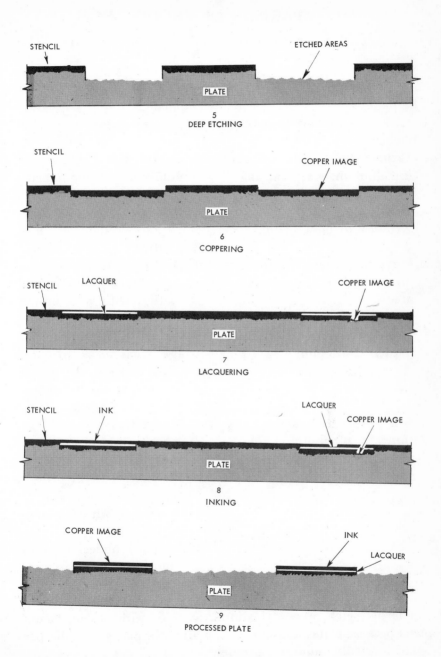

5
DEEP ETCHING

6
COPPERING

7
LACQUERING

8
INKING

9
PROCESSED PLATE

COMPARISON OF PROCESSES

ALBUMIN AND DEEP-ETCH OFFSET LITHOGRAPHIC PLATES

ALBUMIN	DEEP-ETCH
The plate is:	The plate is:
1. Counter-etched or pre-etched.	1. Counter-etched or pre-etched.
2. Coated with a solution of egg albumin, water, and ammonium hydroxide.	2. Coated with a solution of gum arabic, ammonium dichromate, and ammonia.
3. Dried.	3. Dried.
4. Exposed to light behind a negative.	4. Exposed to light behind a positive.
5. Developed to produce a greasy film on the printing areas.	5. Developed to remove the unhardened portions of the coating with a saturated solution containing lactic.
6. Etched to remove partially hardened albumin.	6. Etched slightly in the image areas by a solution which attacks the metal but leaves the light-hardened stencil intact.
7. Gummed, which deposits a thin film of insoluble gum arabic in the grain to desensitize the nonprinting areas.	7. Washed with anhydrous denatured alcohol to remove the etching solution.
	8. Lacquerd after the plate is dry.
	9. Developed with developing ink.
	10. Scrubbed under water to remove the light-hardened stencil.

The deep-etch process is gaining in favor with offset-lithographers because plates last longer than albumin plates, and sharper detail is usually found in halftones.

COMPARISON OF PROCEDURES

LETTERPRESS AND OFFSET-LITHOGRAPHY

LETTERPRESS	OFFSET-LITHOGRAPHY	
Layout or dummy is prepared, and type matter is marked for setting.	Layout or dummy is prepared, and type matter is marked for setting.	
Artwork is prepared, and specifications marked.	Artwork is prepared, and specifications marked.	
Artwork is sent to photoengraver to have original plates made.	Artwork is photographed in the plant to get negatives.	
	ALBUMIN	DEEP-ETCH
Type proof is pulled, proofread, and corrections made.	Repro proof is pulled, proofread, and corrected.	Repro proof is pulled, proofread, and corrected.
Paste-up is made showing position of type and illustration.	Paste-up is made showing position of type and illustration.	Paste-up is made showing position of type and illustration.
Type matter and photoengravings are made up in a galley.	Negatives of type and illustrations are stripped on goldenrod paper.	Positives of type and illustrations are stripped on acetate sheet.
Page proofs are pulled, proofread, and corrections are made.	Contact prints are made for any correction.	Contact prints are made for any correction.
Type forms are imposed in position, and locked in a chase.	Grained offset plate is provided.	Grained offset plate is provided.
Form is made ready so all elements print best.	Negative flats are exposed to plate on vacuum frame.	Positive flats are exposed to plate on vacuum frame.
Locked-up forms are placed on the press.	Plate is placed on press.	Plate is placed on press.

How an Offset-Lithographic Press Operates

The offset-lithographic press does exactly what its name indicates that it does—it *offsets* the image from a rubber-blanketed cylinder—not from the plate—to the paper. The plate prints the image on the rubber blanket.

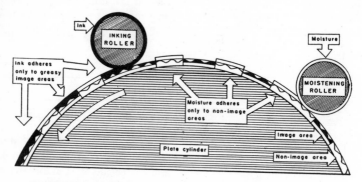

Fig. 9-16. Principle of Offset Plate Inking and Moistening

Grease and water do not mix, and in that principle we have the process of lithography. See Figs. 9–16 and 9–17.

Where the plate is moistened, the ink will adhere, and where the greasy image appears on the plate, the moisture will not adhere. This is how the offset-lithographic press will print from a *plane* or so-called *smooth* surface. In letterpress the *raised* surface of type and plates receive ink. In gravure the image is sunken on the plate.

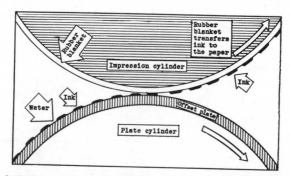

Fig. 9-17. How the Plate Transfers the Image to the Rubber Blanket

Kinds of Offset-Lithographic Presses. Offset presses range in size from very small duplicating machines printing 9¾x14-inch sheets to presses which can print sheets 52x76 inches. Special makes of the larger sizes print in one, two, three, four, or six colors at one time through the press. Most offset presses print single sheets, but special presses will print from a roll, and either rewind the sheets or cut the roll to sheet sizes. Offset presses are made in trade names of ATF, Harris, Miehle, Hoe, Willard, and others. Two popular makes, along with their specifications, are listed below:

Make	Smallest Sheet		Largest Sheet		Speed to:
ATF Little Chief	8x10	inches	14x20	inches	5,000 per hr.
ATF Chief	8x10	inches	17½x22½	inches	5,000 per hr.
ATF Big Chief	11x17	inches	22½x29	inches	5,000 per hr.
Harris	7½x8½	inches	17x22	inches	7,000 per hr.
Harris	10x14	inches	21x28	inches	6,000 per hr.
Harris	10x14	inches	22x34	inches	6,000 per hr.
Harris	17x22	inches	35x45	inches	5,000 per hr.
Harris	22x34	inches	42x58	inches	6,500 per hr.
Harris	25x38	inches	50x68	inches	6,000 per hr.

Fig. 9-18. ATF "Chief 24" Offset Press

Multilith and Davidson Duplicators. These small offset presses offset impressions on sheets from 3x5 inches to 9¾x14 inches at speeds ranging from 3,000 to 6,000 per hour. The printing area on these sheets may be as large as 9½x13 inches. Among the several makes of Multiliths available are: Models 40, 50, and 1250.

Three kinds of plates are used on the Multilith Duplicators. On the paper plate provided for one-run jobs, you can type, write, letter, draw, paint, rule, or trace the image desired in special inks. The plate is then placed in the press without further preparation for printing. Errors can be erased.

A thin, flexible metal sheet can be used on both sides for two different jobs or impressions. The image is placed on the metal plate the same as on the paper plate.

The regular photographic procedure is used for making the usual zinc or aluminum plates as explained in the last few pages.

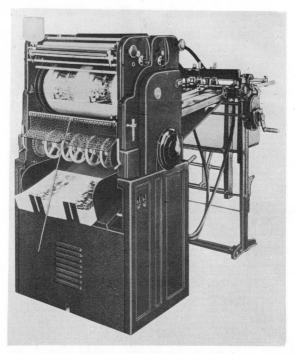

Fig. 9-19. Davidson Dual-Lith Press

Fig. 9-20. Multilith Model 1250 Duplicating Machine

This type of duplicator has found favor with offices for the printing of office forms, sales letters, and kindred work. Among the advantages of the machine, in addition to fast and less expensive work, is that of printing an office form on a paper plate, and then typewriting in certain sections on the plate for the duplicating of short runs on the press. Fine register work is not possible on the duplicators, and it is not considered a print's offset press. Special attachments allow for numbering each sheet lithographed, unbroken perforations along the entire length of the sheet, and a mechanical *jogger* similar to the sheet straighteners on larger machines. Some schools use this machine to illustrate the offset process.

SELF-TEST

This self-test will serve as a review of this chapter. The questions are either true or false, or are asked to create thought and discussion. The numbers following each question refer to the page number on which the correct answer can be found.

1. Albumin plates require positive film. (261)
2. Deep-etch plates require negative film. (261)
3. Repro proofs are usually purchased by the offset house from a trade compositor. (261)
4. Transparent proofs of type are similar to negatives. (262)
5. Why are cellophane proofs of type dusted with a black powder? (262)
6. The stripper does a similar job in offset-lithography to that of the slug-machine operator in letterpress. (263)
7. The stripper works under a light source. (264)
8. Proofs can be pulled of the stripper's work. (264)
9. Goldenrod paper is used in stripping positive film. (265)
10. Why does the stripper use a transparent base for positives in film? (265)
11. Give five reasons for graining offset plates. (265–266)
12. Counter-etching is done to remove oxidation and dirt from the zinc plate. (266)
13. What farm product or its synthetic is used for sensitizing offset plates? (266)
14. An even coating is placed on offset plates on what machine? (266)
15. Explain how you get a tight contact between flat and plate in the vacuum frame. (267)
16. Albumin plates are slightly intaglio. (268)
17. How is an exposed plate developed? (269)
18. Deep-etched plates last longer and give better halftone illustrations. (276)
19. Compare the steps in printing a job letterpress with that of offset by two methods: deep-etch and albumin. (277)
20. The offset press prints directly from the plate to the paper. (278)

21. The offset principle is that grease and water do not mix. (278)
22. Both ink and moisture are used on offset presses. (278)
23. Name three types of cylinders on offset presses. (278)
24. Offset presses run in sizes up to 52-76 inches. (279)
25. Name seven methods in which offset plates can be made without benefit of photography. (280)
26. What steps in making offset plates are eliminated through the use of transparent proofs of type matter? (261)
27. Various types of marbles alone are used to grain plates. (265)
28. Offset plates can be used over again after a plate has been used. (266)
29. The first three steps are identical in the processes of letterpress and offset-lithography. (277)
30. Elements of a form can be moved after the offset plate has been prepared and placed on the press. (277)
31. Name the most popular offset plate. (270)
32. Name the eight steps in making a copper-aluminum deep etched plate. (273)
33. Explain the operation of the following conversion processes: (262)
    (a) Brightype.
    (b) Scotchprint.
    (c) Cronapress.
34. Name nine types of offset plates. (265)
35. Name five kinds of offset presses. (279)

CHAPTER 10

How to Understand the Gravure and Photogelatin Processes

The Gravure Process

THE GRAVURE PRINTER uses positive films of his illustrations and usually glassine paper repro proofs of his type matter. Glassine proofs are made similarly to transparent proofs on cellophane for offset-lithography, as explained on page 262. As explained in Chapter 1 gravure printing is accomplished from a cylinder having a *sunken* image, quite unlike that of letterpress, which prints from a *raised* image, or offset-lithography, which prints from a *plane* surface. The steps in the gravure process are:

Step 1. Carbon Tissue Is Exposed. Carbon tissue is exposed to a screen, which is usually 150 lines to the inch. A positive film in continuous tone (like a photograph) is used for illustrations. The screen is already on the carbon tissue, as explained, so that both type matter and illustrations are screened. Positives of illustrations and glassine proofs are printed next on the carbon tissue.

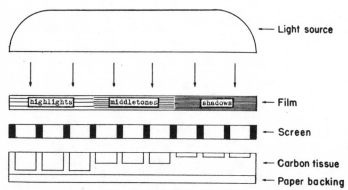

Fig. 10-1. Exposing the Carbon Tissue

284

Upon exposure to the positive film and glassine prints, the gelatin-sensitized coating on the carbon tissue hardens in proportion to the amount of light which comes through the positive film and the glassine repro proofs. See Fig. 10–1.

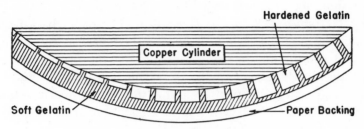

Fig. 10-2. The Carbon Tissue Is Placed on the Cylinder

On the carbon tissue, the gelatin is hardened to the least degree in the shadow areas; to a less degree in the middletones, and to the greatest degree in the highlight areas. The gelatin remains soft where the lines of the screen appear. Gravure screen dots are of the same *size,* but vary in *depth;* quite unlike letterpress and offset-lithographic plate halftone in which the halftone screen varies in size. (Some processes in gravure, like the *Dultgen method,* allow a variation in size as well as in depth of the dot.) The *amount of ink* placed on the paper determines the darkness of the picture.

Gravured printing, when viewed under a strong glass, often shows no screen pattern because the ink spreads slightly when printed, partially obliterating the screen.

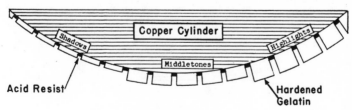

Fig. 10-3. Developing the Copper Cylinder

Step 2. Carbon Tissue Is Placed on the Cylinder. The carbon tissue is now squeegeed onto a polished copper cylinder, which, after it is etched, will print directly on the paper in the printing press.

Gravure cylinders are built up by an electrolytic process similar to the process of electrotyping for letterpress printing. After a job has been run on the gravure cylinder, the old image is turned off in a lathe, the cylinder is again built up to size as explained, and finally turned down again and polished to the correct size.

Step 3. Gravure Cylinder Is Developed. The paper backing and the soft gelatin of the carbon tissue is washed off, leaving the light-hardened gelatin on the copper cylinder. This process leaves a multitude of little gelatin squares of varying hardness. See Fig. 10–3 for an exaggerated illustration of this step. Parts of the cylinder around the edges, which will not be etched, are painted with asphaltum, which resists the etching acid.

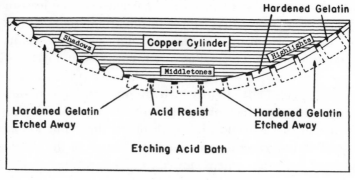

Fig. 10-4. Etching the Gravure Cylinder

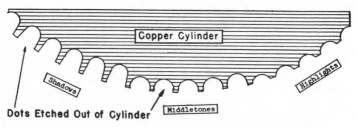

Fig. 10-5. Exaggeration of a Gravure Cylinder After Etching

Step 4. Gravure Cylinder Is Etched. The gravure cylinder is now etched several times. The acid must penetrate the little squares of gelatin before it starts to etch the cylinder itself.

The shadows are etched *deeper* than the other areas because the acid has not so far to go through the gelatin. The shadow dots are etched first, then the middletones, and then the highlights. No etching is done where the gravure screen lines are located because they are protected by the acid resist. See Fig. 10–4.

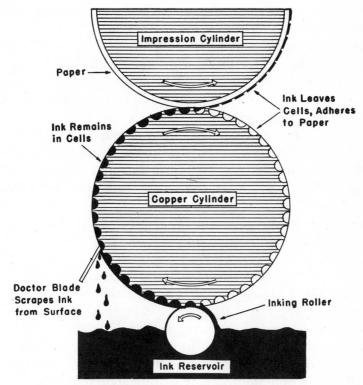

Fig. 10-6. How the Gravure Press Prints

The completed copper cylinder consists of thousands of little cells which have been etched out of the cylinder by the acid. The shadow dots deposit the most ink on the paper because more ink is contained in the shadow, or deeper, cells. The middletone cells deposit less ink than the shadows, and the highlight cells, holding the least amount of ink, deposit the least ink on the paper. The gravure ink spreads slightly upon contact with the paper, and the screen pattern is partially obliterated.

Step 5. Cylinder Is Placed on the Gravure Press. The gravure press is rotary in principle; that is, the press prints one sheet each time the cylinder revolves. Sheet-fed gravure presses are used to print art objects and advertising literature. Newspaper gravure presses print from a *web,* which is a continuous sheet of paper fed from a roll. Color gravure presses print both sides in four or more colors and deliver folded pages into supplements for Sunday editions.

On a gravure press, an inking roller, turning in an ink reservoir, places ink directly on the etched copper cylinder. The ink penetrates the small cells. As the cylinder turns, a *doctor blade* scrapes all ink from the surface or smooth part of the cylinder, leaving the ink only within the small cells. See Fig. 10–6.

When the gravure cylinder contacts the paper, the ink leaves the small cells and adheres to the paper. The ink spreads slightly after leaving the cells, which are etched to a depth of about .0025 of an inch. The press prints on any paper stock other than offset or coated, and is best produced on a No. 1 supercalendered book paper. Press speeds are very high, and the impression cylinder often turns at a speed of 16,000 revolutions per minute.

The Photogelatin Process

As explained in Chapter 1 the photogelatin process is also known as *collotype, phototype, albertype,* and by other names. The printing by the photogelatin process resembles a photograph because it is a continuous tone, and has *no screen.* Copy may be and usually is a photograph, but drawings in wash and crayon are also included. Shadings and delicate strokes reproduce accurately.

A negative is made from the copy as the first step in photogelatin printing. A large piece of plate glass, about $5/16$-inch thick and having ground edges, is cleaned and coated with waterglass, a substance consisting of silicates of sodium or potassium, or both, which is heated until dry. The negative and glass are placed in contact before a strong arc lamp, and the plate is etched in a bath of water and glycerine. Then the glass plate is placed in the press.

The flat-bed press used for photogelatin printing has excellent inking facilities, with as many as 40 rollers to distribute the ink.

Two colors are often used in the same shade; the darker color will ink the darker portions of the plate, while the light shade will ink the lighter parts.

A more modern method of photogelatin printing uses an aluminum plate which has been made light-sensitive. The negative is placed over the plate and subjected to a strong arc lamp. A chemical change takes place in the plate, which makes it repel moisture in proportion to the amount of light which passes through the negative. On the press, the plate is moistened with water and glycerine, then inked. The moistened parts of the plate reject the ink and the dry parts accept it. The plate prints directly on the paper, transferring the ink in inverse proportion to the amount of moisture retained in the plate. Any kind of uncoated paper may be used.

The photogelatin process is economical to use for relatively short runs from 100 to 3,500, and savings result from the fact that expensive plates are not required. A color job can often be printed at less cost than that required for the color plate alone if reproduced by another printing process.

SELF-TEST

This self-test will serve as a review of this chapter. The questions are either true or false, or are asked to create thought and discussion. The numbers following each question refer to the page number on which the correct answer can be found.

1. Gravure plates are made from negatives or positives. (284)
2. Gravure is an intaglio process. (284)
3. The screen in gravure is placed on the carbon tissue before the image of illustrations and type is made. (284)
4. The gravure screen is usually 150 lines to the inch. (284)
5. Cellophane proofs of type are usually used for repro proofs in the gravure process. (284)
6. The gelatin-sensitized coating on the carbon tissue hardens in proportion to the amount of light that comes through the positive film. (285)
7. Gravure screens are usually of the same size in dot. (285)

8. Gravure cylinders are used over and over again. (286)
9. Shadow dots are etched lighter than highlight dots in the gravure process. (287)
10. Etching is done where the gravure screen lines are printed. (287)
11. The deeper gravure cylinder cells deposit less ink on the paper than the more shallow cells. (287)
12. The screen in gravure printing is partially obliterated as the ink spreads and dries. (287)
13. Gravure presses are both rotary and flat-bed in principle. (283)
14. Sunday newspaper magazine supplements are usually printed by the gravure process. (288)
15. Often as many as 40 rollers are found on the gravure press. (288)
16. A doctor blade scrapes ink from the etched-out cells on a gravure press. (288)
17. Cylinders used in gravure printing are etched to a depth of about .250-inch. (288)
18. Supercalendered papers are good for gravured newspaper color printing. (288)
19. Gravure presses often print four colors at one time through the machine. (288)
20. Name three other trade names for photogelatin printing. (288)
21. Photogelatin plates are made of glass or aluminum. (288–289)
22. A very fine screen is contained in photogelatin printing. (288)
23. The most authentic manner in which to reproduce a photograph is by the photogelatin process. (289)
24. Photogelatin plates are comparatively expensive to make. (289)
25. Photogelatin is a short-run process. (289)

CHAPTER 11

How to Do Letterpress Presswork

Kinds of Letterpress Presses

FOUR KINDS of letterpress printing machines are in use today: the *platen* press, the *cylinder* press, the *rotary* press, and the *letterset* press.

The operating principles of each kind of press are shown below in Fig 11–1. Note that the platen press prints *all* of the type form

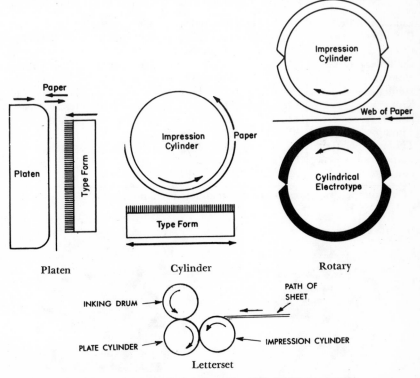

Fig. 11-1. Operating Principles of Four Kinds of Letterpresses

at one time. The cylinder press prints but an eighth to a quarter of an inch of the form at one time. As the impression cylinder turns, the form advances with it. As the cylinder keeps turning after the impression, the cylinder lifts to allow the form to return to its original position. Cylinder presses print one sheet with every second revolution of the impression cylinder. (The cylinder stops revolving on the Miehle Vertical press.)

Letterset (dry offset) is similar to offset. This press transfers a direct-reading image from a plate to paper using an intermediate blanket cylinder. The printing plate is a shallow-etched relief plate, which is placed around the plate cylinder.

PLATEN PRESSES

Name	Inside Chase Size	Platen Size	Hand-fed Speed to	Automatic Speed to
Chandler & Price*	8 x12	9½ x14⅞	3,000 per hr.	————
Chandler & Price*	10 x15	11¼ x18⅛	2,700 per hr.	3,500 per hr.
Chandler & Price*	12 x18	13⅛ x21¾	2,500 per hr.	3,000 per hr.
Chandler & Price*	14½ x22	15³⁄₁₆ x25⅞	1,800 per hr.	2,600 per hr.
Heidelberg	10 x15	10¼ x15	————	5,000 per hr.
Heidelberg	12 x18	13⅜ x18⅛	————	4,000 per hr.
Kluge	10 x15	11⅛ x18	3,500 per hr.	3,500 per hr.
Kluge	12 x18	13 x19	3,000 per hr.	3,000 per hr.
Thompson-National	10 x15	10⅛ x17½	2,000 per hr.	————
Thompson-National	13 x19	13⅜ x25⅝	1,800 per hr.	————
Colt's Armory	14 x22	14¼ x27⁷⁄₁₆	1,800 per hr.	————
Laureate	14 x22	14¼ x27⁷⁄₁₆	2,000 per hr.	————

*Chandler & Price presses are not manufactured now.

Fig. 11-2. *Left:* Hand-Fed Platen Press. *Right:* Automatic Platen Press

Fig. 11-3. *Left:* Rigid-bed Platen Press of the
Colt's Type. *Right:* Small Kelly
Cylinder Press

CYLINDER PRESSES*

Name	Smallest Sheet	Largest Sheet	Hand-fed Speed to	Automatic Speed to
Chandler & Price*	3¼x 5½	12¼x 8½	———	4,800 per hr.
Little Giant*	3¼x 5½	12 x18	———	4,000 per hr.
Heidelberg	4½x 6⅜	21 x28	———	4,000 per hr.
Kelly C*	7 x10	17½x22½	———	4,200 per hr.
Kelly No. 1*	8½x11	22 x28	———	3,600 per hr.
Kelly No. 2*	8½x11	24 x35	———	3,000 per hr.
Miehle Vertical 50	3¼x 5½	14 x20	———	5,000 per hr.
Miehle No. 29	8½x11	22 x28	———	4,500 per hr.
Miehle No. 41	16 x19	28 x41	———	3,000 per hr.
Miehle No. 46	16 x19	33¼x45½	———	2,800 per hr.
Miehle No. 56	19 x25	42 x56	———	2,250 per hr.
Miehle No. 5–0	24 x24	46 x67½	———	1,750 per hr.
Miehle No. 7–0	19 x25	50 x73½	———	1,600 per hr.
Miller Hi-Speed*	4 x 7	13 x20	———	5,000 per hr.
Miller Simplex*	8½x11	20 x26	———	4,500 per hr.
Miller Major	11 x17	28 x41	———	4,000 per hr.
Lee No. 38*	....	24 x36	2,500 per hr.	———
Lee No. 42*	....	26 x40	2,000 per hr.	———
Multipress	2½x 4	9 x12	———	6,500 per hr.

*Many old makes of hand-fed and automatic platen and cylinder presses are not
listed above, but are found scattered about the country, particularly in the smaller
newspaper shops.

Some of the more popular letterpress printing machines are listed in the previous tables which give their sizes and speeds of operation. The sizes listed under "Platen Size" do not refer to the size of sheet that can be printed, because sheet guides must take up a part of this area. Oversize sheets can be printed, however, on hand-fed platen presses, within the limits of the form.

Fig. 11-4. The Dry Offset Process. *Top:* A polyester film negative is stripped from an exposed Dycril printing plate. The plate will be washed out and used on wrap-around and letterset presses. *Bottom:* The plate is ready for wrap-around printing after water is blown from the Dycril plate.

The Chandler & Price and Kluge platen presses have a clam-shell action; that is, the bed and platen advance toward each other on making the impression. These presses, both hand-fed and automatically fed, are used for the general run of commercial printing. See Fig. 11–2. Colt's Armory, Thompson-National, and Laureate platen presses have a rigid bed, and the platen advances to meet it when the impression is made. These presses are used for printing and die-cutting paper boxes and like work. See Fig. 11–3.

Fig. 11-5. Miehle No. 29 (Horizontal) Press

Makeready

The process of *makeready* includes any advance work in getting photoengravings and electrotypes to the correct height-to-paper, placing the form and chase in the press, making the various adjustments necessary on the press, and doing the necessary work to make the type print well on the sheet. *Premakeready* includes those operations done in advance of placing the form on the printing press. Premakeready is often done in the composing room, and includes squaring wood base used under photoengravings, and planing down or building them up to correct height-to-paper.

Reasons for Makeready. In the part of makeready that embraces the operations required to make the sheet print well, the following tasks are done by the pressman:

1. Equalize the height-to-paper of all parts of the type form.

2. Provide the necessary pressures required by the different parts of the type form. Light parts of a printing form of type, photo-engravings, and electrotypes require less pressure than others to print well. For example, a hairline-faced rule usually takes about .002-inch *less* pressure than does type matter. The dark areas of a halftone are usually built up to increase the printing pressure from .001 to .003 more than that required by the high-

Fig. 11-6. Miehle Vertical Press

lights of the halftone. The solid areas of plates and very heavy large types often need from .002 to .004 more pressure to the paper than smaller type faces. This *adjusting of pressures* so that the type, engravings, or electrotypes print to best advantage is most important in the makeready process. Although type height is .918-inch, and *theoretically* all plates would print well at this height, it does not work out this way in presswork practice.

Another important reason for makeready is to *prevent wear* on a type and plate form. Parts of a form that receive too much impression will wear out quickly. This results in plates and type that cannot be used again, and such parts of a form likewise do poor printing after the press has printed a few hundred sheets. With proper makeready procedures, slugs from line-casting machines and foundry type often print well after 50,000 impressions.

Fig. 11-7. 10x15″ Original Heidelberg Platen Press

Printing on letterpress machines without makeready also results in the necessity of using *too much* ink. This results in many attending evils: the smudging of the bottoms of sheets as they are placed on freshly printed sheets (called *offsetting*), sticking sheets in the pile, and general poor quality work on the job in question.

A *perfect* printing form is generally nonexistent, except on rotary presses printing from plates which have been prepared with great care by "premakeready" methods.

Premakeready. Premakeready is that work done to a printing form before the chase containing the form is placed on the press. This work is usually confined to photoengravings and electrotypes, both halftone and line.

Fig. 11-8. Kluge Automatic Press

A *type-high gauge* is used to test all plates. The hand type is often used, although a *Hacker Gauge* is best, which features a dial on which the exact plate height can be tested to one-thousandth of an inch. Plates on wood bases that are either too high or too low are adjusted. Plates too high have the bottoms sandpapered or planed to the correct height. Low plates have to be built up to the correct height by pasting the thickness required on the bottoms of the base, as *underlays,* or between the plate and the base, as *interlays.* Plates fastened to wood bases that rock when tested on a flat surface must be taken from the base and remounted. Any attempts at correcting warped wood usually end in failure. Plates made for use on patent base generally are about .006 low to allow for interlays.

How to Make Ready Type Forms. The following procedure should be followed for making ready type forms on platen printing presses:

1. Ink up the press. This is done by smearing ink from an ink knife (similar to a spatula) across the plate of the press. Ink should be added in *small* amounts. Then the press is operated so that the form rollers distribute the ink over the plate.

Fig. 11-9. Miller Simplex Press

2. Put a new *tympan* on the press. This is the top manila sheet, (usually oiled manila) on which the guides are fastened, and on which the paper is printed by the type form.

3. Place the form, in its chase, against the bed of the press. Make *sure* before the press is operated that the sheet grippers will not come under the type form. *If they do, the form will be smashed.*

4. Add enough packing under the tympan so that an impression is made on the tympan. The packing is the cushion between the type form and the steel top of the platen. The packing usually consists of two *pressboards* (a hard red cardboard) and several sheets of S&SC paper stock. Often two manila sheets are used.

The tympan must be tight, without bulges or wrinkles. If it is not tight, good printing cannot be accomplished. For best work a hard tympan is necessary. Therefore, soft papers like newsprint and antique stocks should not be used in the packing under the tympan. A soft tympan will tend to *emboss* the type impression on the paper used for printing the job. A good platen press packing is about .040-inch thick,

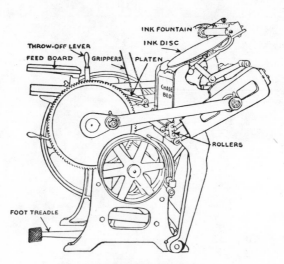

Fig. 11-10. Parts of a Platen Press

Tympan sheets should be cut off at the corners so that the "bales" (steel straps that hold the tympan in place) can clamp it snugly and flat. If the bales are not put back in their closed position, and the press is operated, then the type, bales, and tympan—and perhaps the press itself—will be injured.

Impression Screws. The larger the form, the more impression is needed to print satisfactorily. Because too thick a packing is not practical, platen presses are equipped with impression screws, located under the platen of the press. One screw is at each corner of the platen, and large presses have an extra screw at the middle. Inexperienced persons should move these impression screws only with the assistance of a competent pressman. Maladjustment will throw the impression far out of square with the bed of the press.

How to Set the Guides. After the impression of the form is pulled on the tympan, a lightly oiled cloth is used to remove most of the ink from the platen. The next step is to set the guides, which may be quads (three 12-point three-em quads are usually used), or one of the many makes of gauge pins. Quad guides need paper fenders, Fig. 11–11. Gauge pins have fenders built in, as illustrated in Fig. 11–12. To center a sheet, follow this procedure:

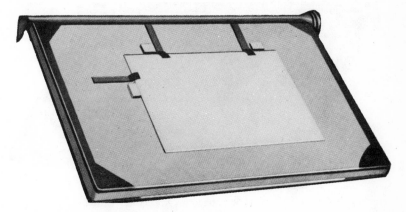

Fig. 11-11. How Quad Guides and Fenders Are Set in Position

1. Place the right-hand edge of the sheet to be printed at the right edge of the impression pulled on the tympan.

2. Fold the opposite edge back until it meets the opposite edge of the impression pulled on the tympan.

3. Draw a line at the fold. This gives the position in which to place the side or left-hand guide.

4. To find the position for the two bottom guides, place the edge of the sheet at the bottom line of the impression pulled on the tympan sheet.

5. Fold the opposite edge back until it meets the opposite edge of the impression on the tympan.

6. Draw a line entirely across the bottom at the fold.

7. On this line, mark the locations for the bottom guides, which are usually about one-sixth the length of the sheet from each end.

8. Mark the position for the side guide, slightly below the center of the sheet.

9. Set the guides on the lines drawn, and at the places marked on the tympan. Glue is used to fasten the quad guides. Gauge pins need no glue, as they have sharp pins which go into the tympan. Some patent guides require a slit cut in the tympan top sheet.

10. Make *sure* that the grippers clear the guides.

11. Place a sheet to be printed against all three guides, and operate the press, so that an impression is made on the sheet.

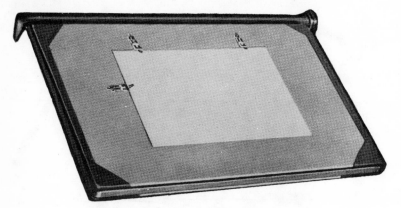

Fig. 11-12. How Gauge Pins Are Set in Position

Pull the impression slowly, so that the press can be stopped if the paper sticks to the type form.

12. Set the right-hand gripper so that it bears down on the right margin of the sheet—but not too close to the impression printed on the paper. Bring the left-hand gripper over to within an inch of the side guide.

Sometimes it is necessary to place a string between the grippers so that it bears against the bottom margin of the sheet being printed. Care should be taken to see that the string clears the form.

13. Compare the margins with each other by folding the sheet. This method is quicker than measuring with a rule. See that the form is squared on the sheet, top and bottom. Comparisons of margins, and also checking for squareness can be done with the use of a rule, lead, or even a card. Place the card at the right-hand margin of the job. Place the right thumbnail on the card where it meets the edge of the paper. Draw the card down the sheet and note the alignment.

14. Move the guides if the sheet is not printed square, or if the margins are off. Remember that *only the paper moves,* and that the type does not move because it is locked firmly in the chase.

15. Adjust the packing so that a light impression is made.

16. Make the quad guides stay in place through the use of gummed kraft paper tape. Fit the tape carefully around the corners of the quads. Gauge pins are tapped *lightly* with the gripper wrench so that their small teeth are imbedded into the tympan. Adjust the fenders in place as shown in Fig. 11–11 when quad guides are used. Pressboard is usually used to make fenders.

If the position is okay, the job is made ready, or *spotted up.*

How to Make Overlays. Follow this procedure for overlays:

1. Place a sheet carefully to the three guides of the press and pull an impression.

2. Theoretically brand new type on a brand new press, if the type is all about one size and weight, will print satisfactorily without makeready once the impression is correctly set. However, type is not always new, and neither is the press. Some type has had a few hundred impressions, and other type has had perhaps a million impressions. The most used type will be *lower* than the new type, and therefore more impression must be given these types to make them print as well as the new types. Other elements of the form, as rules and very light areas, need less impression, as explained. Machine-cast type may not be accurate in height-to-paper, and may need correcting. The job is to get an *even* impression all over the form.

3. Remove the printed sheet from the press, and hold it bottom-side up, at an angle of about 45°. Note the impression which shows on the back of the sheet. Depending upon the condition of the type form, it will be usually noted that some areas of the form are printing with more impression than are other areas. Some areas may be printing too light.

4. Referring occasionally to the printed side of the form, mark out these areas preparatory to pasting bits of thin paper in the thicknesses necessary to make the form print evenly. Fig. 11–13 illustrates the back of a sheet marked for pasting these pieces of paper in position. This is the procedure known as *spotting-up.*

Fig. 11-13. Spot-up Marks Used in Makeready

Spot-up Marks. Although such marks vary with many pressmen, the usual manner in which spotting-up is done in makeready is to indicate those areas which are to take the various thicknesses of paper through the use of signs and symbols.

Meanings of Marks:

T means use makeready tissue, which is a strong paper .001 inch in thickness.

F means use folio, which is a thickness of paper .002 inch thick, or twice that of tissue.

X means to cut out the sheet on which the makeready is being done to relieve the impression a considerable amount there.

S is sometimes used to designate that the paper on which the makeready is being done should be scraped lightly with the makeready knife to relieve the impression slightly.

Fig. 11-13 shows the application of these signs.

5. When the spot-up sheet has been prepared, one sheet of paper is removed from the packing of the press. Then the made-ready sheet is placed against the guides in correct position, and a sheet of the paper for the job is placed over it. An impression is pulled to see what corrections have been made to make the impression even all over the sheet.

The first mark-up is often made on a sheet of carbon paper, so that the marks are recorded on the printed side of the sheet. This is helpful in any markings to be made on any additions to the spot-up.

6. If any further spot-ups are necessary, the same procedure is followed to make ready the form.

Fig. 11-14. Miller 21 x 28 Two-Color Press

7. The makeready spot-up is now "buried in the packing of the press. Place the spot-up sheet or sheets to the guides, and cut the spot-up sheet and tympan through several layers of the packing in such a way that the position can be found in the packing. Three or four right-angle cuts are usually necessary.

8. Find the position on the sheet directly under the top tympan sheet, and place the madeready sheet in register (correct position) through the use of the angle cuts through the packing.

9. Place at least one sheet of pressboard between the top tympan sheet and the madeready sheet. Makeready should never be placed on top of the top tympan sheet, because any paper pasted there will have a tendency to rub off as the job is printed. When quad guides are used, a slight amount of machine oil is often wiped on the gummed kraft tape used to hold the guides in place. This makes for easier press feeding.

How to Make Ready Halftones. Halftone plates in the form of photoengravings and electrotypes of photoengravings usually have highlights, middletones, and more solid areas. Each of these three areas should be made ready so that each receives the correct amount of impression. The plate should be of the correct type height, as explained on page 298.

Electronic Makeready eliminates hand-cutting of overlays. A press proof is placed in the 3M machine as shown in Figure 11–15, and in a few seconds the sheet is delivered with gradations of rise from .001 to .004 inches where additional pressure is needed. A plastic-coated, heat-sensitive material is used.

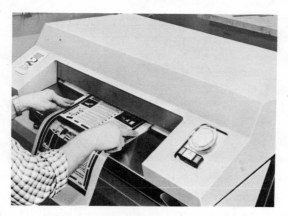

Fig. 11-15. The 3M Makeready Machine

Two-Ply Overlays. Proceed as follows to make a two-ply overlay for halftones:

1. Pull two impressions on S&SC paper stock.

2. Carefully cut the solids of the halftone from one sheet and paste them in perfect register on the other sheet.

3. Cut highlights from sheet on which solids were pasted.

4. To relieve the usual hard edges of the halftone print, cut the edges away about one point from the outer edges.

5. Paste the overlay prepared in perfect register with the makeready of the type matter.

All halftones should be carefully made ready, especially for long press runs, so that the plate does not wear.

Another reason for halftone makeready is to make the impression as good as possible to show up the contrasts of the picture to best advantage.

Three-Ply Overlays. On halftone plates that have several distinct tone values in the highlights, middletones, and solids, this procedure is used for making three-ply overlays:

1. Pull three impressions of the halftone on S&SC stock.

2. Cut the solids from one sheet and paste them in register on one sheet used as a base sheet.

3. Cut the solids and the middletones from the third sheet and paste them in register on the base sheet.

4. Cut out the extreme highlights from the base sheet.

5. To relieve the hard edges of the print, cut away about one point from all sides of the print.

6. Add the overlay in register to the type spot-up sheet.

Vignette Halftones. These are usually made about .916 high, and an interlay made to place between the plate and its base; the halftone dots fade away, leaving no hard edge.

Chalk Overlays. In shops printing a great amount of halftones, a chalk-overlay method of making ready is used to save the tedious job of hand-cutting spot-up sheets. A special paper is pulled with a special ink, and then the paper is etched in a special solution. The highlights are etched out of the special paper to a greater depth than are the middletones. Then the chalk overlay is placed with the makeready of the type matter in the packing of the press.

Scoring. Heavy cover papers used for booklets are usually scored so that they fold smoothly without breaks in the cover stock. This is done best by locking up two 2-point brass rules, about two or four points apart. The press rollers are removed. A piece of linen string is buried under the top tympan sheet, and the rules score the cover stock through their impression.

Die-cutting. Special steel cutting rules are used to die-cut paper and cardboard boxes on platen presses, usually of the Colt's Armory type. No inking rollers are used, and the steel dies are notched in sufficient places to allow the scrap stock to adhere to the board so that the sheets can be easily removed from the press. The scrap is stripped later from the work.

Embossing. This work is usually done on the Universal or Colt's Armory type of platen press because of its great strength of impression. A female die is used on the bed of the press, and the counter die is made by the pressman. Alabastine and dextrine are mixed to make a putty, which is put on a piece of strawboard. The strawboard is glued to the platen where the die will strike. The thickness of the composition is about one-eighth of an inch. A tissue is laid over the composition, and an impression is pulled from the die.

How to Operate the Platen Press

A quantity or *lift* of paper stock to be printed is placed on the feed board of the platen press. (See Fig. 11–10, on page 300.) The lift of stock should not exceed two to three inches of the paper used. *Fan out* the sheets by grasping the lift at both sides between the thumb and fingers of each hand, and tilt the paper so that the sheets will extend over each other on one side of the lift. Place the lift on the feed board so that the sheets project to the operator. This makes feeding easier than if the pile is upright. Sheets that have a tendency to stick together should be *winded;* that is, have air put between each sheet. This is done by grasping the sheets in small half-inch lifts between the thumb and fingers, and bending them downward so that air occupies the space between the sheets.

Feeding a press is the job of placing sheets singly into the press, on the tympan, and against the guides, and then removing the sheets after they are printed. A rhythmic movement is acquired with both hands in pressfeeding. The right hand places the sheets against the guides, and the left hand withdraws them:

1. Grasp the nearest right-hand corner of the sheet with the right hand between the fingers and thumb. Hold the sheet lightly —do not crease the sheet in any manner.

2. With a sweeping motion, strike, the *lower* guides first, and then thrust the sheet against the side guide. Brush the fingers of the right hand over the sheet after it has contacted the side guide, so that the sheet will stay in position against the guides. If the sheet does not strike the guides, thrust back the *throw-off lever* or *trip* to keep the form from printing crookedly on the sheet.

3. While the unprinted sheet is being placed against the guides with the right hand, the left hand is withdrawing the freshly printed sheet. Because the ink on the printed sheet may be smudged, it is necessary to place a finger either on the margin of the sheet or in an open part of the form. If margins are too small, a piece of sandpaper or emery cloth is used to cover a finger to prevent smudging.

For safety, the pressfeeder should stand erect at the press. If he stays in this position, he need not fear having his fingers pinched in the press between the platen and the bed.

Should a sheet fall between the platen and bed, the *pressfeeder lets it go*—he does not take a chance of his hands being smashed in the machine. Most platen presses, particularly in schools, have platen guards to prevent any injury to the operator.

4. Freshly printed sheets are placed on the delivery board of the platen press. To prevent smearing the fresh ink, the sheets are usually allowed to dry where they will on the delivery board. The sheets are *jogged,* or straightened later after they have dried.

5. In addition to feeding the press, the pressfeeder takes care to see that the following duties are performed:

Sufficient ink is kept on the press so that the printing is uniform throughout the run on each sheet. This means that ink must be applied to the ink plate periodically, or that the ink *fountain* must be set to feed a little ink with the printing of each sheet.

The pressfeeder watches the sheets carefully so that if *work-ups* appear he will not spoil the run. A work-up is spacing material that has risen in the form so that it prints on the sheet.

The operator also watches for loose guides, filled-in letters, and halftones, as well as any other troubles. The press should always be stopped when the operator is not in attendance.

Washing the Press. Ink will dry and become gummy on a platen press if left overnight without washing. The form is removed and washed with composing room solvent. Power is shut off, and the rollers run up over the ink plate. A cloth is dampened with kerosene, and the rollers and plate are washed carefully, and then dried with a clean cloth. The rollers are then run off the inking plate so that they do not rest on a flat surface and acquire flat marks.

Printing Ink

Printing ink is made in a great variety of consistencies, colors, and compositions to suit the exact needs of the printing press used and the paper stocks which are being printed on them. Most inks used in commercial printing are in a paste form. News inks used for printing newspapers, on the other hand, are more "runny" and are often pumped to the ink fountains of the rotary presses used.

Ink is purchased in tubes, cans of various sizes, and in large printing establishments it is purchased in steel drums. Caps should be kept on ink tubes to prevent the ink from drying. Cans of ink must be covered to prevent scum from forming and wasting the ink. Good pressmen never dig into the ink cans, but keep the top of the ink in the can level at all times. When ink cans are dug into with the ink knife, it is difficult to "skin" any hardened ink from a partially used can when the ink is used again.

Composition of Printing Ink. Printing ink consists of a *pigment* and a *vehicle*. Black ink pigments usually consist of lampblack or carbon. Colored pigments are derived from animal, vegetable, and mineral sources.

While the pigments furnish the color to printing ink, the vehicle or varnish provides the binder which carries the pigments and makes them adhere to the paper. The more expensive inks use linseed oil as the vehicle. Cheaper inks use rosin oil. Pigments and vehicles are ground together to make printing ink.

Inks dry by absorption into the paper and by oxidation or drying into the air. News ink is an example of ink drying by absorption. Ink dries on coated stock mostly by oxidation. On some printing papers, ink dries both by absorption and oxidation.

Opaque inks are used for normal runs in one color. Where two or more colors are used, transparent inks are used to achieve the effects desired.

Drier. A drier is added to certain inks to make them dry quicker. It is better to test an ink by applying a few pats of it to the stock to be run, and let the ink stand overnight to see that it dries, than to "dope" a good ink with drier. Three types of driers in use are paste, cobalt, and japan.

Japan drier is used for inks printed on the more absorbent papers. Cobalt is used to get quick drying, and paste is for slow drying.

Reducers. These are used to thin out an ink when a thinner ink is necessary for the press run. A reducer may be a varnish, or perhaps a different kind of ink.

SUITABILITY OF INK, DRIER, AND REDUCER TO PAPER STOCKS

Kind of Paper	Ink	Reducer	Drier
Blotting	Book or halftone	Soft halftone	Japan
Machine finish	Book	00 Varnish	Cobalt
S&SC	Book or halftone	00 Varnish	Cobalt
Antique	Book	Halftone	Cobalt
Coated	Halftone	Soft halftone	Japan
Bond	Bond	Halftone	Cobalt
Bristol	Bond or job	Halftone	Cobalt
Cover	Cover or bond	00 Varnish	Paste or cobalt
Cardboard	Job or book	Halftone	Japan
Gummed	Book or job	Halftone	Cobalt
Ledger	Cover or bond	Job or book	Cobalt
Newsprint	News	00 Varnish	Japan
Tag	Bond or job	Halftone	Cobalt

Mixing Inks. On long press runs the safest procedure in securing the correct color, as shown by the layout and the correct ink for the paper to be used, is to take a sample of the paper to the inkmaker, and purchase the ink specially for the job at hand.

When mixing a light color tint, it is best to mix the darker color into the white ink which forms most of the ink.

When mixing color for short press runs, and when there is little time to consult the inkmaker, the following table can be used to determine what colors to use for the color wanted:

For green—use yellow and blue.

For orange—use yellow and red.

For purple—use red and blue.

For brown—use red, yellow, black.

For maroon—use red, violet, yellow.

For olive—use orange and green.

For citron—use green and orange.

For russet—use orange and purple.

SAFETY HINTS

Working in pressrooms is not necessarily hazardous to either life, limb, or health. As pointed out in Chapter 4, on page 181, work in printing shows a good accident and health record.

A careless person, however, can be injured in any occupation. Any piece of machinery can be a hazard if ill-used, or if thoughtless habits are acquired. The following table should be read and heeded by all who work in pressrooms, both in school and in industry.

Hazard	Preventive
Clothing	Loose clothing may be caught in moving parts of presses. Remove neckties, and roll up sleeves and trousers.
Cylinder presses	Do not stand too close to cylinder presses. Be sure that the press switch is locked off before working on the feeder or when adjusting a form on the bed of the press. When handfeeding cylinder presses, never reach for a falling sheet. It is better to lose the paper than to get hurt.
Dim lights	See that work is done under adequate lighting to prevent eye strain.
Fire	Use matches away from press cleaning fluids. Take care to see that paper does not catch fire from the heaters on the press. Keep the gas turned off when making ready.
Lifting and carrying	Get aid when lifting or carrying heavy forms to and from the presses. Always lift with the leg muscles, and not with the muscles of the abdomen. Bend the *knees,* not the *body,* when lifting.
Littered floors	Keep tools and paper off the floor.
Oiling machines	Lubricate machinery when it is *not* running. Do not wash platen presses by pouring the cleaning fluid onto the inking plate.

Hazard	Preventive
Oily floors	Keep floors wiped to prevent slipping.
Paper handling	Take care when jogging paper. Some papers are sharp at the edges and will cut the hands and fingers. Handle heavy lifts of paper with care; lift with the knees, not the abdominal muscles. Do not attempt to lift great weights to demonstrate how strong you are.
Plates	Printing plates, like beveled halftone electrotypes, have sharp edges. Take care in handling them.
Platen presses	Stand erect at all times when feeding a platen press. This will insure that fingers and hands will not be pinched. *Never* reach for a falling sheet, not only between the platen and the bed, but also anywhere around a moving machine.
	Until you become more skillful, do not ink a platen press while it is in operation. The knife may be jerked and cause damage to you and the press. Do not pour cleaning fluid into the press for washing up.
Play	Refrain from wrestling and playing in the shop. No practical jokes on your fellows.
Talking	Refrain from talking to press operators, as it distracts them from their work, and they may be injured when off their guard.
Tools	Take care with the makeready knife. Open blades should never be carried in the pockets; close or sheathe the knife. Make sure that wrenches are tightly on nuts before trying to turn them.
Watching operators	Refrain from watching pressfeeders. Your presence, even without talking, may distract them from their work.

SELF-TEST

This self-test will serve as a review of this chapter. The questions are either true or false, or are asked to create thought and discussion. The numbers following each question refer to the page number of which the correct answer can be found.

1. The platen press prints all of the type form at one time. (291)
2. The cylinder press prints from a flat form on a cylinder. (292)
3. Platen presses range in size from 8x12 to 14½x22 inches. (292)
4. A Chandler & Price platen press has a rigid bed. (295)
5. Hand-fed speed is generally slower on platen presses when compared with automatic presses. (292)
6. Automatic cylinder-press speeds are greater than automatic platen-press speeds. (292–293)
7. Name all operations included in makeready. (295)
8. Explain the reasons for makeready. (295)
9. All halftones should be the same height-to-paper as type. (296)
10. The adjusting of pressures is least important in the process of makeready. (296)
11. Type not made ready properly will cause wear. (297)
12. Explain the disadvantages in not making ready type forms. (297)
13. Premakeready is that which is done before the press run begins. (298)
14. An underlay is placed between the plate and the base. (298)
15. An interlay is between the base and press bed. (298)
16. An overlay is placed in the packing of the press. (303)
17. When inking up, the ink is applied to the rollers. (299)
18. The tympan is the top sheet of the press packing. (299)
19. Why is it necessary to watch the grippers on platen printing presses? (299)
20. A platen press packing is usually .040-inch thick. (300)
21. A packing is usually made up of pressboards and paper sheets. (299)
22. The platen press tympan is held in place by the grippers. (300)
23. Soft packing is better for type than hard packing. (300)
24. The larger the form, the more impression is needed on platen printing presses. (300)

25. Press packings are made flat by cutting off each of their corners. (300)
26. Impression screws are moved for each job. (300)
27. What composing room equipment is often used for platen press guides? (301)
28. What other devices are used for guides? (301)
29. Explain how a sheet is centered to the guides on a platen printing press. (301–302)
30. Guides should be set about one-sixth the length of the paper from the corners of the sheet. (301)
31. Name the machine which now provides electronic makeready. (306)
32. Explain why type forms need makeready, even when all elements are type high. (303)
33. How thick is a tissue? (304)
34. Folio is a paper stock about .004-inch thick. (304)
35. Explain the process of spotting-up. (303)
36. Explain the five steps in making two-ply overlays for halftones. (306)
37. Explain the six steps in making three-ply overlays for halftones. (307)
38. Chalk overlays are used for making ready type forms. (307)
39. Vignette halftones are usually made under type height. (307)
40. Die-cutting is usually done with brass rule. (307)
41. Scoring makes cover paper fold more easily. (307)
42. The pressman makes the female die used in embossing. (308)
43. Fanning out a lift makes pressfeeding easier. (308)
44. Winded sheets are those in a tight pile. (308)
45. One hand is used in pressfeeding. (308)
46. The paper is held at the right-hand corner when feeding. (308)
47. The side guides are struck with the paper when feeding by hand on the platen press. (308)
48. The throw-off lever or trip must be thrust upward when the pressfeeder misses a sheet on a platen press. (308)
49. Name three duties of a pressfeeder other than placing sheets in the press. (309)

50. Platen presses must be washed clear of ink every night. (309)
51. All printing inks are in heavy paste form. (310)
52. A skin forms on printing ink in cans if left open to the air. (310)
53. Ink pigments consist of the color. (310)
54. The vehicle of printing inks is usually linseed oil. (310)
55. Cobalt drier is used on inks printed on coated papers. (311)
56. Japan drier is used in inks for quick drying. (311)
57. Reducers are used in ink to thicken it. (311)
58. When mixing a color tint, the color is added to the white. (311)
59. Why should not operators of presses be engaged in conversation? (313)
60. What simple rules can be followed to prevent being injured on platen printing presses? (313)
61. A paste drier is used for fast drying. (311)

PROJECTS

1. Practice pressfeeding on a platen press. Use no ink or form in learning to get into the rhythm of pressfeeding. (308)
2. Set quad guides for a simple platen press form. (301)
3. Set gauge pins for a simple platen press form. (301)
4. Make a spot sheet overlay for a simple platen press form. (303)
5. Makeready a halftone using the two-ply method. (306)
6. Makeready a halftone using the three-ply method. (307)
7. Makeready a form having rules. (303)
8. Makeready a vignette engraving with an interlay. (307)
9. Wash a platen press. (309)
10. Practice making ready on forms having type and halftones. (303)

CHAPTER 12

How to Understand Paper

Paper and How It Is Made

BEFORE PAPER was invented, *papyrus* was used for many thousands of years in Egypt. Papyrus was made from the thin skins of a kind of rush plant by the same name. Our word *paper* is derived from papyrus. During these early days, *vellum,* a fine calfskin, was also used for writing material.

It is said that paper very similar to the linen paper we have today was invented by the Chinese about the year 100 A.D. The Arabs introduced this rag-made paper to the western world in the tenth century. The Spanish craftsmen who made the first paper gradually located in all parts of Europe during the years 1100 to 1300. Paper, however, had little use in Europe until after the invention of printing about 1450. The first paper mill in England was established by John Tate in 1494. William Rittenhouse set up the New World's first paper mill near Philadelphia in 1690.

Before the development of the papermaking machine in 1804 by Henry and Sealey Fourdrinier in England, paper was made by hand. The hand paper molds consisted of a frame which stretched a fine cloth or fine wire screen with openings large enough to allow water to drain through, but small enough to hold the fibers of paper pulp. The mold was dipped into a vat containing water and paper fibers, and withdrawn. After the mold was violently shaken, the newly formed sheet was allowed to dry in the mold, or removed and placed on a board for drying. Paper was made by hand until about 1860, when the papermaking machines were put into general use in the United States. From this small beginning grew an enormous industry that kept apace with the development of printing.

Paper is manufactured in several states of the United States. New York leads in tonnage production, followed by Michigan, Ohio, Wisconsin, Pennsylvania, Maine, Louisiana, and New Jersey. Southern states are beginning to compete with the Northern states in the production of paper.

Fig. 12-1. Ancient Papermaking   Fig. 12-2. Modern Papermaking

When one considers the many uses we have for paper and paper products, the astronomical figures of production and consumption are understandable. For example, the United States manufactured almost 1,200,000 *tons* of newsprint in a recent year, and imported about 5,000,000 tons more. According to the Bureau of the Census, almost 12,000,000 tons of paper were manufactured in the same year.

In the printing paper field, machine coated paper totalled over 1,200,000 tons, book paper almost 1,560,000 tons, fine papers almost 1,324,000 tons, and coarse paper almost 3,500,000 tons.

Printers order paper by a number of sheets, a ream of 500 sheets, a carton of a number of sheets depending upon weight, or a skid containing many thousands of sheets.

Prices vary in order of the amounts required. In bond papers, for example, a broken package (less than 500 sheets) is higher per pound than any other quantity. Next comes the package price, then the carton price, then a four-carton or 500-pound price, and finally a 16-carton or a 2,000-pound price.

Furnishing paper to printers is a highly competitive business. Paper mills and local dealers vie with each other for the trade. Many new kinds of papers, and improved old lines of stock are continually appearing on the market. Some papers are good for both letterpress and offset lithography; others are made for offset lithography alone. A perusal of a paper dealer's catalog will acquaint the reader with the many varieties, weights, and prices.

Fig. 12-3. Logs Being Chipped

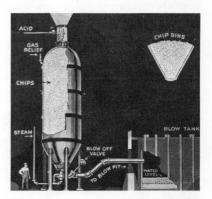
Fig. 12-4. Digesters

Ingredients of Paper. Paper is made from a great variety of vegetable fibers. These "cellulose" fibers are obtained from woods of various kinds, from linen, flax, and cotton; from rags and also from waste printed paper itself.

How Paper Is Made. The ingredients mentioned are reduced to very small fibers through *chipping, digesting, cleaning,* and *beating* processes with various chemicals so that the stuff will matt and interlace properly. These procedures produce *paper pulp,* which is used on the papermaking machines.

On the huge papermaking machine the paper pulp is diluted in great quantities of water and made to flow onto a continuous fine wire screen. The screen shakes as it moves, and this makes the fibers of the pulp matt and interlace. The water drains away and the paper is formed by the many little fibers of the pulp.

The sheet of paper now passes through a series of steam-heated rollers which dry it, and then to the *calendering rollers,* which give the paper the desired finish.

The paper is wound in huge rolls and later cut to sheet size. Some paper is slit to size and rewound for use on rotary presses. Brush-coated paper receives a layer of blanc fixe, casein, and coloring. Coated paper may be either *machine coated* or *brush coated*. After coating, the glaze is brought out with supercalendering rollers. Various kinds of finishes of paper are made to suit the major printing processes of letterpress, offset and gravure.

Watermarks. *Laid finishes* and watermarks, often seen on bond, writing, and antique papers, are put into the paper while it is still wet by a *dandy roll* before the paper is calendered. A dandy roll is made of fine wire, on which the wording or design is in relief. The design is pressed into the wet sheet.

Fig. 12-5. Beater

Fig. 12-6. Calender Rolls

Paper Is Two-sided. Paper has two sides, a *felt* side and a *wire* side, which can be seen on papers other than coated by a close examination. The felt side is the best printing side. On watermarked papers, the printing should be on the felt side, so that when the printed piece is held to the light the watermark can be read the same way that the printing is read.

Laid and Wove Paper. Uncoated papers may have a laid or a wove finish. For wove paper the wire screen is woven like cloth, and for laid paper the wire screen is laid in parallel columns. The wove screen was not in use until about 1750. Wove paper is common; laid paper is not so commonly used in today's printing.

Kinds and Weights of Printing Papers

Printing papers are made in a great variety of surface finishes, thicknesses, and sizes for use in the various processes of printing. Any complete explanation of the varieties of paper is impossible in the limits of this book. However, the most used kinds of papers in printing are explained in the following table.

QUALITIES AND USE OF PRINTING PAPERS

Kind	Quality	Use
Antique	Rough-textured and bulky	Booklets, books, folders
Bible (India)	Fine quality, thin; similar to machine finish	Bibles, encyclopedia, compact booklets
Blanks	Heavy cardboard	Window posters, car cards, boxes, tags
Blotter	Has ink blotting capability	Advertising blotters
Bond (writing)	Strong, firm; sized to take writing ink	Business and social stationery, office forms
Bristol, index	Plain like English finish, tough and thick; takes writing ink	Card files
Bristol, coated	Coated, heavy, rigid	Halftone printing
Bristol, plain	Like English finish, but much heavier	Cards, postcards, displays
Coated	Whiter and smoother than English finish	Fine halftones in advertising printing, books, booklets, magazines
Cover	Finishes in antique, plate, laid, ripple, and coated	Covers for booklets and advertising printing, menus, programs
English finish	Smoother and less bulky than antique, calendered	Magazines, picture folders, books, booklets, catalogs
Gummed	Similar to bond, gummed on one side	Labels, stickers
Ledger	Similar to bond, but much thicker	Bookkeeping records
Machine finish	Similar to English finish	Same as English finish
Mimeograph	Rough, absorbent	Duplicating work
Newsprint	Rough finished, gray	Newspapers, handbills
Offset	Similar to antique, but smoother; or coated	Booklets, books, folders
Supercalendered	Slightly polished and calendered, smooth	Cheaper books, booklets, folders

Paper Suited to Processes. Paper used for printing must be selected with consideration of the process to be used in printing the job. Certain papers are best for letterpress, or offset, or gravure, or copperplate engraving, as brought out in the following table.

PAPER SUITED TO PROCESSES

Letterpress	Antique, English and machine finish, supercalendered, offset, coated, bristols, bond, mimeograph, gummed, ledger, blanks, blotter, newsprint
Offset-lithography	Offset coated and uncoated, antique, bond, ledger
Gravure	Antique, supercalendered, English finish
Copperplate Engraving	Heavy weights in writings, bonds, and weddings
Collotype	English finish

Paper Suited to Photoengravings. Before selecting any paper stock, the printer must take into consideration the type of illustrations to be used—whether they are line or fine or coarse halftone screens. The following table is helpful in this selection.

Paper Permanence. Until recently, the most permanent papers were cotton content. Now some sulphite bond and book papers, called neutral, (having pH value of about 7—midway between acidity and alkalinity) are taking the place of the more expensive "rag" stock.

PAPER FINISHES SUITED TO PHOTOENGRAVINGS

Antique	Line plates by letterpress, halftones by offset-lithography
Bond and writing	Coarse, deep-etched halftones to 100-line, any screen by offset-lithography
Bristols	Line plates by letterpress
Coated	Fine-screened halftones by letterpress
Coated offset	Fine-screened halftones by offset-lithography
Coated one side	Same as for coated and coated offset
Cover, antique	Line plates by letterpress, halftones by offset-lithography
Cover, coated	Fine-screened halftones by letterpress
Cover, coated offset	Fine-screened halftones by offset-lithography
English finish	100- to 120-line screens by letterpress
Newsprint	Coarse-screen halftones, 55- to 85-line
Offset	Line plates by letterpress, halftone screens by offset-lithography
Supercalendered	Fine-screened halftones by letterpress

Sizes and Basic Weights of Printing Papers

Sizes of Printing Papers. The manufactured sizes of printing papers adhere to a set scheme based on the sizes of printing presses, paperfolding machines, and other printing machinery—which in turn are based on the needed sizes of printed matter—that of books, letterheads, envelopes permissible in the mail, etc.

When paper is purchased in large quantities over 2,000 pounds, special sizes may be ordered for a paper mill run to suit the requirements of a particular job of printing. However, standard sizes of paper are stocked for those who cannot wait for the mill to make a special size. These standard sizes are stocked by the paper dealer who supplies the printer and lithographer. Hence bond paper used for 8½x11-inch letterheads is made in a stocked standard size of 17x22 inches, from which four 8½x11-inch letterheads can be cut. Book paper is made and stocked in size 25x38 inches, so that sixteen pages 6x9 inches can be folded from this size.

See pages 324 and 325, "Basic Weights and Sizes of Paper," to learn these standard stock sizes in the various makes of paper stock.

Basic Weight of Printing Papers. The thinner sheets of paper used for books, pamphlets, letterheads, and advertising matter are measured for *thickness* according to *weight*. The thicker papers, like cardboard, are measured for thickness by thousandths of an inch.

Book paper has a *basic size* of 25x38 inches, and all various thicknesses are determined by weighing one ream (or 500 sheets) of the 25x38-inch size. If the ream weighs 70 pounds and is 25x38 inches in sheet size, the paper is *70-pound substance.* If it weighs 50 pounds, it is *50-pound substance,* and so on.

For example, the usual book paper substance weights run as follows: 30, 35, 40, 45, 50, 60, 70, 80, and 100 pounds in size 25x38 inches. Coated book papers run as follows in substance weights: 37, 46, 50, 60, 70, 80, 90, 100, and 120 pounds per 500 sheets in the stocked size of 25x38 inches.

Bond and writing papers have a basic size of 17x22 inches, and all various thicknesses are determined by weighing a ream of the 17x22-inch size.

If the bond paper ream of 500 sheets weighs 20 pounds, the paper is *20-pound substance;* if the ream weighs 16 pounds, it is *16-pound substance,* and so on. The usual bond and writing paper substance weights run as follows: 13, 16, 20, 24, 28, 32, 36, 40, and 44 pounds per 500 sheets in size 17x22 inches.

See the table below for basic weights available in most kinds of printing papers.

BASIC WEIGHTS AND SIZES OF PAPER

Kind of Paper	Basic Weights		Sizes in Inches		
Uncoated as follows:	30	35	22½x35	24x36	25x38*
	40	45	28x42	28x44	30½x41
	50	60	32x44	33x44	35x45
	70	80	36x48	38x50	
		100			
Coated two sides	37	46	22½x35	24x36	25x38*
	50	60	26x40	28x42	28x44
	70	80	32x44	35x45	36x48
	90	100	38x50		
		120			
Uncoated offset	50	60	22½x35	25x38*	28x42
	70	80	28x44	32x44	35x45
	100	120	36x48	38x50	38x52
		150	41x54	44x64	
Coated cover	50	60	20x26*	23x35	26x40
	65	80	35x46		
Uncoated cover	25	35	20x26*	23x35	26x40
	40	50			
	65	80			
	90	100			
Uncoated postcard	94	100	22½x28½ *	28½x45	
Uncoated bristol	90	100	22½x28½ *	22½x35	
	120	140			
	160	180			
	200	220			
Index Bristol	110	140	20½x24¾	25½x30½ *	22½x28½
	170	220	22½x35		
	9	11			

*Basic paper size.

BASIC WEIGHTS AND SIZES OF PAPER *(Continued)*

Kind of Paper	Basic Weights		Sizes in Inches		
Bond, writing, and mimeograph	13 20	16 24	17x22* 22x34 34x44	17x28 24x38	19x24 28x34
Ledger	24 32	28 36	16x21 19x48 28x34 19x24	17x28 21x32 17x22* 20x28	18x46 23x36 18x23 22x34
Coated bristol	*Point thicknesses* 8 10 12 15		22½x28½ *	22½x35	
Coated postcard	8 10 11		22½x28½ *	22½x35	

*Basic paper size.

How to Figure Paper

Equivalent Weights. As explained, paper thickness is determined by weighing 500 sheets (one ream) of the standard basic size in book paper of 25x38 inches. Thus, the term 25x38—70 means a book paper 25x38 inches in size, of which 500 sheets weigh 70 pounds. However, this paper is available also in the same basic weight (or thickness) in size 38x50 inches. The *equivalent weight* for this size is 140 pounds because the sheets are twice as large in area; this is designated as 38x50—140. In the absence of a table which shows the equivalent weights of papers, the following formula can be applied.

Problem: The same weight is wanted as 25x38—70 in the 32x44-inch size. Find the area of the two sheets in inches:

$25 \times 38 = 950$ square inches; $32 \times 44 = 1408$ square inches.

Multiply the area of the ream of unknown weight by the weight of the known ream:

$1408 \times 70 = 98,560$. Divide this product by the area of the given ream weight:

$98,560 \div 950 = 103.7$. For easy reading call this 104 pounds.

See the "Table for Equivalent Weights" on the following pages for quick reference in finding equivalent weights without figuring.

Paper Designated by 1,000 Sheets. Paper is often designated by the 1,000 sheets in basic weight. Example: 25x38—140*M* is the *same* as 25x38—70. The letter "M" stands for 1,000 sheet basis.

TABLE FOR EQUIVALENT PAPER WEIGHTS

COATED TWO SIDES

Basic Weight	Sizes									
	22½x35	24x36	25x38	26x40	28x42	28x44	32x44	35x45	36x48	38x50
37	30½	34	37	41	46	48	55	61	68	74
46	38	42	46	50	57	60	68	76	84	92
50	41½	45	50	55	62	65	74	83	90	100
60	49½	55	60	66	74	78	89	99	110	120
70	58	64	70	77	87	91	104	116	128	140
80	66½	73	80	88	99	104	119	133	146	160
90	74½	82	90	99	111	117	133	149	164	180
100	83	91	100	109	124	130	148	166	182	200
120	99½	109	120	131	149	156	178	199	218	240

UNCOATED

Basic Weight	Sizes									
	22½x35	24x36	25x38	28x42	28x44	32x44	33x44	35x45	36x48	38x50
30	25	27	30	37	39	44	46	50	54	60
35	29	32	35	43	45	52	53	58	64	70
40	33	36	40	50	52	59	61	66	72	80
45	37½	41	45	56	58	67	69	75	82	90
50	41½	45	50	62	65	74	76	83	90	100
60	49½	55	60	74	78	89	92	99	110	120
70	58	64	70	87	91	104	107	116	128	140
80	66½	73	80	99	104	119	122	133	146	160
100	83	91	100	124	130	148	153	166	182	200

UNCOATED COVER / COATED COVER

Basic Weight	Sizes			Basic Weight	Sizes			
	20x26	23x35	26x40		20x26	23x35	26x40	35x46
25	25	39	50	50	50	77	100	154
35	35	54	70	60	60	93	124	186
40	40	62	80	65	65	101	130	202
50	50	78	100	80	80	124	160	248
65	65	101	130					
80	80	124	160					
90	90	140	180					
100	100	. . .	200					

TABLE FOR EQUIVALENT PAPER WEIGHTS—*Continued*

BONDS AND WRITING

Basic Weight	Sizes									
	16x21	17x22	17x28	19x24	19x48	21x32	22x34	23x36	24x28	28x34
13	11½	13	16½	6	32	23	26	29	32	33
16	14½	16	20½	19½	39	29	32	35	39	41
20	18	20	25½	24½	49	36	40	44	49	51
24	21½	24	30½	29½	59	43	48	53	59	61
28	25	28	35½	34	68	50	56	62	68	71
32	28½	32	40½	39	78	57	64	71	78	81
36	32½	36	46	44	48	65	72	80	88	92
40	36	40	51	49	98	72	80	89	98	102
44	39½	44	56	53½	107	79	88	97	107	112

How to Figure Cost of Paper. Paper is usually purchased by the pound, or by the *hundred weight,* or by the ton. Like most material, the cost per pound decreases in proportion to the amount of paper purchased. Certain "penalties" in price are also made for small amounts of paper less than that contained in packages.

To find the cost of a number of sheets for a given job of printing, the following formula can be used to save time:

1. Multiply the number of pieces needed by the weight of 1,000 sheets. Example: 600 sheets 17x22 inches in size are needed in a 20-pound substance bond. (The weight of 1,000 sheets is 40 pounds.)

$$600 \times 40 = 24,000$$

2. Multiply the resultant product by the price of the paper per pound. (In this example the price per pound is 20 cents.)

$$24,000 \times 20 = 480,000$$

3. Point off five places: 4.80000. The answer is $4.80.

How to Allow for Spoilage. Allowance for spoilage differs in the individual printing plants throughout the country. If 500 pieces are cut for a job requiring 500 letterheads, for example, the final number printed will be short because some sheets will be used up in the makeready, in press spoilage, and in the bindery. One suggested allowance for this spoilage on short runs is to add four per cent for each color, and an extra four per cent if the job will be folded on a folding machine. On long press and bindery runs this percentage allowance is lowered to perhaps two per cent.

How to Figure for Cutting Paper. Paper must be cut to the size of any small printed jobs from the larger sheets purchased from the paper supply house. This work is done on paper cutters, and explained in Chapter 13, "How to Do Bindery Work."

Printed jobs are usually planned to a size which cuts without waste from standard size sheets. As an example, Fig. 12–7 below illustrates various practical size pieces that can be cut from a bond standard size sheet 17x22 inches. Examine the illustration and note that the listed number of pieces can be cut from the 17x22 size:

Four pieces 8½x11 inches   Twenty-four pieces 3⅝x4¼ inches
Eeight pieces 5½x8½ inches   Thirty-two pieces 2¾x4¼ inches
Sixteen pieces 4¼x5½ inches   Thirty-two pieces 2⅛x5½ inches

The above sizes are just a *few* of many possibilities in size. These pieces listed above are untrimmed sheets, and usually need cutting to a slightly smaller size after the job is printed. This trim is usually one-eighth to one-quarter of an inch.

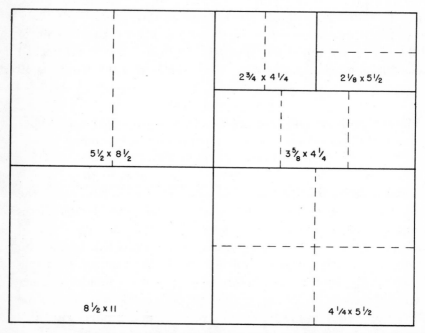

Fig. 12-7. Six Practical Sizes Cut from 17x22-Inch Stock

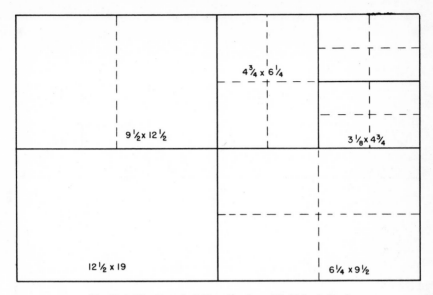

Fig. 12-8. Five Practical Sizes Cut from 25x38-Inch Stock

Fig. 12–8 above illustrates various practical sizes that can be cut from book paper, size 25x38 inches. Examine the illustration and note that the listed number of pieces can be cut without waste from the 25x38-inch size:

Four pieces 12½x19 inches   Thirty-two pieces 4¾x6¼ inches
Eight pieces 9½x12½ inches   Sixty-four pieces 3⅛x4¾ inches
Sixteen pieces 6¼x9½ inches

A few of the many possibilities based on standard book paper sizes are listed below, all cut with a minimum of waste:

PRACTICAL PAPER SIZES

Stock Size	Trimmed Sizes of Booklets			
28x44	2½x3¼	3¼x5¼	4½x7	2½x4⅜
	4½x5¼	5¼x9		
32x44	2½x3¾	3½x5	3½x7¾	5⅛x7
	5¼x7¾	7⅛x10⅜		
35x45	2⅝x5½	3½x4⅛	3½x5½	3½x8½
	4⅛x7¼	5⅜x11⅜	5⅝x7¼	7¼x11⅜
	8½x11			
38x50	2⅞x6	4 x9¼	4½x6	4½x8
	8⅛x12⅜	9¼x12¼		

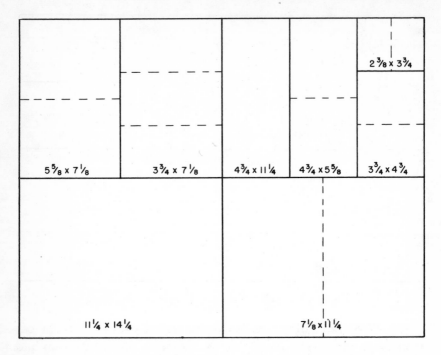

Fig. 12-9. Eight Practical Sizes Cut from 22½x28½-Inch Stock

Practical Bristol Sizes. Figure 12–9 above illustrates various practical sizes that can be cut from bristol size 22½x28½ inches. Examine the illustration and note that the listed number of pieces can be cut without waste from the 22½x28½-inch size.

Four pieces 11¼x14¼ inches   Twelve pieces 4¾x11¼ inches
Eight pieces 7⅛x11¼ inches   Twenty-four pieces 4¾x5⅝ inches
Sixteen pieces 5⅝x7⅛ inches   Thirty-six pieces 3¾x4¾ inches
Twenty-four pieces 3¾x7⅛ inches   Seventy-two pieces 2⅜x3¾ inches

Figure for Cutting Both Ways. To determine how many pieces can be cut from a standard size sheet, figure it both ways of the sheet:

$$\frac{\cancel{6\frac{1}{4} \times 9\frac{1}{2}}}{\cancel{25 \times 38}} = 12 \text{ pieces with } waste \qquad \frac{6\frac{1}{4} \times 9\frac{1}{2}}{25 \times 38} = 16 \text{ pieces with no } waste$$
$$2\times6 \qquad\qquad\qquad\qquad\qquad 4\times4$$

Select Best Stock Size. Stock sizes should be selected so that waste does not occur in cutting the necessary pieces for a given job of printing.

Problem:

For example, a size 8¾x11¼ is needed. Which stock size should be used, the 25x38 or the 35x45 inch?

Solution:

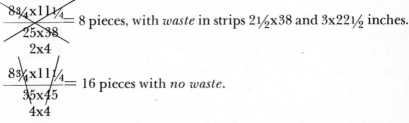

$$\frac{8\frac{3}{4}x11\frac{1}{4}}{25x38}$$
$$2x4$$
= 8 pieces, with *waste* in strips 2½x38 and 3x22½ inches.

$$\frac{8\frac{3}{4}x11\frac{1}{4}}{35x45}$$
$$4x4$$
= 16 pieces with *no waste.*

It will be readily seen that the best size to select for a piece 8¾x11¼ is the 35x45-inch stock, which cuts without waste.

How to Find the Amount of Paper Required. To figure the amount of paper required, in standard size sheets, follow the procedure set forth in the following example:

Problem: How many sheets 17x22 inches are needed for 1,000 letterheads of 5½x8½-inch size?

$$\frac{5\frac{1}{2}x8\frac{1}{2}}{17x22}$$
$$2x4$$
= 8 pieces from each sheet.

Figure spoilage: 4% of 1000=40; 1000+40=1040 pieces needed. 1040÷8 pieces=130 sheets size 17x22 inches needed for the job.

See the table, "Amount of Paper Required," on page 333, to aid in determining the quantity of paper required for a given job.

How to Test Paper for Grain. The grain of a paper must be considered when planning any printed job that is to be folded. Paper folds more easily *with the grain* than *across the grain.* Books fold better and stay open if the grain runs up and down the page. Cardboard posters stand without sagging in store windows if the grain runs up and down rather than across the poster. Folding machines can fold the paper better if the grain runs in the right direction.

Grain is usually indicated on the package of paper stock with an underscore. For example, 20x26, with the underscore under the "26," means that the grain runs in the 26-inch direction.

If the grain of a paper is not known, it can be tested in several ways. Cut off a *square* piece, and bend it between the finger and thumb, *both ways*—the short way and long way of the large sheet. It bends more easily with the grain than against the grain. Another test is to cut strips a half-inch wide and about eight inches long; one strip is cut the short way of the sheet, and the other strip is cut the long way of the sheet. Hold them together, side by side, and note how they bend downward. The piece that bends the least has the grain running the long way of the strip. Still another method is to wet both sides of a sheet of paper. It will curl, when drying, in the direction of the grain.

Effect of Relative Humidity on Paper. The millions of cellulose fibers which make up a sheet of paper respond to even slight variations in atmospheric conditions. The fibers expand when they absorb moisture in the air, and contract when they give off moisture. Paper expands more across the grain than with the grain, and also shrinks more across the grain than with the grain.

When a sheet of paper contains about the same moisture as the air in the room, it is said to be *seasoned* or *conditioned*. This action may take place in as little time as ten minutes.

Relative humidity means the percentage of saturation, or the amount of water vapor contained in the air in relation to the maximum quantity it could hold at the existing temperature. Relative humidity is increased when the temperature is lowered without removing water vapor. Relative humidity is decreased when the temperature is raised without adding water vapor.

When paper shrinks and expands, trouble is likely to occur in the pressroom and in the bindery. The paper may curl, take on wavy edges, and cause misregister on the printing presses doing jobs in color. Printed matter is difficult to manufacture when one color is printed on a hot, humid day, and the second color is added on a dry, cold day. The paper in this case would *shrink in size* enough to cause misregister, especially when printing large sheets. Therefore some pressrooms are equipped with air conditioners.

How to Use This Table. Figure the number of pieces that can be cut from a standard size sheet. Find that number in the extreme left-hand column of the table below. Find the quantity to be printed in the top column. The number opposite that figure will give the amount of standard size sheets required.

AMOUNT OF PAPER REQUIRED

Number Pieces	Quantity of Sheets Needed							
	500	1,000	1,500	2,000	2,500	3,000	3,500	4,000
1	500	1,000	1,500	2,000	2,500	3,000	3,500	4,000
2	250	500	750	1,000	1,250	1,750	2,000	2,250
3	167	334	500	667	834	1,000	1,167	1,334
4	125	250	375	500	625	750	875	1,000
5	100	200	300	400	500	600	700	800
6	84	167	250	334	417	500	584	667
7	72	143	215	286	358	429	500	572
8	63	125	188	250	313	375	438	500
9	56	112	167	223	278	334	389	445
10	50	100	150	200	250	300	350	400
11	46	91	137	182	228	273	319	364
12	42	84	126	168	209	250	292	334
13	39	77	116	154	193	231	270	308
14	36	72	108	144	179	215	250	286
15	34	67	100	134	167	200	234	267
16	32	63	94	124	157	188	219	250
17	30	59	89	118	148	177	206	236
18	28	56	84	112	139	167	195	223
19	27	53	79	106	132	158	185	211
20	25	50	75	100	125	150	175	200
21	24	48	72	96	120	143	167	191
22	23	46	69	91	114	137	160	182
23	22	44	66	87	109	131	153	174
24	21	42	63	84	105	125	146	167
25	20	40	60	80	100	120	140	160
26	20	39	58	77	97	116	135	154
27	19	38	56	75	93	112	130	149
28	18	36	54	72	90	108	125	143
29	18	36	54	72	87	103	121	138
30	17	34	51	67	84	100	117	134

SELF-TEST

This self-test will serve as a review of this chapter. The questions are either true or false, or are asked to create thought and discussion. The numbers following each question refer to the page on which the correct answer can be found, or to the page on which the correct formula can be found to solve certain problems.

1. What is the name of the material that the ancient Egyptians used for paper? (317)
2. The Chinese are said to have invented paper. (317)
3. The Germans were the first to make paper in Europe. (317)
4. What two materials were used in the mold to make paper by hand? (317)
5. Paper was made by hand until about the year 1760. (317)
6. Neutral paper has a high acid content. (322)
7. What state makes more paper than any other, considering tonnage alone? (318)
8. Name five sources of paper ingredients. (319)
9. How is the finish applied to paper? (319)
10. Watermarks are added to certain papers with a dandy roll. (320)
11. The felt side of paper is the best printing side. (320)
12. Uncoated papers are either laid or wove in finish. (320)
13. Name a rough-textured and bulky paper. (321)
14. Name several kinds of paper made to take writing ink. (321)
15. What is the whitest and smoothest paper made? (321)
16. Name some good papers for printing books. (321)
17. What paper is used for printing newspapers? (321)
18. What papers are best for letterpress printing? (322)
19. What papers are best for offset-lithography? (322)
20. What papers are best for gravure printing? (322)
21. What papers are best for copperplate engraving? (322)
22. What papers are best for collotype? (322)
23. On what are the sizes of standard papers based? (323)
24. Thin sheets of paper are measured for thickness according to thousandths of an inch. (323)
25. Thick papers are measured by their weight per 500 sheets. (323)

26. The basic size of book paper is 25x38 inches. (323)
27. The basic size of bond paper is 22½x28½ inches. (323)
28. The basic size of cover paper is 23x35 inches. (324)
29. Substance is paper weight of 1,000 sheets of the basic size. (323)
30. The basic size for bristols is 17x22 inches. (325)
31. Name several good papers for printing magazines. (321)
32. Name the kind of paper usually used for letterheads. (321)
33. An equivalent weight for 25x38—70 paper is 32x44—104. (325)
34. 25x38—60 is the same weight as paper 25x38—120M. (325)
35. The equivalent weight of 25x38—70 is the 38x50—140 weight, in uncoated book. (325)
36. Give the formula for figuring costs of paper. (327)
37. Four percent is usually allowed for spoilage. (327)
38. How many sheets 4¼x5½ inches can be cut from a sheet 17x22 inches? (328)
39. How many sheets 6¼x9½ can be cut from a sheet 25x38? (329)
40. How many sheets 7⅛x11¼ can be cut from a sheet 22½x28½? (330)
41. Is it best to cut pieces 8¾x11¼ from stock size 25x38 or size 35x45? (331)
42. For index cards to be used in a typewriter, the five-inch way on a 3x5-inch size, which way should the grain run? (331)
43. How many pieces are needed for 2,500 sheets, when seven can be cut from the large size? (Use table on page 333)
44. Explain three ways of testing paper to see which way the grain runs. (332)
45. Paper shrinks when it takes on moisture. (332)
46. Paper shrinks more across the grain than with the grain. (332)
47. Paper is seasoned when it contains the same moisture as the air in the room where it is stored. (332)
48. What biggest press trouble is often encountered with changes in relative humidity? (332)
49. How many pieces 3¾x7⅛ can be cut from a sheet 22½x28½ inches in size? (330)
50. How many sheets 4¾x6¼ can be cut from a sheet 25x38 inches in size? (329)

PROJECTS

1. Examine a sheet of paper and mark its wire and felt sides. (320)

2. Using the table on page 321, list the paper or papers suitable for printing:

   a. Booklets and books
   b. Window posters
   c. Card files
   d. Business stationery
   e. Fine halftone printing
   f. Newspapers
   g. Magazines in full color
   h. Postcards

3. List the types of printing plates by letterpress suitable for printing on the following paper stocks. Tell whether coarse or fine screens are suitable if halftones are listed.

   a. Antique
   b. Bond
   c. Bristol
   d. Coated
   e. Coated offset
   f. Antique cover
   g. Coated cover
   h. English finish
   i. Offset
   j. Supercalendered
   k. Newsprint
   l. Writing

4. List the basic weights, and underscore the basic paper size, of uncoated book papers listed on page 324.

5. List the basic weights, and underscore the basic paper size, of coated book papers listed on page 324.

6. List the basic weights, and underscore the basic paper size, of bond papers listed on page 325.

7. Collect a sample, printed or unprinted, of the following kinds of paper, and write on each what paper it represents:

   a. Newsprint
   b. Bond
   c. Bristol
   d. Coated
   e. English finish
   f. Antique
   g. Gummed
   h. Ledger
   i. Blotter

8. List the equivalent weights for a coated 50-pound substance of 25x38-inch size for the following sizes of paper, using the table on page 288: 32x44, 35x45, and 38x50.

9. List the equivalent weights for a 20-pound substance 17x22-inch size for the following sizes of paper, using the table on page 327: 17x28, 19x24, 22x34, and 23x36.

10. Using the formula given on page 327, find the cost of the following number of sheets of the full-size bond paper, 20-pound substance bond: 800, 1,000, 2,300, 5,000, and 7,500.

11. Repeat project 10 for 60-pound paper for 500, 750, and 1,000 sheets.

12. Figure the number of sheets necessary for spoilage allowance for 10,000 letterheads, run in two colors, using the percentages listed on page 327. Letterhead size is 8½x11 inches.

13. Figure how many sheets 5x9 inches can be cut from a sheet 22½x28½ inches. Figure this two ways. (331)

14. Figure how many sheets 8x12 inches can be cut from a sheet 32x44 inches. Figure this two ways. (331)

15. How many sheets 8½x7 can be cut from a sheet 17x28 inches? (331)

16. How many sheets 19x24 inches are required to make 3,000 pieces 3x6 inches? (331)

17. Determine the grain of a piece of paper in three ways: (331)
    a. By cutting a square
    c. By moistening
    b. By cutting strips

18. Using the table on page 332, determine the number of sheets required for the number of pieces needed as listd below:
    a. 1,500 pieces with two out of a sheet.
    b. 2,500 pieces with six out of a sheet.
    c. 3,000 pieces with 18 out of a sheet.
    d. 35,000 pieces with 10 out of a sheet.
    e. 4,000 pieces with eight out of a sheet.

CHAPTER 13

How to Understand Bindery Work

Methods of Fastening Sheets

BEFORE the process of binding was practiced, the Egyptians pasted papyrus sheets together, which formed rolls often as long as 18 feet. About 6,000 years ago the manuscripts were written crosswise on the roll and later were divided into columns written lengthwise of the roll. When parchment made from animal skins was later used for making books before the invention of printing from movable type, the sheets were folded once to form four pages. Each four-page signature was then tied together and covered over-all with leather. Thus the first bookbinding was done.

After the invention of printing from movable types, about the year 1450, the bookbinding trade grew along with the new practice of letterpress printing. For many years printed sheets were folded by hand, and books were bound by hand. In 1876 the *Philadelphia Times* installed the first folding machine invented by Stephen D. Tucker. About the same time other machinery was developed, and finally all modern necessities were fully entrenched: stitchers, sewing machines, power cutters, gathering machines, gluing machines, casemaking machines, casing-in machines, backing machines, and folding machines.

Fig. 13-1. Early Bookbinding

338

Printed sheets may be bound together in many different ways. Illustrated and explained on the following pages are the major methods used today, with an explanation of their particular advantages and disadvantages.

CONVENTIONAL BINDINGS

Conventional bindings are used for books of a more permanent nature, and to which sheets cannot be added or removed. These are the *saddle-wire, side-wire, sewn soft cover,* and *sewn case-bound.*

Saddle-Wire bound booklets are the simplest and cheapest in form and are used for small thicknesses, usually from eight to 32 pages, although saddle-wire bindings are often seen on magazines printed on thin papers up to 200 pages. Such bindings seldom hold up with great use, however, and are therefore temporary. The cover and pages are held by two or more wire stitches on saddle-wire booklets, which allow them to lie flat and open for ease in reading. Also, such books may be folded over onto themselves. The inside margins may be very small, and bled illustrations (pictures which run off the margin) may be used. Most small advertising booklets, programs, catalogs, and other printed matter are bound by the saddle-wire process, so-called because the sheets are bound through the middle over the saddle of a stapling or stitching machine. See Fig. 13–2.

Fig. 13-2. Saddle-Wire Binding

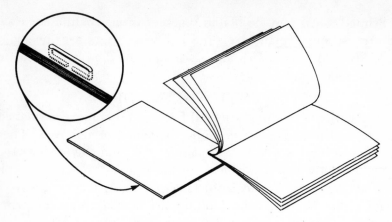

Fig. 13-3. Side-Wire Binding

Side-Wire bound booklets are simple and cheap in form, and are used for books of any thickness that can be stitched, usually under one inch. The cover is usually glued on in one piece to the backbone. One disadvantage in side-wire binding is that the book will not lie open for ease in reading, except in very large sizes, and must be held open. The inside margin must be larger than that used in saddle-wire bound books: One advantage is that a two-page sheet may be included, as well as odd-sized pages. See Fig. 13–3.

Sewn Soft Covers are more expensive than saddle-wire or side-wire styles, but are much more permanent. Each signature is

Fig. 13-4. Sewn Soft-Cover Binding

sewed together, and signatures are sewed to signatures in an un-
limited quantity by book sewing machines. Double stitches are
used; this prevents one book stitch to unravel when the books
are cut apart later. Book sewing can be accomplished on machines
in any manner that can be done by hand. The covers are usually
glued on in one piece to the front and back of the sewn book.
The book lies flat when open, and the inside margin can be small.
Bled pages are possible, and the backbone can be printed.

Sewn Case-bound is best when permanence is wanted, and
therefore is the most expensive. Books of any size and any number
of pages may be sewn and case bound, but large and heavy books

Fig. 13-5. Sewn Case-Bound Book

must be if they are expected to endure much handling. Most
school textbooks feature this binding style. The case of the book is
usually tough binder's board covered with cloth. The book lies
open for ease in reading, and the inside margins may be small.
Bleeds can be used through the backbone of the binding. The
front cover and backbone are usually stamped in metallic ink like
gold or silver. Sewn books usually have rounded backs, which are
lacking in the other styles.

Perfect Binding is a recent development designed to eliminate
the expense of sewing and case-binding books. The process uses
no sewing or stitching. A glue is used that keeps its strength and
resiliency for long periods of time. The book is not rounded.

LOOSE-LEAF BINDINGS

The main feature of loose-leaf bindings is that sheets may be added or removed, which cannot be done in other types of binding. Another advantage is that sheets may be selected and bound to suit the needs of a particular reader, as in catalogs where the reader is interested in only a part of the products manufactured by the advertiser. Sheets may be torn out without spoiling the binding or releasing other pages. Presswork runs may be saved by printing all color pages in one form. This is made possible because the book need not be printed entirely in signatures (folded sections of the book), and pages can be assembled in any manner for loose-leaf books.

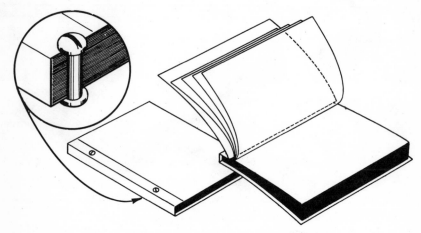

Fig. 13-6. Binding Post Type of Loose-Leaf Binding

Binding post loose-leaf binders have a disadvantage in that they do not lie flat when open. A large margin is necessary at the binding edge. In this type the binding post is exposed, and new pages are not easily added because of the time it takes to unscrew the binding posts. However, readers are discouraged from taking out sheets, which has certain advantages. See Fig. 13–6.

Binding post with tongue cover styles are similar to the binding post type, except that the binding posts are concealed, which makes a better looking binding. A heavy paper of great strength should be used, and folded back as shown in Fig. 13–7.

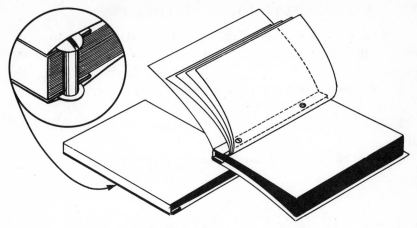

Fig. 13-7. Binding Post with Tongue Cover Loose-Leaf Binder

Ring binders are the popular type, and in general use especially in schools and colleges. The sheets lie flat when the binder is open, and no large margin is necessary at the binding edge; hence more of the area the page can be used. Various makes of ring binders allow sheets to be taken out and other sheets put in with the greatest ease of any binder. It will be found that this type of binder will hold a given amount of sheets, and that sheets will tear out if the binder is overloaded. The binding post types, however, can be filled to the limit of the length of the binding screws, and then longer binding screws may be substituted. See Fig. 13–8.

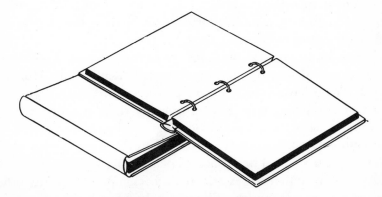

Fig. 13-8. Conventional Ring Binder

MECHANICAL BINDINGS

During the past few years the *mechanical* type of binding has risen in the estimation of purchasers because of these general good features:

1. Odd-sized sheets and pages may be used.
2. Books always lie flat when open for reading.
3. Most mechanical bindings are rugged to stand harsh handling.
4. Good color schemes on the binding material are possible.

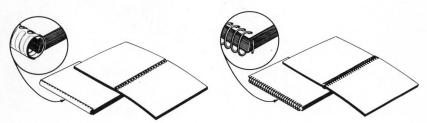

Fig. 13-9. *Left:* Plastic Binding   *Right:* Spiral Binding

5. Some mechanical bindings may be printed.
6. Sheets may be added to some mechanical bindings.
7. Sheets can always be torn out without affecting the other pages.
8. Books need not be printed in signatures, that is, in sections of four or eight pages or more; this often saves the number of color press runs in printing the book.
9. All pages have complete visibility; no part of the page is concealed because of the binding used.
10. Certain mechanical bindings are of the loose-leaf type. Some of these are Multo, Streamliner, Swing-O-Ring, Tally-Ho, and Tubak. Some have a few rings of plastic or wire, and others are of the multiple ring type, having as many rings as shown in Fig. 13–9 above. Other mechanical bindings are being introduced.

Plastic binding, Fig. 13–9, consists of a cylindrical device which holds the sheets with a multitude of plastic rings, which may be in colors. The cylinder makes a sturdier backbone than many other types of mechanical binders. The plastic backbone may be printed.

A stiff or soft cover may be applied without affecting the rigidity of the book. Opposite pages register well on this type, because the pages are bound in alignment. The binding will not fold over on itself, which is a feature of the spiral type of binding shown below. Sheets can be added to plastic bindings.

Adhesive or "perfect" bindings are exemplified in magazines such as *Reader's Digest,* by thick telephone books, paper back books and mail order catalogs. They include books too thick to bind side-wire and when perfect bound will lie flat when open. In manufacture, the signatures are gathered and trimmed on folds. The backs are milled to make them rough, lint is removed and glue applied to the compressed backs on automatic machines. "Pull-on" paper covers are usually used and the books are trimmed on three sides. (See Fig. 13–10.)

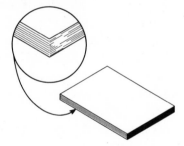

Fig. 13-10. Adhesive or "Perfect" Binding

Spiral binding is made of a simple wire coil which runs through small round holes punched in the sheets. The wire coils are often covered with colored plastic. A strong, nonflexible backbone is possible only if a stiff cover stock is used. Spiral type bindings fold over on themselves. Opposite pages are out of register with each other, which means that any double-page illustrations will be out of register when the book is open. See Fig. 13–9.

Other Mechanical Bindings. Plastic and Spiral bindings are representative of many similar types not shown here. Others of a similar nature are Aligno, which features wire loops spaced at intervals; Circla and Cerflex, which have flat plastic rings; Wire-O, which has double-looped wires; Flex-O-Coil, which has coils of three wires; and Overwire, which has a wire coil within the cover.

How Paper Is Handled in the Bindery

How Paper Is Folded. Very little folding is now done by hand except in very small printing establishments, and then only short press runs are hand-folded. The reason for this is obvious: A hand folder will make three folds in a sheet of paper (making a 16-page signature) in about three and one-half hours per 1,000 sheets. The same work can be done on a folding machine in about 30 minutes! On small-sheet single folds, a folding machine may turn out 10,000 per hour. By hand, this would take about 16 hours.

Whether by hand or by machine, printed sheets are folded *to register,* meaning that the printed pages are exactly in alignment (on top of one another) regardless of how the edges of the paper fold. Paper edge to paper edge may not give this needed register. Bone folders about 10 inches long are usually used in hand folding to save undue wear on the thumb, and to crease the folds properly. After hand folding, the signatures are kept in a neat pile.

The "buckle-type" folding machine illustrated below in Fig. 13–11 is a Baum Decuplet, which takes a minimum sheet size 4x6 inches and maximum size 22x28 inches. It can make ten folds on one sheet, in a variety of ways.

Modern job folders operate with lightning speed, and paper is

Fig. 13-11. Baum 22x28-Inch Decuplet Folding Machine

fed much in the same way sheets are delivered to the guides on printing presses. The sheets are carried along from the feeder on rollers set at an angle, which keep the sheets to a set side guide. Other steel rollers then run the sheets into a pocket called a *plate*. As the sheets can go only as far as a set guide allows them, they buckle or bend at a given set point, and are engaged between a set of steel rollers which fold them. Subsequent folds are made the same way, parallel or at right angles to the first fold.

Some large book folding machines operate with a knife action which delivers the sheets to the folding rollers. These machines will do many jobs, such as delivering two separate 16-page signatures or inserting one in another to deliver one 32-page signature.

How Paper Is Jogged. Jogging is the term applied to straightening sheets which have been delivered from the press in a helter-skelter manner to prevent smearing of freshly-printed ink. To jog:

1. Take about an inch of the paper or less to a table.

2. Raise the far edge and stand the paper upright.

3. Grip the sides between the thumb and fingers *loosely,* then bend the sheets.

4. Now grip the sides of the sheets *tightly,* and straighten the lift of paper. *This will place air between the sheets.*

5. While air is between the sheets, thrust inward with both hands. Vibrating electric jogging machines are in common use to aid in this work. The trick to getting the hang of jogging is learned by practice.

How Paper Is Stored. Paper is delivered wrapped in reams, and in packs of one-hundred and two-hundred-and-fifty sheets, depending upon the kind of paper. It is also delivered in large quantities in wooden cases, or wrapped on large wooden skids. Paper should always be laid flat. If it is delivered in cases, the case should be laid flat, or the paper should be removed and laid flat on a shelf. If the paper is allowed to stand upright, it may develop wrinkles which will retard press feeding. Large sheets of paper can be easily carried if taken in easy lifts, and loosely folded to make three layers.

To keep paper stock from getting dirty, it should always be kept in a clean place, and the covers should be kept intact until the paper is to be used.

How Paper Is Cut. Paper is cut to size on cutting machines, by both hand and power. The smaller hand-lever paper cutter, shown in Fig. 13–12, is used in small printing shops where cutting is not a major problem. The electrically-powered paper cutter, shown in Fig. 13–13, is used in the larger printing establishments.

Paper is usually cut to smaller sizes, as explained in Chapter 12, before it is printed, and again after it is printed, in the case of books and booklets. Trim is either one-eighth or one-quarter inch.

The back gauges on the larger cutters can be divided into three parts, one for cutting the first trim, one the second, and one the third. In this way cuts on three stacks of booklets can be done at the same time, and with one stroke of the knife.

When using either a hand-lever or power cutter, care should be taken to see that the top and bottom of the pile of paper stock is protected by a piece of *straw board,* a cheap form of cardboard. This will prevent the top sheets of the pile from being marred by the sections of the clamp which hold the paper in position for cutting. It also protects the bottom sheets from getting rough edges.

Fig. 13-12. Hand-Lever Paper Cutter

Small lifts should be cut on the hand-lever cutters, because large lifts are too difficult to cut.

Most power cutters are equipped with controls which occupy both hands of the operator, so he cannot be injured by the knife.

One operator should work on the hand-lever cutter. If two work on the machine, there is little protection for either operator.

Care should be taken on hand-lever cutters not to bring down the clamp *too tightly,* as this may mar the top sheets. Loose clamping will allow sheets to slip. Power cutters usually are equipped with automatic clamps.

How Paper Is Padded. Some office forms and the handy "scratch pads" are glued at the top edge to keep them in a single pile. This process is called *padding* or *tabbing*. The printed pieces are carefully jogged, and often trimmed slightly at the binding edge.

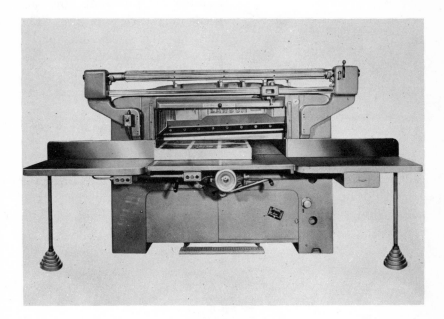

Fig. 13-13. Power Paper Cutter

Padding glue is painted on the binding side, after the printed job has been aligned in straight piles, and weighted at the top with a heavy object, such as a brick or type metal cast. The weight should be heavy enough to compress the sheets well. Padding glue is either the cold or the heated type. The cold type is always ready for use. A double container is generally used for heating the hot type.

Sheets of straw are usually placed at intervals between a given number of sheets, usually 50 or 100. After the padding glue has dried, the weight is removed, and the pads cut apart with a sharp bindery knife made for this purpose.

To insure a clean job, the form is often printed a quarter of an inch oversize. Then, after the padding operation it is trimmed down to the required dimensions.

How Paper Is Punched or Drilled. Pages for use in loose-leaf books must be punched or drilled in the bindery. Small printing offices use the paper punch, Fig. 13-14, on which holes can be made in about six sheets at a time. A number of punching dies are used, in a variety of sizes. The most popular size is one-quarter inch. Care should be taken to see that sheets are put to the guides; otherwise the work will be spoiled.

Fig. 13-14. Paper Punch

Where a large amount of work is done, it will be found that the paper drill is best to use.

Paper drills utilize hollow drills of various sizes, which bring the paper chips up through the drill and into a container at the back of the machine. These power-driven machines make light work in binderies.

Fig. 13-15. Paper Drilling Machine

How Paper Is Stitched. Booklets may be wire-fastened with
either staplers or stitchers. Staplers use made-up staples fastened
in an inverted **U**-shape, and stitchers use a coil of wire. The size of
the stitchings may be adjusted for
the thicknesses of work. Staplers
fasten work up to one-quarter
inch, and the stitchers fasten
printed matter up to one inch.

Both staplers and stitchers are
adjustable to do saddle-wired or
side-wired books.

Usually the work is fed from
the right side of the machine, and
two or more staples or stitches are
used. Care must be taken to see
that the work is fed correctly to
the guides in side-wire binding,

Fig. 13-16. Stitching Machine

and snugly over the saddle for other work. Stitchers are electrically-
powered, and a clutch is engaged with a foot treadle. Staplers are
either hand or foot-powered.

How Paper Is Round Cornered. To prevent the corners of certain cards, tickets, or booklets (that require severe handling) from
bending, they are often rounded after folding, stitching, and trim-
ming. This operation is done on a round-cornering machine, which
has different sizes of cutting bits to suit the size of the particular job.
These machines are either foot or hand-powered, and the newer
paper drills have attachments for this type of bindery operation.

Gold Stamping. Gold stamping of covers is a bindery operation
which requires the use of brass type, or a special heat-resisting plate.
A special press is used on which the heated type or plate is pressed
against a sheet of gold leaf which has been laid on the cover. Later
the waste gold leaf is wiped away, leaving the lettering or illustration printed on the cover. Imitation gold foil is often used, and
some work is done in aluminum and other metallic substances.

How Paper Is Perforated. Simple sheet perforating can be accomplished on the printing press, and is often done on inexpensive printing. Round-hole perforating, however, must be done in the bindery on straight or rotary perforating machines. This is similar to that seen on sheets of postage stamps.

Fig. 13-17. Rotary Perforator

For press perforating, a steel perforating rule is locked up with the type. To protect the press rollers, the area of the form, not including the perforating rule, is underlaid with a piece of pressboard. The form is unlocked and planed down so that the rule is *lower* than the type. In this way the form rollers of the press do not bear down on the sharp rule. The rule is built up so that it cuts the paper in the makeready process.

Both round-hole and slot perforators are used, and are available in rotary makes that allow fast production. Straight perforators are usually foot-powered, and the rotary makes are usually power-driven. See Fig. 13–17.

Ruling Machines. The blue, red, and other colored lines found on bookkeeping forms and index cards are pen ruled on special bindery equipment. A woolen cloth feeds liquid ink to the pens, and the paper is carried along on a flannel belt under strings. Several colors are possible in one impression. A striker lifts the pens and drops them at any desired point on the paper, which is fed to a guide by hand or is automatically delivered. Another type of ruling machine prints the lines by means of a disc. Some ruling machines slit and perforate the sheets while ruling the lines.

SAFETY HINTS

As pointed out in Chapters 4 and 11, working in printing establishments is not necessarily hazardous to life and limb. The following table presents a few of the hazards which exist, however, and some suggestions on how to keep safe.

Hazard	Preventive
Clothing	Loose clothing may be caught in moving parts of bindery machinery. Remove neckties, and roll up sleeves and trousers.
Dim lights	See that work is done under adequate lighting to prevent eye strain.
Folding machines	Do not stand too close to folding machines. Be sure the machine is turned off before any adjustments are made—never put the hands on a folder which is operating.
Lifting and carrying	Get aid when lifting or carrying heavy lifts of paper or cases. Always lift with the leg muscles, and not with the muscles of the abdomen. Bend the *knees,* not the *body,* when lifting.
Littered floors	Keep tools and paper off the floor.
Oiling machines	Lubricate bindery machinery when it is *not* running.
Oily floors	Keep floors wiped to prevent slipping.
Paper cutters	Operate a paper cutter *alone.* On hand-lever cutters, make sure that the handle is brought back *all of the way* after making a cut, and that there is no danger of the knife falling.

Hazard	Preventive
Paper cutters *(continued)*	Use *both hands* to operate the trip on power cutters. Keep hands away when the knife falls.
Play	Refrain from wrestling or playing in the bindery. Play no practical jokes.
Stitchers, staplers, round-cornering machines, etc.	Keep the fingers and hands away from the moving parts of all bindery machines. Operate all such machines alone, and do not indulge in conversation.

SELF-TEST

This self-test will serve as a review of this chapter. The questions are either true or false, or are asked to create thought and discussion. The numbers following each question refer to the page on which the correct answer can be found.

1. Saddle-wire bound books have stitches aligned on the fold. (339)
2. The entire page on saddle-wire books may be seen. (339)
3. Saddle-wire books must be held open for reading. (339)
4. Side-wire booklets are limited to about 32 pages in size. (340)
5. Covers are usually glued on saddle-wire books. (340)
6. Two-page sheets may be included in saddle-wire books. (340)
7. Signatures are sewed to signatures on sewn bindings. (341)
8. Books sewn by hand can also be sewn by machine. (341)
9. The entire page area can be seen on sewn books. (341)
10. Case-bound books have soft covers. (341)
11. The most permanent binding is case bound. (341)
12. Book backbones can be printed or stamped on saddle-wire binding. (339, 341)
13. Name the advantages of loose-leaf books. (342)
14. What can be added to the binding post cover to hide the screws? (342)
15. What binding is best for quickest changing of sheets and pages? (343)
16. Binding post styles are limited in the number of sheets that can be placed in the book. (343)
17. Any sized sheets can be used in ring binders. (344)

18. Give as many of the ten general features as you can of mechanical bindings. (344)
19. Plastic bindings can be folded over on themselves. (345)
20. A stiff cover should be used on plastic bindings. (345)
21. Bleed illustrations on double-page spreads are out of alignment on spiral-bound books. (345)
22. Spiral bindings are made of a simple wire coil. (345)
23. Folding machines can fold a sheet three ways about seven times as fast as the same work could be done by hand. (346)
24. Books are folded paper-to-paper for accurate register. (346)
25. Small folders operate with the buckle principle. (347)
26. Large book folders operate with the knife principle. (347)
27. Jogging is accomplished by beating the sheets on the table. (347)
28. Name three ways in which paper is delivered to the printer. (347)
29. Wrinkles may be put in paper by storing sheets flat. (347)
30. Book trim is usually from one-quarter to one inch. (348)
31. Back gauges on most cutters can be divided to make three different trims at the same time. (348)
32. Bottom and top sheets can be spoiled in cutting by failure to put straw board on the stock. (348)
33. The paper clamp on paper cutters must hold the paper with great pressure during the cutting. (348)
34. Jogging is unnecessary when padding. (349)
35. Both cold and hot padding glue is used. (349)
36. Paper punching is faster than paper drilling. (350)
37. Hollow drills are used on paper drilling machines. (350)
38. Stitchers use made-up stitches fastened together. (351)
39. Staplers fasten thicknesses of one-half an inch. (351)
40. Flat and saddle-wire books may be stitched on stitchers. (351)
41. Gold stamping uses hot type. (351)
42. Round-hole perforating is done on printing presses. (352)
43. Rotary perforators are faster than straight perforators. (352)
44. Ruling machines print lines on paper in many colors at one time through the machine. (352)
45. Ruling machines use both discs and pens. (352)
46. Power cutters require both hands to operate. (348)

47. Paper is jogged by placing air between each sheet. (347)
48. Books too thick for side-wire binding are "perfect" bound. (345)

PROJECTS

1. Using any kind of 8½x11-inch paper stock, fold paper-to-paper with two right-angle folds, and with the resultant eight-page signatures:
   a. Saddle-stitch a 32-page booklet.
   b. Side-stitch a 48-page booklet.
2. Using the cutting machine, trim the books made in project No. 1 to size 4x5 inches. Do not mark the top or bottom sheets on the paper cutter.
3. Punch a number of sheets to fit a standard three-ring 8½x11-inch binder. Set the punch or drill in the correct positions.
4. Using 17x22-inch paper of any kind, fold paper-to-paper with three right-angle folds, and with the resultant 5½x8½-inch signatures:
   a. Saddle-stitch, with cover, a 32-page booklet.
   b. Side-stitch a 64-page booklet, and place a wrap-around cover made up of any contrasting colored stock. Glue on the cover.
   c. Trim each booklet one-quarter of an inch on three sides.
   d. Number each page.
5. Practice jogging paper as explained on page 347.
6. Cut bond paper stock for a quantity of scratch pads, and pad them on a narrow edge.

CHAPTER 14

How to Choose a Career in the Graphic Arts

THE APPROXIMATELY ONE MILLION graphic arts workers in the United States are proud of their contribution to education, to the development of science, and to the advancement of society. About a third of the employees are craftsmen, including over 233,000 compositors, linecasting machine operators and pressmen.

Without the use of printed products business and industry would cease to function. Work in the graphic arts is satisfying, creative, exciting, and remunerative. The work is interesting because no two jobs of printing are alike, and its wages are the second highest of all manufacturing industries.

Printing is a stable industry. The graphic arts worker is less affected by business declines than the labor force in manufacturing as a whole, and his pay check is far better than the average. Salaries ranging from $8,000 to $25,000 a year are quite common.

The graphic arts employ a great variety of talent. Printing utilizes the skills of photography, chemistry, electronics, and physics. Those who like machinery can find a challenge in the mechanical marvels found in all departments of a printing office. Artistic talents are needed in layout and design, and in the work performed by the lithographic color artist. Skills in English and mathematics can be applied in proofreading and in estimating costs. Practical psychology is applied by those who meet the public as printing salesmen.

Career opportunities abound in the graphic arts. The industry needs almost double the number of apprentices now in training in order to replace men due for retirement soon.

The tables on page 358 from the U. S. Census Manufacturers indicate changes in establishments, all employees and production workers in 1954 (or 1958) and 1963.

CHANGES IN ESTABLISHMENTS, EMPLOYEES, AND PRODUCTION WORKERS

Source: *1963 Census of Manufacturers*, U.S. Department of Commerce, Bureau of Census, Major Group 27.

		ESTABLISHMENTS	ALL EMPLOYEES	PRODUCTION WORKERS
NEWSPAPERS	1963	8,331	306,439	160,061
	1958	8,279	295,622	154,656
	CHANGE	+52	+10,857	+5,405
PERIODICALS	1963	2,630	67,730	12,257
	1958	2,332	66,749	11,711
	CHANGE	+298	+981	+546
BOOKS, PUBLISHING AND PRINTING	1963	936	46,812	11,810
	1958	883	38,502	11,023
	CHANGE	+53	+8,310	+787
BOOK PRINTING	1963	683	36,101	29,641
	1958	791	28,625	23,732
	CHANGE	−108	+7,476	+5,909
MISCELLANEOUS PUBLISHING*	1963	1,374	22,551	9,798
	1958	1,104	19,301	6,538
	CHANGE	+270	+3,250	+3,260
PRINTING, EXCEPT LITHOGRAPHIC	1963	12,109	170,215	136,118
	1954	12,073	200,233	157,567
	CHANGE	+36	−30,018	−21,449
PRINTING, LITHOGRAPHIC	1963	6,822	121,072	91,538
	1954	2,924	77,717	60,178
	CHANGE	+3,898	+43,355	+31,180
COMMERCIAL PRINTING, EXCEPT ENGRAVING	1963	18,931	291,287	227,476
	1958	16,792	279,290	219,056
	CHANGE	+2,139	+11,997	+8,420
ENGRAVING AND PLATE PRINTING	1963	580	9,022	7,126
	1958	528	9,047	7,228
	CHANGE	+52	−25	−102
MANIFOLD BUSINESS FORMS	1963	502	28,796	21,259
	1958	----	23,618	16,883
	CHANGE	----	+5,178	+4,376

EMPLOYMENT SIZE OF ESTABLISHMENTS, 1963—AVERAGE NUMBER OF EMPLOYEES (FROM SELECTED STATISTICS)

	Total Estab.	Total Employees	1–4	5–9	10–19	20–49	50–99	100–249	250–499	500–999	1000–2499	2500–higher
PRINTING, EXCEPT LITHOGRAPHIC	12,109	170,215	7,081	2,115	1,509	876	298	148	50	20	10	2
PRINTING, LITHOGRAPHIC	6,822	121,072	3,195	1,226	1,062	854	271	160	48	3	2	1
PRINTING, EXCEPT LITHOGRAPHIC, GRAVURE	171	15,193	51	24	17	29	16	18	9	3	4	–
PRINTING, EXCEPT LITHOGRAPHIC, LETTERPRESS AND SCREEN	11,938	155,022	7,030	2,091	1,492	847	282	130	41	17	6	–
ENGRAVING AND PLATE PRINTING	580	9,022	252	122	101	82	10	11	1	–	1	–
MANIFOLD BUSINESS FORMS	502	28,796	103	51	98	104	72	47	23	3	1	–
	32,122	499,320										

*Miscellaneous Publishing does not indicate whether printing was carried on.

About 65 different types of activities are found in the Graphic Arts. They are classified here into five separate Units:

1. The Composing Room
2. Jobs in Letterpress
3. Jobs in Offset-Lithography
4. Bindery Work
5. Professional Positions

These positions are discussed on the following pages. They are defined, typical examples of work performed are given, required knowledge, skills and abilities are listed, and comments are made upon the minimum requirements for entrance into the work.

In general, Graphic Arts work is clean. Many advances in techniques and procedures have eliminated the old-time print shop which was so dirty. Although ink is freely used, it runs only on the presses and not onto the personnel of the pressroom.

Wage scales, generally, are roughly the same for many of the positions but vary according to locality. The pay for journeyman work compares favorably with the scale for other skilled work, and premium wages are often granted to highly exceptional men in the crafts.

The industry can be entered through many different paths. One lies through graduation from high school, followed by training on-the-job in an apprenticeship. Another is found in graduation from a vocational school or department where, in many instances, credit is given for apprenticeship time. And another is in graduation from a college or university which provides major courses in printing management, design, and layout, or industrial engineering. Apprenticeships run for four, five or six years, depending upon the craft. The industry is open to receive those who have talents coupled with the will to use them. All talents and interests have a place in the 65 different occupations of the graphic arts industry, and each has its own opportunity and reward.

Composing Room Jobs

Compositor. *Definition:* The compositor sets type and assembles the products of type composing machines into pages for books, newspapers, commercial printing of all kinds, and advertising. He may be classed as a "make-up man" in a newspaper composing room, where he assembles advertisements and news columns. He may also be required to design and lay out his own arrangements, particularly in the smaller shops.

Examples of Work Performed. Depending upon the type of work printed by the shop, he will perform one or more of the following activities:

Makes a rough sketch of the customer's copy to guide him in setting type for a job.

Sets type from type cases, slug lines on Ludlow Typographs and operates a variety of cold type devices.

Makes up jobs, advertisements and newspaper pages, by assembling slug lines or monotype-set material, and by following the layout provided.

Distributes type and materials back into cases. Locks up forms for various kinds of letterpress printing presses.

Operates saws, mitering machines, and kindred tools of the composing room.

He may operate one or more of the cold type composing devices —from a VariTyper to a Photon, or paste up photoprints of type and illustration to prepare copy for the offset process.

Required Knowledge, Skills, and Abilities. Considerable knowledge of the techniques employed in setting type.

Skill in exact justification of hand-set and assembled typographic materials.

Ability to read instructions as well as copy, and to follow rough or detailed layouts.

Ability to stand for several hours without fatigue.

Ability to operate composing room equipment, such as proof presses, saws, miterers, and the like.

Minimum Requirements. Completion of a five-year apprenticeship as a hand compositor, or the equivalent.

Layout Man. *Definition.* The layout man draws and writes exact typographic specifications to scale for the other workers in the shop, in order to instruct them in the production of a printed job.

Examples of Work Performed. Works with the salesman or customer to determine the target for the job to be laid out and designed.

Establishes the basic design for a printed job, or the format for a folder, booklet or book.

Selects type faces and arranges them in relation to the illustrations.

Makes a detailed layout, marking specifications to the printer as to type to be used, measures to be set, space between lines, size of margins, indicates positions for illustrations, and copyfits manuscript into type lines accurately.

Required Knowledges, Skills, and Abilities. Thorough knowledg of typographic art, and its relationship to illustration.

Thorough knowledge of the type faces available in and outside the shop, and of their use in all types of book, advertising, and commercial printing.

Skill in the accurate use of the printers' system of measurement.

Ability to copyfit manuscript within reasonable tolerances so that it will fill a predetermined area.

Minimum Requirements. Sufficient layout experience to meet the requirements of the individual shop. This may be gained through experience as a hand compositor, or graduation from an art school which specializes in design and layout, followed by several years more of experience in practical layout and design.

Proofreader. *Definition.* The proofreader checks the galley and page proofs to determine if they coincide with the copy furnished by the customer. In addition, he checks for errors which may have occurred in the original copy, and queries his findings to the customer. He usually reads from the original copy to another proofreader who holds the proof, and in this activity he is known as a copyholder. Occasionally he alternates with the proofreader to alleviate any monotony. However, the copyholder is generally a learner.

Examples of Work Performed. Enunciates clearly when reading copy and calls all marks of punctuation.

Scans the proof while listening to the copy-holder, and marks any errors with standard proofreading marks and symbols.

Required Knowledge, Skills, and Abilities. A thorough education in English.

Skill in finding errors in spelling, punctuation, and typographical layouts. His training must teach him to detect the slightest errors made by compositors and machine operators.

A thorough knowledge of word division.

A thorough knowledge of the mechanical nature of typecasting machines.

Minimum Requirements. Good eyesight and a thorough knowledge of the English language.

Linotype-Intertype Operator. *Definition.* The linotype operator manipulates the keyboard of the machine according to the copy to be cast in line form. In the smaller shops he may take care of the maintenance of his machine if linotype machinists are not employed.

Examples of Work Performed. Sets straight matter and/or display lines for all classes of printed matter.

Changes magazines, liners, and makes other adjustments of the machine for the work to be composed.

Required Knowledge, Skills, and Abilities. Knowledge of the processes of letterpress printing.

Skill in the manipulation of the keyboard for fast composition.

Ability to divide words correctly.

Ability to read accurately and at high speed.

Minimum Requirements. Completion of a five-year apprenticeship in a composing room, including one year as a linotype operator, or completion of a school course in linotype operation and maintenance.

Monotype Operator. *Definition.* The monotype operator works on one or both of the machines used in the monotype system of composition. One is the keyboard, which punches a control ribbon for use in the caster. Caster operators run the ribbon through the caster, and then set up and make adjustments to the machine.

Examples of Work Performed. Sets a keyboard for controlling the punches in the ribbon. Makes adjustments on the caster.

Required Knowledge, Skills, and Abilities. Ability to keyboard straight matter and intricate tabular or mathematical work.

Knowledge of the processes used in letterpress printing.

Skill in the manipulation of the keyboard for fast composition.

Ability to divide words correctly.

Ability to make adjustments on the keyboard and caster.

Ability to read accurately and at high speed.

Minimum Requirements. Completion of a five-year apprenticeship in a composing room including one year as a monotype keyboard operator or caster operator. Alternatively, four years of experience in the composing room after one year of training at a monotype school.

Jobs in Letterpress

Pressroom Positions. *Definitions.* The positions in the Pressroom include the press-feeders, the cylinder and rotary pressmen. Feeding the press by hand has been replaced largely by more speedy mechanical feeders. The great size of the cylinder machines now demands that an assistant pressman be present. Pressmen may be specialists in any one of the type of presses, but transfer to another is not too difficult since the new techniques of operation are easy to learn.

Examples of Work Performed. Adjusts the machine for new work, and makes the job ready. He builds up solid areas and cuts down the light areas, using such aids as tissue paper and mechanical overlays.

Ensures that the amount of ink flows from the fountain to the press rollers.

Makes periodic checks to see that sheets are being fed at the correct rate.

Loads the feeders and removes sheets from the delivery.

Knowledge, Skill, and Ability. Thorough knowledge of the mechanics of the press operated. Thorough knowledge of the principles, methods and procedures used in laying ink on paper by the letterpress method.

Skill in determining the extent of makeready needed to prevent undue wear on plates, even if it is still doing adequate presswork jobs.

Ability to get good production from various makes of presses.

Minimum Requirements. Completion of a four- to six-year apprenticeship on the type of press operated.

Platemakers. Platemakers include photoengravers, electrotypers and stereotypers. Their functions are similar to those of the Offset platemakers except in their techniques.

Electrotyper. *Definition.* The electrotyper must know all the tasks performed in his process, even though he only works in one area of the activity. He must know how to place the type forms on a molding press, so that an impression can be made in plastic or lead molds. Then he must deposit a metal shell on the mold. After he has stripped the type from the mold and backed it with metal, it can be finished and mounted type high, or beveled for plate high. His requirements include the completion of six years of apprenticeship.

Stereotyper. *Definition.* The stereotyper makes molds of type

forms, or of engravings, in papier maché for a matrix press. After drying, the mold is used to cast a stereotype plate, type high, or it is shell cast for mounting. It could also be curved to fit the rotary press cylinders. Special machinery is often used to perform the work, particularly in large newspaper plants. The stereotyper is required to know all the operations of the process, and his training must cover a five- or six-year apprenticeship.

Photoengraver. *Definition.* Photoengravers may perform all of the operations required in making letterpress original plates, or may specialize in just one field of activity. For instance, the *camera man* makes line or halftone negatives, using color filters and halftone screens, and then develops the work. The *printer* makes a print for the negative on a zinc or copper plate. The *etcher* takes over these plates and, through a chemical process, etches out the non-printing areas in them. The *finishing* operations follow, which include touching up the plate with hand tools, routing away dead metal, blocking type high, and proofing. Rotogravure photoengravers perform similar operations working from positives to make intaglio plates. Six years is the usual apprenticeship period for photoengravers.

Jobs in Offset-Lithography

Pressroom Positions. *Definitions.* Offset pressmen operate a variety of presses from small machines to the four-color, perfecting rotary equipment. Their positions are roughly comparable to those in the letterpress establishment. The sheet feeding devices are quite similar, for example, even though they employ a plane instead of a raised surface. By contrast, the stripper arranges the offset pages of lithography with film, while the letterpress "stone man" locks up forms by arrangements of type masses or pages.

Positions include offset-lithographic pressmen on all sizes of presses, from 14-inch to 76-inch sheet size, and positions on web offset presses. Photographers make negatives in black-and-white or through color separations. Strippers work in film or paper, and in color halftone. Platemakers sensitize the plates, and place them in position with negatives or positives to make offset plates. Lithographic artists perform the work of dot etching, Ben Day, tusching, and opaquing.

Processes and methods in the offset-lithographic trade are ever changing. New plates and "dry offset" prints are brought into the market, improved and presensitized plates are devised by lithographers, and new processes like three-color work are advancing offset techniques continually.

Platemakers. *Definition.* The major fields of offset-lithographic tasks are in camera work, lettering, platemaking and presswork. The *camera man* usually specializes in either black-and-white or color work, and develops his own negatives and positives. *Artists* retouch negatives to lighten or intensify certain areas in order to achieve the correct color tone values. The work is done by hand

with chemicals and dyes and is highly skilled. *Strippers* arrange the negatives in order when making a "flat," which is a similar function to that of the makeup man in letterpress printing operations. *Platemakers* use the "flats" to make plates which wrap around the impression cylinders of offset-lithographic presses. They make the plates sensitive to light and expose them by placing them in vacuum frames, or photocomposing machines, with the negatives resting on top. After exposing them to arc lamps, they are developed and fitted on the press for printing.

Bindery Jobs

Definition. Bindery work includes many processes and procedures, from the simple cutting of paper and the stapling of booklets, to the operation of intricate and electronic three-way book trimmers, collators, gathering machines, gluing machines, and book sewing machines. Hand binding can still be found, particularly in account books and fine editions, and pen-ruling machines are still included in the bindery category. Workers may be specialists on one machine, or may be required to operate folding machines, cutters, and other equipment as well. Their duties will depend upon the scope of the bindery department.

Examples of Work Performed. Operates cutting machines, perforators, stitchers, folding machines, marbling and gilding devices, gold stamping presses, round cornering machines, paper punches and drills, rounding and backing machines, signature-sewing ma-

chines, casing-in machines, gluers, pen-ruling machines, and kindred devices.

Most repetitious work is generally done by women, but the heavy or intricate work is still performed by men.

Knowledge, Skill, and Abilities. Considerable

knowledge of all of the bindery operations carried on in the establishment.

Skill in the operation of machines to prevent spoiled work.

Ability to understand written and verbal orders.

Minimum Requirements. Completion of a four-year apprenticeship in bindery operations.

Professional Positions

Certain professional positions have been collected under this heading, although their work differs slightly. Their operations are all fairly similar to the work of the journeymen already discussed.

The Foreman. Foremanship assumes several prerequisites: the foreman must have a greater knowledge than the men who work under him; he analyzes work and organizes his men to perform the necessary tasks; he acts in a supervisory capacity; he ensures that economy is practiced; he instructs his men in their duties; and he operates his department in an efficient manner.

The foreman of any department must adapt his men and machines for the best production, and check often to see that progress is made on the work in the plant. He is the intermediary between the men and management, and he negotiates on wage scale adjustments and on working conditions. He hires, fires, promotes, and demotes. He does not have to be tough, but he must be firm in his dealings with his employees.

The foreman must be a leader, and command the respect of his men. This makes his mastery of the technical manipulations a prime necessity. He should be able to do anything that his men can do, and do it better. He should be able to get work done without being a "driver."

Years of experience in the work being supervised are required, as well as the ability to accept new processes and methods, and to keep up with technical changes.

The Typographer or Layout Counselor. The layout counselor is usually a free lance (not employed by any one establishment) who advises his clients in the planning and layout of typographic work.

The Owner-Operator. The owner-operator is usually a craftsman who had become proficient as a plant superintendent or foreman,  and who has established his own business. If his plant is small, he may do some or all of the work himself; if large, he will hire others to take some of the responsibility. It should be remembered that an owner, though often called a "printer," may be a businessman and not a working printer.

The Printing Engineer. The printing engineer customarily sets up an office as a consultant for letterpress and lithographic plant owners. His job is to guide them in applying modern engineering principles to their work. He acts in an advisory capacity, or he may take over the management of a plant for the length of time necessary to bring about the suggested changes. The printing engineer may be a graduate mechanical engineer who has specialized in the graphic arts.

The Production Superintendent. Plant superintendents and production managers are the overseers of the foremen of the various departments of the printing or publishing business. They have often risen from the position of foremen. In addition to knowing the varied aspects of the business, they have to keep up with new trends in production methods and deal with the labor unions. A great responsibility rests upon their shoulders in correlating and integrating each department. Such men are valuable and earn from $8,000 to $25,000 per year.

Jobs in Sales and Estimating. Sales and estimating may go hand-in-hand as companion duties. In the larger printing establishments, it is more likely that an estimator would work in one duty only. Sales opportunities abound in the printing business, and sales representatives should have sufficient knowledge of the  type of work undertaken by his plant to advise customers on processes and methods. This is particularly true of the estimator, who must visualize each separate operation to be performed on a job, from the setting of copy, through the final bindery. He must know how long operations take and calculate their hour cost, in order to establish the probable cost of the finished work.

The printing salesman investigates the needs and requirements of his clients, and suggests layouts and formats to aid his prospective customers. He brings to his printing office the necessary work to keep the plant in operation. He should know the principles of advertising and sales psychology, and should be able to work with all kinds of people. He should know most of the processes and methods used in his own plant and in competing firms.

The Graphic Arts Teacher. The graphic arts teacher is usually a teacher in a high school or in a college, either in industrial arts or in vocational education courses. He may be a specialist in composing room or pressroom, for example, or he may be an all-around man who can teach many different operations.

Graphic arts teachers must be skilled in two professions: (1) that of teaching, which they learn in teacher-training colleges and universities, and (2) that of the Graphic Arts. As Vocational teachers preparing young men and women for jobs, they are usually required to have completed at least seven years of working experience in the actual trade taught.

How to Get a Job

Graduates of vocational and other printing schools generally secure employment by one of these means.

1. By applying at employment and school employment bureaus.
2. By answering or placing newspaper and magazine ads.
3. By inquiring about openings and calling at printing plants.
4. By contacting those who know of openings.

A printing school graduate should not apply for a job for which he is not qualified. He should not claim to be able to perform skills he cannot accomplish. He must admit that he is starting in the trade. But he should not, in any case, belittle his training or be too modest in stating the duties he can adequately perform. When the subject of school training comes up between the prospective employer and employee, the graduate should sell him the idea that his school is a good school, and prove it by references to catalogs and the amount of work accomplished. After all, a student gets out of schooling only what he or she wants to put into it.

In large city shops a man may be employed in one department all the time, like the workers in the composing room or pressroom. In small plants, he may be expected to change about and perform a dozen or more duties. Hence, an applicant should keep the type of shop clearly in mind when seeking for employment.

Speed is an important consideration in mechanical duties. Employers think in terms of *time,* which is *cost* to them. They want to know not only what the applicant can *do,* but how *fast* he can do it, and how *well* the job will be done. They realize that a man must know how to make adequate and correct layouts; but they are not interested in one who takes a half-day to make one for a simple job. They are interested in speed on a typesetting machine, but a speed of 3,000 ems an hour is useless to them if half a galley must be reset because of errors.

Written applications should sell employers on personal interviews. Employers hesitate quite often to employ a man they have never seen and never questioned. They like to "size up" an applicant. To secure a personal interview, the applicant for a graphic arts job should write a good letter of application, or call on the telephone for an appointment.

The way to get a better job is to prepare for it. One method of getting a job, and then perhaps a better one, is to get adequate preparation in a good graphic arts school. High-school graduates with proper credits may enter one of the post-high schools devoted to training men and women for the graphic arts.

If the high-school printing graduate finds it impossible to enter higher schools, he can make progress in learning about printing through various other means:

1. Many books are printed in the graphic arts, and many are listed in this book as references at the close of each chapter. The larger libraries stock many titles.

2. The embryo printer should subscribe to one or more of the best printing trades journals:

    a. *Inland Printer/American Lithographer,* Chicago, Ill.

    b. *Printing Magazine/National Lithographer,* Oradel, N. J.

    c. *Graphic Arts Monthly,* Chicago, Ill.

    d. *Printing Production,* Cleveland, O.

3. Large city school systems offer evening courses in many of the graphic arts subjects, and many of their day courses are also offered at night.

4. An organization, bearing the slogan "Share Your Knowledge," is the International Association of Printing House Craftsmen. Many of the local clubs of the International Association are located in large cities in the United States. Some have junior memberships which allow membership to printers who are not foremen or superintendents. The monthly magazine, *The Share Your Knowledge Review,* is packed full of new ideas and old in the graphic arts, and it is worth reading to keep informed of the daily developments in the graphic arts.

SELF-TEST

This self-test will serve as a review of this chapter. The questions are either true or false, or multiple choice. They are designed to create thought and discussion. The numbers following each question refer to the page on which the correct answer can be found.

1. Job security in the graphic arts is below the average of manufacturing industries. (357)
2. No artists are ever employed in the Graphic Arts. (357)
3. A scarcity of apprentices exists in the graphic arts industry. (357)
4. Wage scales in the graphic arts vary according to locality. (357)
5. The length of apprenticeships vary between crafts. (359)
6. One of the most important abilities of the linotype operator is to divide words correctly. (362)
7. Lithograph artists perform the work of dot etching, Ben Day, tusching and opaquing. (365)
8. Professional engineers sometimes specialize in printing-plant layout and management. (368)
9. Most plant superintendents were once foremen. (368)
10. Graphic Arts teachers usually work for seven years in their trade before beginning to teach. (369)

Glossary of Graphic Arts Terms

A

Acid Resist: Any coating that does not allow the etching away of a portion of a plate by acid.

Agate: Body type of 5½ points; newspaper advertisements are measured in agate lines.

Albumin: White of egg.

Albumin Plate: A lithographic press plate used for short runs on less exacting work, for runs under 50,000.

Alive: Type after it has been set, before it is ready for distribution.

Alkali: A compound which has an action opposite to that of an acid; a mixture of alkali and acid will neutralize one another and weaken the stronger.

Alley: Floor space between two type cabinets.

Antimony: One of the ingredients of type metal.

Antique: A rough-surfaced paper stock.

Arabic Numerals: 1234567890.

B

Backing-up: Printing the reverse side of a sheet.

Balance: A pleasing arrangement of type masses.

Bank: A stand to hold type and spacing materials.

Base: Transparent support for light-sensitive coatings, as film, glass or paper. See *Patent Base*.

Basis Weight: The name given to a sheet of paper in terms of the weight of 500 sheets in a certain size.

Beard: The beveled space below the face of a type.

Bearers: Type-high ledges on a press to insure the rollers turning; strips of wood or metal placed inside the ends of platen press chases; type-high strips of metal placed around and within blank space in a type form prepared for electrotyping.

Bed: The part of a press on which the form is placed.

Ben Day Process: A mechanical method of producing a shaded effect on a line plate.

Beveled Rule: Rule on which the printing surface is on one side rather than the center, so that perfect joints can be made.

Binder: A cover for sheets; one who does bindery work.

Bindery: A shop where books are assembled.

Blanket: Fabric coated with a rubber or synthetic compound which transfers the image from the plate to the paper on offset-lithographic presses; the impression surface on newspaper rotary presses.

Block: A hardwood or metal base for letterpress plates; a woodcut.

Block Letter: "Gothic" or sans serif type faces.

Blow-up: An enlargement.

Body: The size of type from the bottom of the descenders to the top of the ascenders, excluding leading.

Body Type: Type used for straight matter composition; regular paragraph type for newspapers and books.

Bond: A strong and translucent rag or sulphite paper.

Book Paper: A class of paper used for making books; includes coated, sized and super-calendered, antique, machine-finish, etc.

Border: Characters or lines cast in individual types or strips used for panels.

Brace: Character used to group type matter. ⁓

Bracket: Characters used to enclose words, figures, etc., from the text. [   ]

Brass Rules: Strips of brass used to print lines.

Brass Spaces: Spaces 1-point thick in various point sizes.

Brayer: A handled inking roller used in proofing.

Bristol Board: A fine grade of cardboard.

Broadside: A large specially-folded advertising sheet.

Brochure: A booklet.

Bronze: A fine metallic powder used to give brilliant glossy effects in gold and silver, etc.; glassine proofs of type are bronzed to give opacity in gravure printing.

Bundling: Compressing book signatures to make them lie flat in bookbinding.

Butted: Slugs of type lines placed end to end to form one line, when specifications call for type lines over the maximum of the line-casting machine, usually over 30 picas, or 5 inches.

C

Cabinet: An enclosed chest used to hold type cases.

Calender: A paper-making machine which gives the finish to paper.

California Job Case: The most popular type storage case.

Cap: Capital letters in the type font. A 14x17-inch sheet of paper.

Caption: A heading or title.

Carbon Tissue: A light-sensitive, gelatin-coated paper stock used in gravure plate-making.

Car Card: A large card advertisement used in street cars and buses.

Case: A shallow tray divided into compartments, used to hold type.

Casein: An albuminous substance used for sizing paper.

Case Stand: A framework used to hold type cases.

Cast: To force metal into a mold against matrices, as in line-casting machines.

Cellulose: A fibrous substance used to make paper obtained from cotton, linen, hemp, and wood.

Cellulose Acetate: A transparent sheet, insoluble in water, used for films, reproduction proofs of type, and a base for deep etch stripping in offset-lithography.

Centered: Placed in the center of a sheet or line.

Chalk Overlay: An overlay mechanically made; used in making ready halftone plates in letterpress printing.

Chapel: An organization of union workmen in a printing shop.

Chase: An iron or steel frame in which type forms are locked for letterpress printing presses.

Chroma: The degree of intensity from black to white.

Circulars: Advertising matter in the form of letters and handbills.

Clean Proof: A term used when few errors are found on a proof of type.

Closed Shop: A shop in which only union workmen are employed.

Coated Paper: Smooth or dull finished with a fine surface, used for printing halftones.

Coating: Making an offset-lithographic plate sensitive to light. Plate whirler is used and a solution is poured onto the middle of the plate while it spins.

Collating: Examining the folded signatures of a book in the process of gathering to see that all sections are in order; often confused with gathering.

Colloid: Egg albumin in water, gum arabic, casein, glue, and gelatin.

Colophon: An inscription in a book telling of the manner in which it has been printed, and by whom.

Color Filter: A sheet of colored glass used in excluding certain colors in color photography.

Color Form: The form making the second color in a job of printing.

Column Rules: Strips of rule used between columns.

Combination: Combining of more than one job into a flat in offset-lithographic stripping; the combining of line and halftone work in platemaking.

Composing Machine: Device used to produce single types and lines of type on one slug; the Intertype, Linotype, and Monotype machines.

Composing Stick: A receptable in which single types are assembled and justified by hand compositors.

Composition: Setting and arranging types; the product of type either hand or machine-set.

Compositor: One who sets type.

Condensed: A term used for thin type faces.

Contact Print: A print made by placing a transparency against a light-sensitive material and shining a light through it. The image formed is the same size as the negative image.

Continuous-Tone Negative: A negative made in a camera without the use of a screen; has no dot formation.

Copperplate Engraving: Work done from either copper or steel engraved dies, engraved intaglio. The ink on the completed job appears intense in color, and stands out from the surface of the paper or card.

Copper Spaces: Spaces one-half point thick, in various point sizes.

Copy: Material furnished by the customer for reproduction; typewritten manuscript or art work.

Copy-Cutter: One who divides copy into "takes," or small sections, which are given to compositors to set in newspaper shops.

Copyholder: One who holds copy and reads aloud to a proofreader.

Counter-Etch: The chemical cleaning of an offset-lithographic plate to free it from excessive oxide, graining mud, and finger marks.

Cover Papers: Heavy, decorative papers used for covering pamphlets, etc.

Creasing: Breaking fibers of heavy paper and cover stock with blunt rule in a straight line, so that fold resulting therefrom will not break the fibers too much and cause an uneven fold.

Crop: To cut down in size, as directed by crop marks.

Crop Marks: The cross marks at the outside of a photograph or art work, usually placed on the mounting of the copy, to designate the area of the copy to be used.

Cut: Term often used to denote a photo-engraving, electrotype, or stereotype in letterpress, and any picture in offset-lithography.

Cut Cards: Cardboard die-cut to standard and exact sizes.

Cut-off Rule: A rule used to separate advertisements in newspapers.

Cutting Rule: Steel rule sharpened to cut out designs on a letterpress.

Cylinder Press: Style of letterpress machine which prints by the action of a cylinder on a flat type form.

D

Dampeners: Rollers that distribute dampening solution to printing plates on offset-lithographic presses.

Dandy Roller: A wire cylinder used on papermaking machines that make wove or laid effects on the texture, as well as the watermark, as in bond, ledger, and antique book paper.

Dashes: Straight lines in en and em widths in type and matrix fonts. Not to be confused with hyphens used for dividing words.

Dead: Type ready for distribution; plates after printing has been accomplished.

Deadline: Last day or hour in which copy, artwork, or electrotypes are acceptable.

Deckle-Edge: An untrimmed feather edge on paper.

Deep-etched Plate: An offset-lithographic plate used for long runs on more exacting work, and where color correction is desired. The ink-carrying areas are slightly recessed below plate surface.

Density: Opaqueness of a negative; opaqueness of the image on a positive.

Densensitizer: To treat an offset-lithographic plate chemically so that the work areas will not accept ink.

Developing: To make a picture appear by treating a film chemically; rubbing-in an offset-lithographic plate with a greasy developing ink.

Developing Ink: A black substance which produces a greasy film on the printing areas of an offset-lithographic plate, and prepares it for receiving the ink.

Devil: The youngest apprentice in a printing shop.

Diamond: 4½-point type.

Die-stamping: Intaglio printing done by means of a die and counter die; blind or color stamping of a book front cover.

Diphthong: Two vowels joined, as æ, œ.

Dirty Proof: A proof of type containing many errors.

Display: Type composition in the larger sizes; that type matter which first attracts the eye.

Display Type: The largest and specially designed type faces used to attract attention.

Distribution: The placing of type and materials back into type cases and racks.

Doctor Blade: The knife pressed against the gravure press cylinder which wipes away the ink from the surface of the cylinder.

Dot Etching: The process by which a color retoucher changes the tone values on a halftone negative or positive.

Drier: A substance added to assist it in drying.

Dummy: Pages of a planned book, catalog, or booklet put together to assist in determining the specifications.

Dump: The place where type matter is placed.

E

Electrotype: An electrolytically formed duplicate of a type form or photoengraving.

Em: The square of the type body of any size; often used as alternate of pica—meaning 12 points.

Embossing: Impressing letters or artwork in relief, as on book covers.

Emulsion: The suspension of light-sensitive silver salt, generally in a gelatin solution; used for coating plates, films, etc.; the same coating when dried.

En: One-half the width of the em.

Enameled Paper: Paper coated with clay, glue, and other substances, having a glossy finish; a gloss-coated paper.

Engraving: A photoengraving; the process of cutting designs into a plate for the purpose of making impressions on paper.

Enlargement: A blow-up; an image which is made larger than the original.

Envelope Corner Card: An address printed at the left of an envelope.

Etch: Acid solution mixed with the dampening fountain water to help control the ink on an offset-lithographic press.

Etching: The fixing of the image area in offset-lithography so that bare areas will accept only water, and printing areas will accept only ink; the eating away of metal, as in photoengraving.

Expanded: A thick type face.

Exposing: Making an image on a light-sensitive coated plate or film, from a negative or positive, with a light source.

Extra-condensed: A very thin type face.

F

Face: The part of a type that makes the impression; reference to a type face style, as a "book face."

Family: A group of related type fonts in a series, as the "Caslon Family."

Farm Out: To sublet a process in printing, as the binding, composition, or presswork.

Feeder: A device for automatically delivering the sheets of paper to a press; a person who hand-feeds sheets to a press.

Feet: The two lower projections of a piece of hand-set type; "off its feet" refers to types or slugs that do not print correctly because of their being out of a true vertical position.

Fixing: The process of removing unexposed and undeveloped silver halide from a plate, film, or print.

Flat: The stripper's completed work in offset-lithography; negatives or positives properly assembled on a lithographic layout and ready for plate making.

Flat Bed: A press which prints from a flat form, as from type or photoengravings.

Flong: A paper matrix used in stereotyping.

Flush: To the end of either side; or end of a line of type, as "flush right."

Focal Plane: Rear section of a camera which supports the ground glass, stayflat, or vacuum back.

Folio: Page number.

Font: An assortment of letters and characters of any one size and style of type.

Forwarding: The process of binding a book after the sheets are fastened together.

Fountain Solution: Water made slightly acid with chemicals that react to balance excessive greasiness from ink depositing itself into the grain of the plate in offset-lithography.

Furniture: Pieces of wood or metal used to fill out large blank spaces in a type form. Metal furniture is used for large blank spaces within a type form, as well as for locking up forms for the press. Wood furniture is used only for locking forms.

G

Galley: A shallow metal tray in which type is placed for assembling or storage.

Galley Press: A proofing machine for type and plates.

Gathering: Assembling the signatures or sheets of a book or booklet, often confused with collating.

Gauge or Gage: A measuring rule in picas.

Gauge Pin: A piece of metal used to hold sheets in position on letterpresses.

Gelatin: A substance derived from animal tissue, bones, hoofs, etc. Sensitized gelatin is used in *screenless illustration printing*—collotype and photogelatin. The process reproduces illustrations in continuous tone.

Goldenrod Paper: A support for negatives used by a stripper in making flats for the albumin process of platemaking in offset-lithography. The masking goldenrod paper prevents the exposure of the plate in the blank areas.

Gordon Press: A style of hand or automatically fed platen press.

Grain: The direction in which the fibers lie in a sheet of paper; see *Graining*.

Graining: Roughening the surface of a metal offset-lithographic press plate by means of marbles and an abrasive to increase its water-carrying capacity during the press run.

Gravure: Printing from an etched-out or sunken surface; an intaglio method.

Grippers: Iron fingers on the cylinder of a press which hold the sheets while they are being printed; the iron clamps which hold the paper against the platen on a platen press.

Gudgeons: Metal wheels used on press roller stocks.

Guide: Sheet-feed gauges against which paper is fed on printing presses.

Gum Solution: Gum arabic in water to form a 20% to 30% solution, used to preserve plates in offset-lithography.

Gumming-up: Coating the nonprinting parts of offset-lithographic plates, but not the images, with gum, to desensitize the nonprinting parts.

Gutter: The margin of a book toward the binding edge.

H

Hairline: The fine and delicate lines in a type face design or in an illustration; hairline rule is the thinnest made in letterpress.

Hair Spaces: Half-point, and one-point spaces made in various point sizes used to letterspace words and to justify lines of type.

Half-Diamond Indention: When successive lines are indented each slightly more than the ones above in type composition.

Half-Title: The title placed at the head of the first chapter of a book.

Halftone: Picture in which the gradation of tone is reproduced by a graduation of dots, produced by the interposition of a screen during exposure.

Halftone Positive: One made in a camera from a continuous tone negative with a screen interposed between the photographic plate and the lens.

Halftone Screen: A grating of opaque lines on glass, producing transparent apertures between intersections. Rulings range from 50 to 300 to the inch.

Harmony: The state of a pleasing relation between parts of a piece of printing.

Harris Press: An offset-lithographic printing press.

Head: A type heading; the top of a book page or job of printing; the title of a newspaper story.

Hell Box: A place where broken or worn-out type and material is placed.

Highlight: The bright part of a halftone represented by considerable opacity in the negative and by nearly clear paper in the print.

Hypo: The most common fixing agent used in photography.

Hypotenuse Oblong: A book page proportion in which the depth is 50% greater than its width.

I

Imitation Embossing: See *Thermography.*

Imposing Table: The flat stone or metal-topped table on which forms are locked up in chases.

Imposition: The proper placing of page forms in a chase.

Impression: The pressure of type forms or plates on the paper in a printing press.

Impression Cylinder: The cylinder that carries the paper while it is being printed.

Indent: To space before a line in type composition.

Inferior: Figures or letters below the line, smaller than the type used, as $_{123}$.

Initial Letter: The large letter used at the beginning of a book page. "Up" means the initial is aligned at its bottom with the bottom of the first line of type. "Down" means that the top of the initial letter aligns with the top of the first line of type.

Ink Fountain: A device to feed the correct quantity of ink to the printing rollers on a press.

Insert: An extra sheet placed within a book.

Intaglio: Cut-out or etched-out pictures or type from a plate, as in steel-plate engraving or gravure printing.

Intertype: A keyboard machine which casts a line in one piece.

Italic: Slanting type.

J

Job Compositor: A typesetter who sets commercial printing.

Jobber: A press used for small work.

Job Font: A small assortment of type in any one size and style.

Job Printer: A printer who does small commercial printing, such as letterheads and envelopes.

Job Ticket: Usually an envelope containing copy and art work, on which directions are given for the printing of a job; used in printing shops.

Job Type: Type faces used in printing commercial work.

Jog: To straighten sheets of paper.

Journeyman: A printer who has completed his apprenticeship.

K

Kelly Press: A two-revolution letterpress.

Kern: The part of the type face that extends over and from the side of the type body.

Key: A device for operating quoins.

Key Plate: The plate used to guide the register of subsequent color plates in color printing.

Kraft: A tough wrapping paper.

L

Labor Saving: Any printing material, such as leads and slugs, cut to assorted sizes.

Laid Paper: Paper having parallel lines watermarked at equal distances.

Lay of the Case: The arrangement of letters and characters in a type case.

Layout: A full scale drawing of a proposed press sheet, divided into individual units of the job, containing measurements needed to position correctly the work areas in the unit, in offset-lithography; a drawing containing specifications of a proposed job in letterpress or lithographic printing.

Leaders: Periods or dots at intervals to lead the eye in tabular matter, contents pages, etc.

Leads: Thin strips of metal used to space between lines of type, 1, 1½, 2, 3, and 4 points thick.

Legend: Explanatory type matter under an illustration.

Letterpress: Printing from a raised surface, as type and photo-engravings.

Letterspacing: Spacing between letters in a line of type.

Lift: When each piece of type in a form stays in place after being locked in a chase, it is said to "lift."

Ligature: Two or more letters tied together in design and cast in one piece of type, or made on one matrix, as fi, fl, ff, ffi, ffl. In hand-set type ligatures prevent the breaking of kerns.

Light Face: A term used for type faces having less impression space on the face.

Line Copy: Original copy in the form of printed, written by hand, typewritten, or drawn by hand.

Line Cut: See *Line Engraving.*

Line Engraving: A printing plate made up of black-and-white, non-screened.

Line Gauge: See *Pica Rule.*

Line Negative: Negatives made from line copy and for use in making a line plate, without printing through a halftone screen.

Linen Finish: Paper or cardboard having a finish similar to that of linen cloth.

Lining: The aligning of type faces at the bottom of the letters in different sizes.

Linograph: A keyboard linecasting machine, not now manufactured.

Linottype: A keyboard machine which casts a line in one piece.

Lithography: Printing from a stone, now superseded by the offset-lithographic process.

Live: A printing form still in use.

Logotype: Several letters or a whole word cast in one piece of type; the stereotype or electrotype used in newspaper advertisements giving the name of the advertiser.

Long Primer: The old name for 10-point type.

Lowercase: Small letters in type, or on slugs.

Ludlow-Typography: A linecasting machine for which the matrices are hand-assembled.

M

Machine Composition: Any type composition done mechanically, as on the Intertype, Linotype, or Monotype.

Machine Finish: A smooth paper used in printing books.

Makeready: The shimming up of certain parts of the letterpress type form so that heavy and light areas print with the correct squeeze-to-paper.

Making-up: Arranging set type and slugs into a type form.

Master Layout: A ruled sheet, usually on white paper, which serves as a guide for stripping identical flats in offset-lithography.

Matrix: A mold in which type characters are cast in linecasting machines and in individual type making: plural matrices; the paper mold used in stereotyping.

Middletone: Intermediate tones between the shadow and the highlight in halftone illustrations.

Miehle: A flat-bed letterpress of the two-revolution type; also trade names for presses made to produce by any process.

Miehle Vertical: A printing press, letterpress, in which the type form stands vertically.

Misprint: A typographical error.

Mold: That part of a linecasting machine or monotype in which the line or type is cast against the matrix.

Monotype: A series of machines which cast individual letters for type cases to be set by hand; body type cast and set as wanted; rule, border, leads, slugs, and spacing material.

Mortise: The cutout portion of an electrotype or photoengraving, mounted, in which type is set.

Mutton Quad: An em quad.

N

Neck: The part of a type between the shoulder and the face.

Negative: Film resulting from photographing copy in a camera. Work areas are transparent on the negative, and the white areas are opaque.

News Cases: A pair of type cases in which the caps are kept in the upper case, and the lowercase letters are kept in the lower case. Now practically extinct.

Newsprint: A cheap paper made from wood pulp.

News Stick: A composing stick with a fixed measure.

Nick: A notch in type which acts as a guide to the compositor.

Nonpareil: The equivalent of 6 points; a size of type now called six-point.

Numbering Machine: A type-high printing machine which is locked with type in regular printing forms, and prints numbers in consecutive order, forward or backward as wanted.

Nut Quad: An en quad.

O

Offset: The smudging of the bottom of a sheet on the press delivery from a print on top of the sheet directly below it; often used also as a shortening of the term "off-set lithography."

Offset-Lithography: Making an impression from a plane surface onto a rubber blanket, and then making an impression from the rubber blanket onto the paper; same as offset and planography.

Oldstyle: A type style having diagonally-sloping serifs.

Onionskin: A thin, translucent paper, usually used in carbon paper work.

Opaque: Water soluble paint used to block out areas on negatives and positives to make them nontransparent.

Opaquing: Applying an opaque to a photographic negative or positive in order to stop completely the transmission of light where desired.

Open Matter: Type lines very widely spaced.

Optical Center: The center of a rectangle as it appears to the eye; two-fifths from the top of the rectangle.

Outline Halftone: A halftone plate in which the background is cut away.

Overlay: In letterpress makeready, a piece of paper placed in the packing to make part of the form print more heavily in that place; in offset-lithography, the transparent or translucent covering on the copy on which directions or work to be overprinted are placed, in the preparation of artwork.

Overprinting: Double-printing or surprinting work on an area that has already been printed upon, in platemaking.

Overunning: Setting type backward or forward in making corrections, as when copy is left out, or added in the paragraph.

Oxide: Result of a union of a substance and oxygen.

P

Pamphlet: Several sheets of paper stitched together.

Panel: A square or rectangular design made up of rule or border.

Patent Base: Steel base used to make electrotypes type-high, so that wood bases need not be used.

Pearl: An old size of type, now 5 point.

Pebbling: A process of graining or crimping gloss-coated paper after printing halftones to give an antique paper effect, now generally out of date.

Perfecting: A press which prints both sides of a sheet of paper once through the press.

Perforating Machine: A machine used to punch small holes, close together, to facilitate tearing.

Photocomposing Machine: See *Step and Repeat Photocomposing Machine.*

Photoengraving: The process of making line and halftone letterpress printing plates by the action of light on a film.

Photogravure: See *Gravure.*

Photolithography: See Offset-Lithography.

Phototypecomposing Machine: A keyboard device for assembling images of type faces photographically on film, rather than in metal type forms.

pH Value: A method of indicating acidity or alkalinity in a fountain solution, by number, on offset-lithographic presses. Scale is from 1 to 14 with 7 as the neutral point. Below 7 is acid and above 7 is alkali.

Pi: Mixed and jumbled handset type and slugs and spacing material; pi lines often inadvertently get into print when the linecasting machine operator runs matrices taken from lines in composing, and then finishes out the line with the common "etaoin shrdlu," etc.

Pica The standard unit of measurement for printing material; 12 points; an old name for 12-point type.

Pigment: The substance used for coloring in printing ink.

Pin Mark: The round mark made by a pin that ejects a type from the mold in casting handset type.

Planer: A smooth-bottomed hardwood block used with a mallet to knock type to its feet on the imposing table.

Plate: Flat letterpress plates such as electrotypes, photoengravings, stereotypes, etc.; offset-lithographic plates are thin and are wrapped around the cylinder of an offset press; plates used in die stamping by intaglio methods.

Plate Cylinder: The cylinder on a rotary press which holds the printing plate or curved electrotypes.

Platen: The flat part of a platen press facing the bed, on which the tympan is placed.

Platen Press: A style of letterpress which makes impressions from a flat surface.

Point: A unit of measurement in printing material and type; .014-inch on linecasting machines, and .0138 in foundry type; any mark of punctuation, as the period, comma, etc.

Point-Set: Letters of a type font which are cast to point multiples.

Point System: Refers to the point as a unit of measurement; see *Point.*

Positive: The reverse of a negative. The work appears on the copy the same as it does on the positive film.

Pre-etch: To clean and desensitize an offset-lithographic plate.

Press: A machine for making printed impressions.

Press Feeder: One who hand-feeds a printing press with the sheets to be printed; the automatic attachment which feeds sheets to a press.

Press Gripper: The distance the front edge of the plate is inserted into the clamps on an offset press plate cylinder; the metal fingers which hold the sheet fast in the impression cylinder.

Pressman: One who operates printing presses.

Press Proofs: Proofs made on regular printing presses, as when taking reproduction proofs.

Primary Colors: Yellow, red, and blue.

Printing Ink: A nonfluid, pasty substance used in letterpress and offset-lithographic processes. Newsprint ink and gravure ink is more fluid.

Process Engraving: See *Thermography.*

Process Plates or Process Printing: The printing from a series of plates, two or more, in halftone, which makes varying colors possible from the usual four colors: yellow, red, blue, black.

Progressive Proofs: Proofs of color plates used as a guide for the pressman, and furnished by the engraver or platemaker.

Proof: The first print of a type form or engraving or offset-lithographic plate, examined and read to detect errors.

Proof Press: A machine used to make proofs of type matter and plates.

Proofreader: One who examines proofs and marks errors for correction.

Proofreader's Marks: Signs used by proofreaders to denote errors for correction.

Proof Roller: See *Brayer*.

Proportion: Comparative relationship between the elements of a piece of printing.

Pull a Proof: To make a print for reading proof.

Pulp: The mass of material used to make paper.

Punch: The original die used in typefounding; the die used to impress characters and letters in matrices used in linecasting and monotype machines.

Punching Machine: A machine for making holes in paper, now generally out of date, and superseded by a paper-drilling machine which features a hollow drill.

Q

Quad: Blank type used to space out at the ends of lines in type composition, and to indent paragraphs.

Quadder: Short name used to denote special linecasting machine equipment which centers, sets flush left or flush right automatically, without keyboarding.

Quoin: A small wedge or expanding device used for locking type forms in chases in letterpress.

Quoin Key: The tool used to manipulate quoins.

Quotation Furniture: Small sizes of metal furniture used by compositors.

R

Rack: A framework used to hold type cases.

Railroad Furniture: Metal furniture similar in shape to railroad rails.

Raised Printing: See *Thermography*.

Ready Print: Inside sections of newspapers bought already printed with feature articles, advertisements, etc.

Ream: Five hundred sheets of paper.

Register: The adjustment of forms or plates so they will print in correct position over another form or plate, as in color printing.

Reglet: Wooden 6 and 12-point slugs, used in locking up type forms for letterpresses; not generally used within a type form because of inaccuracy.

Relative Humidity: Reference to the amount of water vapor which the air holds compared with what it could hold, at the given temperatures, if it were saturated.

Relief Printing: Letterpress, from type, electrotypes, photoengravings, and stereotypes.

Retouching: Corrective treatment of a negative, positive, or copy.

Reverse Plate: A printing plate in which the black-and-white have been reversed.

Revise Proof: Any proof taken of printing types or forms or plates after the first, as "1st revise," "2d revise," etc., used to determine if corrections have been made and on which additional corrections are made.

Rollers: Inking and dampening rollers used on presses.

Rolling-up: To cover an offset-lithographic plate with a thin layer of developing ink.

Roll-Leaf Stamping: A process of stamping gold, silver, or other colors on covers of books, stationery, and like work.

Roman Numerals: A system of notation, little used at the present day; I means 1, V means 5, X means 10, L means 50, C means 100, D means 500, and M means 1,000.

Roman Type: The regular style of type used commonly for books and newspapers; a straight letter as differentiated from italic, etc.

Rotogravure: The process of intaglio (gravure) impressions on a rotary press.

Roughing: See *Pebbling*.

Router: A device used to cut away dead metal from letterpress plates, as electrotypes and stereotypes.

Rule: Strips of brass or type metal used to print lines in letterpress; a pica ruler; straight lines cut into negatives to reproduce lines.

Ruling Machine: A device used to pen-rule lines in colors on paper, used in blankbook work.

Running Head: The title of a book, chapter, or section of a book printed at the head of each page.

Running Title: See *Running Head*.

Run-in: Proofreader's mark "run-in" when they do not wish type matter to be paragraphed.

Run out: To make hanging indention.

S

Saddle-Stitch: To fasten a pamphlet by stitching it through the middle fold of the sheets.

Safety Paper: Paper treated usually by printing a design in a light tint, which protects the sheet against forgery.

Salts: Sodium carbonate, calcium chloride, ammonium dichromate.

Sans Serif: Type having no serifs; the so-called American "gothic" types.

Saw Trimmer: A machine designed to cut slugs and other material to point size.

Scale: A list of wages or prices; a device used in copyfitting, in typesetting, and layout.

Scaling Copy: Calculating the percentage of enlargement or reduction of artwork; determining proportional width or depth of artwork to needed depth or width.

Score: To create paper or cover stock to facilitate folding without breaking the fold.

Screen: Plate glass with cross-ruled opaque lines used in cameras to break continuous-tone illustrations and artwork into halftone screens; refers also to the number of lines to the inch on printed illustrations. Offset screens are generally 120, 133, or 150; letterpress screens run from 50 to 175 generally, depending upon the roughness of the paper stock used; gravure screens are generally 150.

Screw Chase: A chase used in newspaper offices with screws on the top side to tighten the form, rather than quoins.

Scumming: When the nonprinting parts of an offset-lithographic plate picks up ink or becomes dirty.

Section: A signature or group of signatures.

Sensitive Material: An emulsion attached to a film, paper, or dry plate base.

Sensitizers: Materials which make other substances responsive to light, as dichromate potassium and ammonium make solutions of albumin, glue, gelatin, and casein sensitive to light.

Sensitizing: Making a plate sensitive to light. In offset-lithography, coating the plate with bichromated albumin solution; in the deep-etch lithographic process, coating the plate with bichromated glue or gum.

Serif: The short cross-lines at the ends of the main strokes of certain styles of type faces.

Setting a Stick: Adjusting a composing stick to pica measure or half-pica measure.

Shadow: Shaded or darker portions of a halftone.

Sheet-wise: Pages imposed in two forms, that is, the same form does not back up itself.

Short And: The mark &, or ampersand.

Short-Stop Bath: A solution of acetic acid used in producing line negatives; it neutralizes the alkaline developer on the negative and so helps to preserve the acid of the fixing solution.

Shoulder: That part of a type not covered by the face.

Show Card: A large advertising placard.

Side Head: A heading set to the side of the main type composition.

Side Stitch: The fastening of pamphlet sheets together sideways.

Signature: A folded section of a book after being imposed and printed; a letter or figure appearing at the bottom of the first page of a signature to guide the binder; dots or squares are often used, printed at the fold, to aid in collating.

Signature Mark: See *Signature*.

Signature Press: A machine used to press signatures together to expel air from between the sheets.

Size: A sticky yellow ink used in bronzing and flocking. The metallic gold and silver dust adheres to the sticky ink when dusted.

S & C: Sized and calendered paper; a smooth-finished paper stock.

S & SC: Sized and supercalendered paper; a glossy paper stock.

Skeleton Chase: A large iron chase, with dovetail slots into which crossbars fit, used in making small area prints on large sheets of paper.

Slitter: Device used to cut paper as it passes from printing press.

Slug: A lead over 6 points thick; a line cast on a linecasting machine.

Small Caps: Smaller sizes of capital letters provided in a type or matrix font.

Smashing: Pressing signatures together so that they will lie flat in binding.

Solid Matter: Type composition not leaded.

Solution: A combination of a liquid and a solid substance.

Sorts: The types in a compartment of a type case or storage box; matrices not usually contained in a line-casting machine magazine, but which "run pi," that is, to a chute and stacker at the right side of the magazine.

Space: Metal blank used in spacing between words in type composition.

Spaceband: A device used to provide equal spacing between words on linecasting machines.

Square Four: Four pages imposed so that when printed on both sides and cut, two sections of four pages each are made.

Standing Matter: Type composition, photoengravings, and other plates held over for another printing.

Stamping: Die stamping or embossing.

Steam Table: Equipment used for drying wet matrices in stereotyping.

Steel Engraving: See *Copperplate Engraving.*

Step-and-Repeat Photocomposing Machine: A device for the printing of the same image in register many times on the same plate, for gang or multiple printing.

Stepover: Procedure of repeating the exposure of an offset-lithographic flat by stepping it along the gripper edge.

Step-up: Procedure of repeating the exposure of an offset-lithographic flat by stepping it back from the gripper edge.

Stereotype: A letterpress printing plate cast from a paper matrix.

Stick: See *Composing Stick.*

Stipple: A printing surface on plates which consists of fine dots.

Stock: Paper.

Stone Man: A workman who imposes and locks up forms in printing plants.

Straight Matter: Body matter or plain paragraph type composition.

Stripper: One who makes flats in an offset-lithographic plant. He arranges and affixes the negatives or positives on the goldenrod paper or acetate sheet, following the instructions on how the job should appear when lithographed.

Stripping Table: A light table; a glass-topped table, with a light source beneath the glass, on which a stripper works.

Sub: An abbreviation for substitute workman, used in printshop chapels.

Subhead: A secondary title or heading, usually printed in a contrasting type face.

Supercalendered: Extra-smooth paper stock, not coated.

Superior Figures or Letters: Small figures or letters cast on the extreme upper part of the type body, for reference purposes, such as [123, abc,] etc.

Sweating-on: A process of fastening a printing plate on a metal base.

Symmetry: The arrangement of type mass elements over a given axis, so that a division through that axis will divide it into halves.

T

Tabular Matter: Lists of words or figures in columns, usually separated by blank space or rules.

Tack: Stickiness, as in printing ink.

Text: Straight type matter in a book.

Thermography: The process of dusting freshly printed sheets with resinous powder; when heated, the powder fuses, forming a raised surface of the print, simulating copperplate engraving, usually used on business and calling cards, and like work.

Thick Space: Usually the 3-em space.

Thin Space: Usually the 4 and 5-em space.

Tint: A very light color, usually used for backgrounds for type matter and illustrations.

Tint Block: A solid or screened background for printing tints.

Tissue: A very thin paper, usually .001-inch thick, used in letterpress makeready.

Transpose: To change a word or letter or group of words or illustrations from one place to another.

Tusche: Greasy, water-soluble black liquid applied to plates with pen or brush, for repairing the image when broken or missing on offset-lithographic plates.

Two-Line Letter: An initial letter covering two lines of the text matter.

Two-Thirder: An advanced printing apprentice.

Tying-up: The process of wrapping type forms with cord to keep them from being pied.

Tympan: The paper that covers the platen or impression cylinder of a letterpress.

Type: Printers' letters, in metal to sizes of 144-point and wood in larger sizes, having a character cast or cut in relief at one end.

Typefounding: The manufacturing of types.

Type Louse: A mythical bug, for which naive novices search for and never find, to their chagrin, in print shops.

Type High: The standard height of type and mounted letterpress plates; .918-inch.

Typographer: A master typographical designer of printed matter.

Typography: The art of printing design.

U

Underscore: To set a rule under a word or sentence in type composition.

Underlay: A piece of paper placed under a form in letterpress printing makeready.

V

Vandercook Press: A make of proving machine used by letterpress printers and trade composition houses for pulling proofs for reading and for photographic reproduction.

Varnish: A substance used in making printing ink; the vehicle; used also to give a gloss-coated effect to printed work.

Vehicle: See *Varnish*.

Vignette: Halftone plates in which the background gradually fades away.

Virkotype: A thermograph machine.

W

Washington Press: A style of large platen press, now obsolete.

Watermark: A faint design or lettering pressed into paper while the paper is still wet during the manufacture.

Wax Engraving: The process of making letterpress printing plates of rule work by engraving in wax and then electrotyping.

Web: The length of paper being fed to a press from a roll rather than in sheet sizes.

Webendorfer: A make of offset-lithographic press.

Weight Font: Type purchased by weight, usually in multiples of 20 pounds, rather than by the job font.

White Space: That part of printed matter not covered by type and illustrations.

Wood Cut: An out-of-date method of hand and machine carving illustrations.

Work-and-Turn: Imposing all pages of a section or signature of a book on one form, and then turning for a second printing by the same form on the other side.

Wove Paper: Paper having the appearance of a piece of cloth, having fine lines running each way of the sheet.

Wrong Font: A wrong face of type in a piece of type composition.

Z

Zinc Etching: A printing plate for letterpress made by photography and the chemical processes of acid; either line or halftone.

Index